MONEY,

MURDER,

GIRLS . . .

The case seemed to have everything—except an end!

Names of new women bobbed up every day. "There was a married woman up on Fifth Avenue . . ." Sergeant Sol Fuchs of the 17th went to check it out. What did she know of Serge Rubinstein?

"Serge Rubinstein? The fellow that was murdered? Why I don't know anything about him. I never met him."

"We heard different."

"What do you mean?"

"What I mean is that six months ago you and a certain blonde and Serge spent four hours in bed together, that's what I mean."

The woman looked at the sergeant intently. "Will this go no further?"

He assured her it would not. So they talked.

There were many such married women at good addresses denying any liaison at first but ending up, each and every one, by saying yes, they had been with Serge and another woman and that it had been so disgusting, ugh—but they wouldn't have missed it for anything.

The Life and Death of Serge Rubinstein

GENE SMITH

MB
A MACFADDEN BOOK

THIS BOOK IS THE COMPLETE TEXT
OF THE HARDCOVER BOOK

A MACFADDEN BOOK ... 1963

MACFADDEN BOOKS are published by
MACFADDEN-BARTELL CORPORATION
205 East 42nd Street, New York 17, New York

Library of Congress Catalog Card Number 62-7681

CONTENTS

WHEN THE SUBJECT OF THIS book was found murdered in his bedroom it was said by the detective in charge of investigating his death that there was no more applicable case for the use of the old joke about narrowing the list of suspects down to 10,000. The author, who thinks he has a pretty good idea of who caused that murder, has not interviewed 10,000 people while conducting his research, but he is quite sure that if he had, at least 7500 of his interviewees would insist that their names not be used. Certainly a great number of people who knew Serge Rubinstein do not want the fact advertised. For that reason—because he has had to promise anonymity to so many people—the author will content himself with simply expressing his thanks to men who never knew Serge Rubinstein in life: the members of the New York Police Department who investigated his death and who have been, almost without exception, wonderfully cooperative in helping prepare this book. Primarily his thanks are due to the detective in charge, Assistant Chief Inspector Edward Feeley, a kind gentleman. The discerning reader will be able to tell, reading the book, who else gave information and private thoughts to the author. In any event, it is the author's hope that it can be said about him that he is one of the few persons who ever wrote a line about Serge Rubinstein that did not repeat old myths and mad fantasies dreamed up, in great part, by the man about whom the line was written. The author has nothing against Rubinstein, whom he never met, but it is his hope that if nothing else, the truth will be served by this work.

"I Am Serge Rubinstein"

ONE DAY IN MIDDLE 1953 a young man living in an apartment house on the East Side of New York City heard noises outside his door that were identifiable as those made by a lady in distress. A woman was screaming for help, and banging on a solid surface with her fists.

The young man opened his door and stepped out into the hall. The noise was coming from the apartment next to his. Behind that apartment's closed door a woman was crying "Help me! Somebody please help me!" and pounding on the door. He said, "What's the trouble in there?" and the banging stopped. A woman's voice sobbed, "I'm locked in. I can't get out."

"I'll get the janitor," he said.

"No—please don't leave me alone," she said. "Please help me get out."

"I'll try," he said, and went back to his apartment and got a screwdriver and hammer. Then he went to work on the door of her apartment—in which he had a certain proprietary interest. For the woman inside was the sub-tenant of a friend of his who had recently gone on a trip after asking the young man to keep an eye on things.

After a while he loosened the lock. The door opened. Out stepped a girl dressed all in black, with a string of pearls around her throat. She was in her early twenties. She swept by him. "I have no time to thank you," she said. "I'll thank you another time." And she was gone. She was quite lovely.

Some three or four months went by. And although the young man kept his eyes open for her, he did not see her again. She did not send a note to thank him, or invite him in for coffee. He had gallantly gone to her rescue and she was ignoring him.

One night he rang her doorbell. She appeared and repeated her scanty thanks, but that was all. She did not invite him in. Still he did not give up and when one day a friend and the friend's girl dropped in to see him, he decided he would invite his next-door neighbor to go out with them for a drink. "I'll pull her out," he told the others. He did just that. When she kept saying, "I don't go out;

8

I have a friend," he grabbed her hand and dragged her into the hall.

They went for a drink and then back to her apartment where they sat, all four, listening to her record-player. After a while her telephone rang.

"The young man next door is here," she said into the phone. "He's here with some friends. Yes, they're just leaving. Yes, of course—I'll call you back." An hour later the phone rang again. "Yes," she said, "they're still here, listening to records. They're leaving very shortly."

They left. But now the ice was broken and the young man and the girl next door became friends. They never dated in a formal way, but often he would go to her apartment and after a while they took to having breakfast together several times a week—muffins and eggs. She would call him to say the muffins were getting burnt and he would go next door.

She was a quite beautiful girl, much addicted to talking about the virtues of helping people, of doing good. He thought her a kind of Florence Nightingale of the spirit. She never spoke of her personal life. But often as they sat the phone would ring and she would say yes, yes, the young man was with her and they were listening to these records of that symphony, or were hearing this program on the radio, or talking about such and such a subject. "My friend knows all about you," she would tell the young man. "He understands."

So passed some four or five months. They were pals. On weekend nights they had their own lives and rarely saw each other. But sometimes they met in the hall and she would be all elegance and black dresses and the smell of perfume drifting behind her, and pearls on her neck. He never knew a man to come to her apartment to pick her up. She left the building alone and sometimes he heard her coming back very late, but always alone. She did not seem to work, yet he never asked about that.

One night she telephoned him. "A California friend of mine is coming over tonight," she said. "I used to know him on the West Coast when I was trying to get into the movies. He's an actor. But look—I can't be alone with him. Please come over. You know I can't be alone with anybody."

"Jesus Christ," he said.

"Please come," she said. The young man went.

They sat in the apartment and had a few drinks. After a while, as usual, the telephone rang. "My friend from next door is here with another friend," she said into the phone. "They won't be long, yes."

They sat for an additional hour. They had a few more

drinks. The phone rang. She answered and, quite high, she used her friend's name: Serge.

The actor jumped up. "Is that Serge?" he asked. "Serge, that White Russian? I have to talk to him, good old Serge." He grabbed the phone from her. "Serge," he said, "oh, Serge, oh, boy. We're having an orgy, we're all getting out of our clothes and running around the room. You should see. Come over and join us." The man on the other end hung up.

"Who was that?" asked the young man.

The actor told him: Serge Rubinstein. The young man thought, Rubinstein—financier, international manipulator, man of mystery. "Listen, get out of town," he told the actor. The actor laughed. "I'm leaving," the young man announced, thinking to himself that he knew the girl's friend was a jealous man and that now, of course, this jealous man would be furious, and that when a Serge Rubinstein was furious it was not a time to hang around.

"You're a coward," the girl giggled at him. He told her good night and left as she and the actor prepared to go out for a few more drinks.

He went back to his apartment and a while later the girl rang his bell and came in and threw open the cape she wore and flipped it off and kicked away her shoes. "Give me a drink," she said. "Oh, these actors, they're such romantic men. And you, you're such a pip-squeak."

"Listen," he answered, "better get out."

"Why?" she asked and at that moment there was a loud, heavy ring, a very long buzz from his doorbell. It went on. No one had ever rung his bell that way. It went on, a long, long drone.

He said to the girl, "Quick, go into the bathroom and lock the door and keep your mouth shut and don't come out no matter what you hear." She ran into his bathroom.

He went to his door and opened it.

All in black, black overcoat, black Homburg, holding a cane in his hands, a short, heavily built man stood there.

"Tell her to come out," the man in black said quietly.

The young man looked at him.

"It's all right," the man in black said. "She can come out."

"I don't know what you're talking about," said the young man.

"I am Serge Rubinstein," said the man. "I am Serge Rubinstein and the young lady from down the hall is in there. She told me so."

"Please go," said the young man.

The other's voice was very quiet. "Do you hear me? I am Serge Rubinstein."

10

The young man owned a sense of humor. He leaned against the door. "Have you got a card?" he drawled.

"Please tell her to come out. You know who I mean, don't you? The young lady from next door who is now in your apartment? The woman in your home?" He was very quiet. The young man was thinking that you had to respect the fellow's conduct. He wasn't getting excited; he wasn't yelling. "The doorman told me she is in your apartment," said the man.

"Mister," said the young man, "why don't you mind your own business? I don't have to tell you anything." He closed the door. Some ten minutes passed. There was silence outside the door. The young man told the girl to come out.

"I heard," she said to him. "You were wonderful."

"Look," he said, "I'll go out, take a walk, have a drink. You stay here and don't move." They were whispering together. But she was putting on her cape and shoes. "Oh, you were wonderful," she said.

"Don't go out," he said. But she went by him and opened the door.

The man was right by the door.

The man grabbed the girl and started throwing punches. But they were not landing on the girl with great effect; he was throwing them as you throw a baseball, with a lot of wrist action. The girl turned away and the man slammed her neck. She cried out and staggered, but made for her apartment. He followed, still striking out at her.

The young man looked on. He figured he could jump in and be a hero, or he could call the police, or he could let the girl get beaten up. He decided on the third course. After all, he reasoned, at least he's not using the cane and after all, they liked each other. This was their way, she was his girl. And anyway, she was a big girl and could defend herself or scream for the cops, or for the doorman. The young man closed his door.

For half an hour he heard sounds of occasional muffled violence from the other apartment. Then there was silence and he heard the door of the apartment close.

A moment later there was a tap on his door. It was not from a hand; it had to be from the cane. The young man went and stood silently by his closed door.

The man on the other side was talking to him.

"Hey, loverboy," the man said, very quietly. "Hey, lover." He wasn't raising his voice at all. "Lover—I pay the rent, I support her, I do everything and you're her lover. I want to deal with you.

"I want to deal with you. I have a dossier on you. I know everything about you." He went on talking, and the young

11

man, quite safe behind his door—at least no shots were being fired into it—thought to himself it was kind of pathetic, his paying all the bills and thinking someone else was getting everything. The man talked on, charging the young man with sleeping with the girl every day in the week while he, the man in black, paid for the whole set-up. Then there was silence and he was gone.

An hour later the girl called. "Come on in," she said. Her face was swollen. "It wasn't a bad beating," she said. "Let's have a drink."

That night the calls began. The first was at four o'clock in the morning; when the young man picked up the phone no one was there. An hour later the phone rang again. The next night there were three calls. After the last one, at five o'clock, the young man called the girl. She told him she had gotten a call at about two minutes to five.

The calls kept coming, three or four a night. The young man wrote a letter to a mansion on Fifth Avenue: "Mr. Rubinstein: By nature I am a fairly tolerant and good natured guy. I find my tolerance and good nature threatened by you and your behavior . . . You have recklessly breached any decent regard for you by your outrageous disregard for my personal privacy and peace of mind . . ."

The calls did not stop. They kept on, in twos: one to the young man; one immediately before or after to the girl. The young man toyed with various counterattacks—he would answer her phone and have her answer his; both would let their phones ring on; one would answer and the other would not—but she would have none of that. So he had to content himself with picking up the phone and cursing into it: "Hello, you Russian bastard . . . hey, con-man, hey, crook . . ." Sometimes there would be a quick feminine gasp, and he decided a telephone service was being utilized for some of the calls. But most of the time there was silence.

He called the police and they asked, what can we do? He got his number changed but still the calls came. He got an unlisted phone. The calls did not stop. He thought of leaving the phone off the hook but was afraid to: Suppose an emergency arose with someone in the family and he couldn't be reached? So the calls went on.

Then the girl next door told him she was moving out; her friend had ordered it. She left. He had liked her although he found it hard to understand her attitude which was not that she was a serf or vassal, that my god, he's after me, but rather that this is the way he is, this is the deal.

The calls stopped as soon as she was gone. A year went by and the young man began a romance and became engaged to the woman now his wife. Then one evening his ex-neighbor called him. "Serge and I are going to get married," she announced. "We're downstairs and we just had some drinks and we're on our way to the opera. Serge wants to come up and shake hands and have you wish us luck. He appreciates the situation now."

"Put him on," said the young man. He heard whispering and the girl got back on saying they just wanted to come up for a minute.

"What's the point?" asked the young man. "I wish you luck. I wish him luck. Be well. But why come up?"

"Please, for my sake," she said.

"All right," he told her. "I'll be in front of my door. Don't come into the apartment." They came up. The young man had his door open and when he heard the elevator stop at his floor he left his fiancée and went and stood in the doorway.

Again he had to admire what the man did. When the young man put out his hand it was brushed lightly aside, his shoulder was quickly pushed and the man was walking past him and into the apartment. The young man turned and went after him as he went into the living room and, as if he knew every bit of furniture in the room, silently sat down at the young man's desk. The ex-neighbor slipped into a chair.

Serge Rubinstein sat at the desk. His hat—a Homburg— was still on. "This girl is pregnant," he said, indicating the ex-neighbor. "You have been intimate with her. You have made her pregnant. We have absolute proof you did it; we have absolute proof she is pregnant. You are the father of her unborn baby. What are you going to do about it?"

There was a stunned silence. He got up from behind the desk and went and stood over the young man's fiancée. "I know all about you," he said to her. "You are from Phildelphia. Your father's first name is Alfred." He named the place her father worked, and where she had gone to college, and the day of her birth. "This man has made this girl pregnant," he said. "Your fiancé. What are you going to do?"

The fiancée pushed back into her chair. Her eyes rolled and it appeared that she was about to faint.

The young man sprang forward. "You're a lying son of a bitch!" he screamed. "I'm going to kill you! I'll kill you!" He grabbed at the black overcoat. "You get the hell out of here!"

The visitors walked toward the door. The ex-neighbor had

not said a word; the fiancée stayed in her chair. The young man followed the couple to the elevator and when the car came up he said to the operator, "If this son of a bitch ever shows his face around here ever again, you let me know. I'll beat his brains in and call the police." The elevator took the visitors down.

The young man returned to his fiancée. An hour later the doorman and the elevator man came up. "Jesus," they said. "He's been paying us five dollars a week apiece to keep an eye on you," they told the young man. All in all six elevator- and doormen were involved. It was $30 a week and it had been going on for many months.

Later still, the ex-neighbor called to apologize. She said she had not known what had been about to happen.

A month later Serge Rubinstein was found dead, murdered. As the young man's door had been open during the visit to his apartment, his yelling had been heard by several persons on his floor. And the elevator man remembered what he said. And the police found his letter in Serge Rubinstein's files. So it was that Detective William J. Whelan of the Manhattan East Homicide Squad came one day to the young man and said, "You told him you were going to kill him."

The young man, along with many, many others, had become a suspect in the case of Homicide committed upon Serge Rubinstein, who was, as the Police Department's Uniformed Force Form 61 pointed out, Male, White and 46, and who began life in a cradle identical in every way to that of the son of Czar Nicholas II, in the fortress city of Kronstadt, near St. Petersburg, in Russia.

Chapter One

Mitka

General Vladimir Sukhomlinov, the Russian Minister of War, had in 1916 fallen upon very bad times. For six years he had been in charge of the Imperial Army and had, before the beginning of the Great War, brought in much-needed reforms, improving equipment and raising officers' pay. But he had done it by foregoing the construction of expensive fortifications along the German frontier, and to those not of his coterie there was something sinister about that. When the war came the general's reluctance to build new frontier fortresses was remembered, and it began to be said in the salons of those interested in such matters that General Sukhomlinov, in addition to his wholly normal and expected sale of war contracts, was also selling out to the German enemy.

There seemed to be a good reason for the general to be much in need of moneys over and above what his position paid him. He possessed a beautiful wife, younger than he, who lived in an exceedingly extravagant way. It was the aged Sukhomlinov's pleasure to satisfy her every whim. A divorcée, she had met him when she was a schoolteacher in Kiev and he was military governor there.

In early 1916, the general's enemies moved against him. His wife's brother was murdered during a visit to a house of ill fame; his wife's lover, a colonel of the frontier guard, was shot. In addition, his principal fiscal agent was carefully shadowed. The agent, whose main duties for the general consisted in negotiating on his behalf for larger bribes from war contractors, was, like Sukhomlinov, a married man. His wife was Vera Sukhomlinov's best friend. The agent's name was Dimitri Rubinstein; his wife was the former Estelle Fichtengolz of Kharkov.

Dimitri Rubinstein met his wife when he was a student at the University of Kharkov. He was a poor boy making ends meet by tutoring other students. She was the daughter of a prosperous grain merchant running a business that had been in the family for generations. (Family legend had it that Peter the Great regularly purchased Fichtengolz grain.) When the couple announced their desire to marry, Stella's parents were not happy. They felt Dimitri was too unsettled, a charge she answered by saying that life with him would always be interesting. As the family already possessed one

15

daughter who had not found a husband, they were not anxious to end up with a second in the same circumstances. They gave in and even helped out by paying for Dimitri's studies at law school following his graduation from the university.

Dimitri did not practice law long. Instead, using his wife's dowry, he became a moneyman. The early years of his marriage were ideal for taking up such an occupation, for after centuries of economic dozing, Russia was awakening to the advent of modern capitalism. To double an investment in one year was not unusual and stock companies often paid as much as 20 per cent per year in dividends alone.

Dimitri bought real estate in the booming towns, some of which were doubling their populations every five years. He put up apartment houses and went into the insurance business in a very large way. Equally important, he began to cultivate aristocrats in need of easy loans.

In a way this was difficult but in a way it was easy because it was a traditional course for such as Dimitri Rubinstein. He was Jewish and, because of it, many roads in Russia were shut to him. He could not own agrarian land, he could not sell many articles, including liquor, he could not live in interior Russia without special permission and he was at the mercy of officials enforcing the weird and cumbersome laws, many of which were interpreted, now and then, as calling for the sudden exclusion of all Jews from a given town or area.

The way out of all of this was to become important to powerful members of the nobility, a time-honored custom celebrated by a Baltic saying which holds that "every Baron should have his Jew." Dimitri, however, was not satisfied by mere Barons. With his rapidly growing fortune, he was in a position to lend money to the highest of the high. Grand Duke Constantine became a regular borrower. So did Grand Dukes André and Boris.

With such involvements, it was not hard for the moneylender to move from the Pale of Settlement, as the areas open to Jews were called. He went with his wife to a suburb of the capital, the then-styled St. Petersburg which later, when the war came, was to be rechristened Petrograd—a more Russified name—and which now is Leningrad. From the suburbs he went to a thirty-room former Czarist castle in the best section of the city, on the same block where lived members of the highest nobility.

He and his wife maintained what in America is called an open house, but which in their time was called by a German term meaning an open castle. They gave gigantic parties. And to these parties were invited the Grand Dukes in debt to the master of the house. These gentlemen gave

16

every evidence of being unhappy to be found in the home of a Jew, and would appear for a moment, say good evening and be gone into the night. But that they would be there was known beforehand and constituted almost a royal command performance obligating other lesser members of society to be in attendance. With the other ladies and gentlemen came contacts for Dimitri Rubinstein. That this Prince had been in his home, that this Countess had drunk his champagne, meant that certain things went easier for him. Government officials came to see things Dimitri's way; business dealings were brought to him for his approval. And soon he was known all over Russia as an exceedingly rich man—perhaps the richest Jew in the country. But with his wealth, his palace, his connections at such high levels, there also came notoriety. He became the subject of a good many newspaper articles. One of them, still remembered by many who lived in St. Petersburg just before the First World War, was written by a celebrated columnist. The article was titled "We Keep Up a Woman," and although Dimitri and Stella Rubinstein were not mentioned by name, all of Petersburg—or at least all who made it their business to be acquainted with such matters—recognized who was being written about. In a café called The Wild Dog, where artists and writers gathered to entertain themselves, a song was written dealing with the columnist's story.

What had happened, according to the article and song, was that Dimitri had taken a mistress. Stella objected. Her husband explained that the girl meant nothing to him but that his position as banker, as president of insurance companies, as important man, demanded that he have a mistress —"Rothschild has one, so must I." Comforted, Stella took a liking to the girl. Wherever the Rubinsteins went, they took the girl with them and when she would arrive at their house in an elegant carriage with driver and footman, Stella pointed her out with great pride. The climax came when Stella took the girl to the family's box at the opera. During the intermissions, when the gentlemen would walk about and visit and the ladies would stay to be called upon, Stella introduced the girl to all who came, saying, "This is our protected girl." The Wild Dog song celebrated the unusual relationship—Stella and her girl.

This did not amuse Dimitri and he took the recommended way out of the difficulty, which was not to get rid of the girl and/or his wife, but rather to buy secretly into one of Petersburg's biggest newspapers in order to assure that more favorable news about himself would appear in print. He bought a large share of the *Novoye Vremya*. Almost at once word of this transaction leaked out, to the accompaniment of a tremendous hubbub. It was quite within the recognized scheme of things for influential Russians to pay regular monthly stipends to editors and reporters, and for the Imperial Government to wholeheartedly support several Paris papers, but for a Jew to suddenly walk into the life of the *Novoye Vremya* was quite another matter. Dimitri had overstepped himself. Stella was later to say it was his worst single mistake.

His popularity was not aided when, not long afterward, he was involved in a messy episode in a railroad car. Off on a business trip, Dimitri peered into a private compartment and seeing there a beautiful woman, wordlessly opened the door and flung himself upon her. It was said a considerable number of 100-ruble notes had to be passed out in all directions to avoid serious consequences of the passionate leap. Naturally the matter was fine material for disapproving gossip.

But regardless, the man's fortune was growing larger. He became St. Petersburg consul for a Balkan country—purchasing the post, as was the custom, from the responsible authorities of the country's government. He got control of several more banks and through them was able to go into large-scale stock market speculation, an endeavor just then coming into fashion in Russia. He got a Grand Duke to be a director of one of his banks, which did not hurt the institution's business, and he was made unofficial fiscal agent for several other nobles, who entrusted him with funds to invest in the stock market. He established contacts with financiers in other countries. He was an enormously successful man—later it was to be said that his fortune was the equivalent of $200,000,000—but his reputation was not as high as his finances. There was always something shady about the stories of his operations, something that savored of the back-alley method, the undercover deal. He was universally referred to as Mitka Rubinstein, the diminutive being insulting in tone. Opposed to Misha, which would have indicated affection, or Mishinka, which connoted love, the name Mitka had about it a distinct tinge of distaste and even contempt.

It was not, however, completely his fault that many of his business doings were based on bribery and "arranging" matters. Russian absolutism, harsh upon all citizens save those few who administered it, was particularly cruel in its application to the Jews. Russia was governed by an administration which looked upon its subjects as cattle to be herded. The country's citizens were in existence, it was frankly held in official circles, to provide revenue for their betters. And the betters ruled according to their own whims. The standard answer by officials to peasants protesting any arbitrary move was, "I am your God and your Czar." At a higher level, the same tone prevailed: Mitka Rubinstein was a good long way from being one of the Dark People, the peasants, but for him, also, there was no legal appeal from a ruling handed down by one of that group from whose innermost circles he was barred by virtue of his religion. There was only one way to get around the rulings based on the stupid and petty laws cornering citizens in a barbed-wire existence: bribery, the sole habeas-corpus of Russia.

This was an understood feature of Czarist life. The administrators were not well paid and it was fully expected that most of their personal revenue would derive from "arrangements" and "side issues." New laws and restrictions were continually promulgated so that new exemptions could be made—for a consideration.

Mitka Rubinstein was an expert at living in this slippery society, which demanded a remarkable ability to transfer loyalties as well as funds. In order to keep his palace and be a self-appointed member of the grandeur of Old Russia, to have the great parties and eat sitting on antique chairs from silver-laden tables, surrounded by servants in braided livery, it was necessary, mandatory, imperative, to have friends. His Imperial Highness the Grand Duke Constantine had inborn prestige that was unshakable, and withal heavy debts, while Mitka Rubinstein from Kharkov had an immense social non-acceptability, also inborn, withal ample supplies of good rubles. When you combined the two pluses and minuses of both men, you arrived at a situation where a Grand Duke was able to pluck a diamond ring from his finger and offer it to one of the charmers at Monte Carlo in exchange for her favors for the night, and a Jew was able to live on the best block in the Russian capital.

Also part of the situation, a side issue as it were, could be the friendship of such as General Vladimir Sukhomlinov and his pretty Vera. The side issue was to particularly prove a pleasant experience when the general controlled the army purchasing of a country possessing perhaps the largest gold reserves in Europe. A great deal of money could be made arranging contracts and buying and selling materials. Of course, when the war came Dimitri supported it in his way, which was to make giant donations to organizations helping wounded soldiers and shipping gifts of food to men at the front. But as in the case of a good many men of wealth in every country, soldiers killing each other far away offered a means of making more and more money. And in the lives of the Russian society people of these the last years before the Dark People rose up in revolution money was needed, for sensing that all this might soon be coming to an end, the parties were ever more glorious, the hunting trips more extravagant, and the balls more luxurious.

Mitka was in the forefront of all of this, in his way. He lacked entrée to a great many other palaces, but yet his own home attracted the owners of those barred places.

Then one day Sukhomlinov was arrested and charged with malfeasance, corruption, treason. The army police came for him and he found himself, like the French aristocrats of that country's Revolution, being carted through the streets to be shown to a public which jeered and hooted. The general went to a cell in the Fortress of St. Peter and St. Paul. The jail chosen for his fiscal agent was in a nearby city, Pskov.

Chapter Two

Stella

Stella Rubinstein was not a pretty woman. Her movements were graceless and all her life she suffered from a weight problem. In addition, she did not speak well; she was always confusing words and then mouthing them out in a fashion that made people think she was grinding her teeth or chewing on something while she talked. But she was not stupid. For all that fashionable St. Petersburg called her Madame Mitka Malaprop, she was a steady reader and lecture-goer. When during July and August she and her husband went to Carlsbad to take the baths, she was often pointed out by the Germans and Czechs as an example of how intelligent wealthy Russian women were.

She was an active woman, always rushing to the opera and shops (where she was known as the woman who always said she spent more money on clothing than anyone else in Russia), to concerts, to parties. It was well for her husband that she possessed this intelligence and ability to act. For when the word came that Dimitri was in prison, likewise General Sukhomlinov, and that the world appeared to be coming to an end, Stella knew what to do about the situation and immediately did it.

She took in hand a great sum of money and made for a building in an unfashionable section of Petrograd and went up several flights of steps and down a long musty hall which led to a large and crowded apartment.

This was the home of Grigori Rasputin, the famous Mad Monk then at the height of his immense power. In his apartment each day he sat holding court surrounded by women in velvet and diamonds, officers in Guards uniforms, and peasants wearing mud-covered boots. Mumbling incoherent bits and snatches of the Bible, whispering of life in his native Siberia, of the beauty of the trees and flowers and the simplicity of the country folk, dropping bits of sugar from filthy fingers into the tea of his visitors—this was deemed a kind of blessing of the waters—he was the actual ruler of Russia. He had come to this position by virtue of the semi-hysterical cast of mind of the Czarina, the former Princess Alix of Hesse-Darmstadt, now the Czarina Alexandra Feodorovna. She was accounted at least partially insane even as a young married woman and her condition had not improved with the years. A mystic-minded soul, she had at one time or another consulted numerous occult practitioners of whom the most important was Rasputin, the itinerant holy man (self-ordained) who washed irregularly—*very* irregularly—drank almost continuously, and possessed unlimited ability to seduce any woman coming his way. (He preferred women of the upper classes because, he said, they "smelled better" than any others.) This dramatic person came the Czarina's way shortly after the birth of a son, heir to the Throne, who suffered from hemophilia and general nervousness. As Rasputin seemed the only person who could calm him when he was agitated—he would mutter spells and chants and look at the child with hypnotic eyes—he soon became indispensable to life in the Czar's household. It was not only his aid to the boy that made him so meaningful to the Czarina. It was also his wild philosophical-religious orientation which fed her own strong inclinations in such directions. She believed he could predict the future, that he was in constant contact with the Beyond, that he symbolized all that was good in the strange and mystic land she conceived Russia to be. She came to depend upon him in all matters, as in parallel fashion her weak and irresolute husband depended upon her.

Rasputin was the right person for the petitioning Stella Rubinstein to see. No Grand Duke could help her now, for the matter of her husband's imprisonment was too tied in with important trends in the war, with the very life of the monarchy, for anyone save the Czar to be effective in dealing with Dimitri's freedom or continued incarceration. Certainly there was no legal way to deal with the matter, for there was no legality as the West understands the term. Legality did not exist in Russia, either for the nobility, which was above law, nor for the radicals at the other end of the scale, who lived by terrorism and bank robbing.

Rasputin received her. It is possible the two had met before, for Mitka was one of what were called the monk's "clients" and had often given Rasputin money in exchange for tips about what the government was going to do next in a

21

given situation. Although the monk was not interested in amassing a fortune, he did need operating funds, and these were supplied by such as Dimitri or other highly placed men equipped to take advantage of inside information. Later on, after the monk's death, and after the Rubinstein family left Russia, it was to be said that Mitka was Rasputin's main financial adviser, but this was an exaggeration of the relationship between the two. It was not the only lily-gilding indulged in by those who fled the Dark People running wild in the streets.

During the meeting, money was certainly passed between Stella and Rasputin. And when one considers the monk's normal approach to women, it is likely that other, more personal, activities were undertaken by the two. If such was the case, Stella was only one of hundreds of women who tarried with the monk, whose scrambled mumblings generally included discussions of how poor mortals must seek redemption of the spirit by debasement of the flesh.

But there was nothing secret about Stella's visit. All her friends knew of the pilgrimage to the shrine of the holy man and she often talked about it (in generalities) during later years. She could be quite proud of what she had done, for her visit, coupled with one by Vera Sukhomlinov, soon caused two new names to frequently crop up in converse between the Czarina and the Czar. One was Vera's last name and the other was Stella's.

We know today exactly what the Czarina said to the Czar about Dimitri Rubinstein because it is all in writing. The two were forced to communicate via the mail because of the Czar's foolish insistence that he take to the field to command the Imperial Army. While he did his limited best, she stayed behind, attending to matters at home and consulting with Rasputin, whom she referred to as Our Friend, before she made a move. The letters between Nicholas and his wife were written in English, which was the language in which they generally spoke to each other. (Educated Russians of those days reserved the country's tongue for servants.)

It is fortunate for an English-speaking reader that the letters are written in his language, for their essence cannot be captured by translation. How would one render in another language such phrases as "Me loves oo" or "Wify misses her big Huzy" or "Manny man, boysy boy, oodles of kisses from me to you"—all of which and many more of similar sentiment are laced through the Imperial writings?

On September 22, 1916, some five months after the arrests of their husbands, when the uproar about the War Minister was somewhat forgotten, the donations of Vera and Stella began to pay off. On that day the Czarina wrote the Czar from the Imperial Palace at Tsarskoe Selo, outside Petrograd: ". . . . Then Our Friend said, 'General Sukhomlinov should be set free so that he should not die in jail, otherwise things will not be smooth. One should never fear to release prisoners, to restore sinners to a life of righteousness; prisoners until they reach jail become through their sufferings in the eyes of God nobler than we.' "

Four days later, referring to an incoming Minister of the Interior, a half-mad old fellow now believed to have been suffering from an advanced case of syphilis, she wrote: "Protopopov has asked to see you—won't you tell him to let Sukhomlinov out, he says it can of course be done at once . . . And also speak to him about Rubinstein to have him quietly sent to Siberia, not left here to aggravate the Jews. Protopopov quite agrees with the way Our Friend looks on this question. Protopopov thinks it was Gutchkov [1] who must have egged on the military to catch the man, hoping to find evidence against Our Friend. Certainly he had ugly money affairs—but not he alone."

The next day again referring to Protopopov, from whom a disagreement with anything Rasputin said was highly unlikely, he owing his appointment as Minister of the Interior to the monk: "Speak to him about Sukhomlinov, he will find means of doing it—the old man will die else in prison & we shall never be at peace about it. Then speak about Rubinstein, he will know what to do." She ended the letter with a list of six things for Nicholas to do. Point One was: "Sukhomlinov, order to find a way to get him out." Point Two: "Rubinstein to send away."

By October 31, she had decided against sending Mitka away—which would have in no way "aggravated the Jews" —and was agitating for him to be handed over to Protopopov. The urgency in her tone speaks of the desire of the monk to fulfill the bargain made with Mesdames Sukhomlinov and Rubinstein. The Czarina wrote: "Lovy dear, Our Friend begs you absolutely to have this Sukhomlinov story stopped. Telegraph this: 'Having got acquainted with the preliminary investigation in the case of the former Minister of War, Gen. Sukhomlinov, I find that there are absolutely no grounds at all for the charges, and therefore the case should be discontinued.' Then about Rubinstein, the man is dying.[2] Wire or

---

[1] Ex-president of the Duma (Parliament) and chief enemy of the Czarina and Rasputin.

[2] Mitka may have been dying to get back to his palace; in other respects his health was of the finest.

give Alexiev [3] the order at once to wire to Ruzsky [4] to give over Rubinstein from Pskov to the Minister of the Interior (best you wire yourself) then he will do all at once."

Her next letter, November 1, ended with: "Ever yr. very own Wify. Hope you wire about dying Rubinstein."

Two days later, beginning with "Sweetheart, beloved One," she said: "Lovy, have you had Rubinstein given over to the Minister of the Interior—otherwise he will die, still at Pskov. Please, dear. Now, lovebird, I must end, the man must go. Blessings and kisses without end from yr. very, very Own."

The next day Mitka was set free. The general had left his cell a couple of days earlier. Both went back to their homes, the general to his Vera, Dimitri to his Stella, her mother, who lived with them, her sister, who also lived with them, and to his two sons: his elder, André, and his younger— Serge.

Chapter Three

Revolution

When the Russian Revolution had run its course a great and beautiful dream took hold of many of those who had fled from the mobs shooting down Nevski Prospekt and wandering through the Winter Palace. The dream was that before, before all of that, the red flags and dead officers in the gutters, they who had fled had lived their lives in a special way that no one in Paris or Rome could ever know: that at dinner they had eaten fish and fruits and meats far better than what the West could serve, that at the drinking parties of the officers—at the end of the night the Colonel was tossed up and caught—the champagne was finer, the brandy smoother. Everything was better. There was stag hunting with huntsmen and flaring torches and winding horns, Caucasian festivals with great bonfires burning in the hills and wild music sounding for the gypsy dancers, wonderful *zakuska* (hors d'oeuvres) at suppers after the balls where the Grand Duchesses danced the night through, the blazing diamond stars on their red ribbon Orders of Catherine the Great catching the light from the many chandeliers hanging from high ceilings.

Beyond the great gates of the palace with its noblemen buttoning gloves and twisting mustache ends, with footmen carrying braziers of incense down long corridors, was Russia,

[3] The Chief of Staff at the Czar's headquarters.

[4] The general commanding the Northern Front, which included the city of Pskov.

with steeplechasers rising to the barrier before the Imperial Pavilion, with great roses growing in vines on the roofs of Crimean mansions, with hall porter and sledge driver and peasant. "We wish good health to Your Excellency!"

So the dream, true for a good number of those who fled. There is a Russian song which says that things past are always sweet; what will have gone by will be sweet to us.

If the memory of a fall from high estate (which became the more impressive after leaving it) did not apply to all who after the Revolution learned in far-off places to call themselves Count, Prince, owner of many acres, at least it applied to Dimitri and Stella Rubinstein and their entourage. This group was composed of two children and four adults. For Dimitri Rubinstein always used to say he married three women: Stella, her sister Eugenia, and their mother. The mother, quite old, wrote poems. After she died her "The Pink Carnation" was set to music by the Russian composer Alexander Grechanivov; he dedicated it to Genia. Genia herself, so different from Stella, was to live on when all the others, grandparent, parents, both sons, were dead. All her long life she had but one interest: music. She had no romances, no real life beyond her visits to the opera and the teachers who gave her singing lessons almost to the day she died.

One great experience belonged to the sweet, butterfly type of person Genia always was. Once at the Imperial Opera in Petersburg, the Maryinski Theatre, she was invited to sing the title role in Serov's *Judith* opposite Russia's greatest singer, Feodor Chaliapin. At the time of the great proposal Genia was a student who had never sung with an orchestra or stood upon a stage and when one thinks about it it does seem strange that she should have been asked to sing with the immortal Chaliapin. Some of those who did think about it knew Genia's brother-in-law and they decided that Dimitri must have donated something very large to a favorite charity of the singer. But in any event—and it was a story Genia still loved to tell half a century after the event—the more she thought about singing opposite Chaliapin, the more terrified she became. Finally she flung up her arms and fell back in a dead faint. "So I never got to sing with him!" she would cry out years later and with tears in her eyes and elbows akimbo she would put her hands to her face and sway back and forth. No one who ever met her stayed the first fifteen minutes in her company without hearing of the famous drop to the Maryinski floor. (But her faint wasn't the complete end of the world, for Chaliapin grew fond of her and even gave her his picture with a kind inscription on it: *"To a sister-soul of an artist."* And he often came to the Rubinstein home.)

Even as Genia talked of her great moment, so did Stella,

forever looking back, remember her great pearl necklace, her beautiful clothes, how the wet nurse she used for her sons was regularly employed by several Grand Ducal families, and of course how those sons spent their first moments in the cradle exactly duplicating that of the Czar's son. As far as her marriage itself, half a century later, it was hard to say whether she and her husband were happy together during those their great days. But it is easy to say what their marriage was in its relationship to the outside world. Each offered the other a great amount of aid in facing that world, which was Old Russia. Stella must have been happy to be married to so eminent a man and Dimitri must have been happy to have a wife who so fully understood the position they both were in, which was to be operatives caught between many struggling factions seeking a place in the sun during the twilight of Czarism. Were they to slip, all the power and money would go almost at once—God knows disaster of a permanent type was close at hand when Stella went to Rasputin—and they would be what were the overwhelming number of Jews in the Russian Empire—fearsome, unsettled, always as the saying went with one foot booted, ready to flee, and existing with the most tremendous uncertainty and with the picture of the traditional government-sponsored pogroms well in mind. Other Jews in their synagogues forced by law to end all services by saying "Bless the Czar" might instead under their breaths say Damn, but it was a slight revenge and protection. Dimitri and Stella were better armed, for where Grand Dukes Constantine and Boris and André had been, the pogroms were not apt to come.

For such as they who were among the few fortunate Jews raised above the lowest level where lived the vast majority, for they of the moneyed Jewish intellectual class, it was the most typical characteristic to seek the power of influence and of name, to be able to get your box at the opera and money out of the country (a call from the right person to the right office: "The banker Rubinstein comes to see you; do everything for him"), to have, if for only a moment, a Prince and Grand Duke in your home.

To live in Petersburg when other Jews were in the Pale meant to be safe from the frequent "punitive expeditions" sent to quell disturbances, which saw columns of soldiery appear with bayonet and rifle. "Ninety-five per cent of those killed were Jews," Nicholas casually wrote to his mother after one such expedition along the Moscow-Kazan railroad line where the colonel commanding lived up to his orders to "take no prisoners and act mercilessly." To the cossack troopers sabers and whips were meant, after all, for those who, as the Czarina was fond of remarking "showed Christ no mercy."

Dimitri and Stella functioned all their lives in Russia in such a power-oriented atmosphere, where there were numerous stories of past Czars who regularly slapped their ministers in the face, who in turn slapped their underlings until it reached down to the peasant who beat his wife. Nicholas was not a man to slap ministers around, for the famous Romanov brusqueness was not a physical matter with him, but the tradition of force physical or mental did not die because the Czar was not handy with his fists. It had been in Russia too long.

Serge Rubinstein was only a month past his tenth birthday when he saw Russia for the last time, but as psychologists figure, he was old—formed. He had seen his world and understood it. Many years later there was a story he often used to tell with the great vivacity and zest which were always his. He had been walking near his home, he would say, when he came upon a street fight. One man was beating another. A group of onlookers had gathered and one of them addressed the man doing the beating. "Go ahead, harder," the spectator shouted. "Beat him harder; he is much stronger than he looks. *I know because he is my friend!*" The grown Serge Rubinstein would laugh after he flung out the punch line. In Russia you are the ally only of the strongest, he would explain. You must not believe Russians are consistently friendly. "I know it because he is my friend. . . ."

But the time came when no power position counted, nor rank, nor even money. Revolution was upon Russia. Czar Nicholas II abdicated his three-hundred-year-old throne and lived to see the day when the Grand Duke Cyril marched with a red flag hanging from his buttonhole and then, after a while, went with the Czarina and their children to his fate in a cellar at Ekaterinburg where an execution squad did its duty with rifle and bayonet. In February 1918, Dimitri, still reluctant to believe, took leave for Sweden, flying across the frozen water in a sledge. The women and two boys stayed behind through the difficult days of spring. Food was scarce and now and then there was shooting in the streets. They went to their country home where Stella worried about her Petrograd palace and its treasures. They came back—Stella wanted to put everything in the basement vaults—and as they entered their home a file of ragged Bolshevik soldiers followed them past the deserted gatekeepers' posts. Stella's arms were filled with the family gold plate when she saw the first soldier. There was no conversation. She had delivered the plate to the Dark People.

They stayed on in Petrograd. Their car was taken and their coach horses, all save one skinny, sickly animal. Chaliapin was singing, though, and to Genia that was still important and so they drove through the deserted streets to hear him. An Imperial Army ex-colonel was along for protection, a revolver in his hand. He held one arm around Genia to make sure her coat was secure. "I am only risking my life," he said, "but should you lose your coat you would be risking your voice." Genia never forgot it.

Chaliapin was touched to see them and the next day he came for dinner. The markets were long since closed and the food in the iceboxes confiscated and they were trading velvet curtains for a pound of butter, a carpet for a bit of flour brought by peasants from outside the city. But Dimitri's friends in Sweden had that day gotten through a package of food and so they dined well for the last time in Russia. The family nurse produced two bottles of champagne she had hidden under her clothing in an old trunk, so they were able to drink this last time to yesterday. They sat by a boiling samovar into the dawn. But by then it was time to go forever. Dimitri returned and in June they were gone, to Sweden. Money was sewn into their coats; around the boy Serge's neck, on a leather thong, hung a giant emerald later sold for the equivalent of $20,000. But at the frontier they were stopped and Bolshevik guards arrested Dimitri. Later, Serge was to say that his brother André denounced their father to the guards, but later there was nothing Serge would not say about André. Dimitri was taken away but Stella was still Stella. She had defeated the usual way of life of Czarist Russia; now she would defeat Revolutionary Russia. The troops were going to execute Dimitri right there by the halted train but Stella reached their commander with that which made him take pause and change his mind. Dimitri was released; they went on their way past the frontier and away from what had once been home. In later years Stella was to amend the story and say the commander had as a youth worked in a bakeshop in the city of her childhood where each day he saw her passing by only to remember her in 1918 when he took occasion to let her husband go.

But they were safe, whatever the reason. Sweden was not home but Dimitri had good connections there. He would not have been a good banker, had he no money abroad. He also owned a share in a Swedish insurance company which forty years later would still be paying a monthly remittance to Stella's New York bank.

So now they were refugees, *émigrés*. Persons in exile was the term they used. All over Europe now, while the Rubinsteins settled in Sweden, the gentry of Russia were on the run and on the make. Money gone, untrained for anything but the life of aristocracy, they filtered into Western Europe and China to found their White Russian colonies. In Paris the men came to dominate two professions: taxi-driver and gigolo. The cabbies, of course, were not Count or Prince to the fares ordering them to drive to Maxim's. But inside Maxim's and the great hotels other Russians held forth to the rich women going to *thé dansants* seeking someone young and handsome and most elegant and fluent in several languages. And on the Mediterranean cruise ships the reception officers anxious to dance with the tourist ladies were always sure to find ready listeners to their stories of the great summer reviews of the Imperial Army at Krasnoe and of the dances in the Winter Palace's Salle de Nicholas. Princess and Countess and wife of Governor-General modeled clothes. But the Rubinsteins were luckier.

Chapter Four

Vienna

Scandinavia has a life all its own, different from Europe or European Russia, and Stockholm was not for Dimitri Rubinstein and his party. They lingered there a year and a half as travelers passing through, ever looking backward to where they had come from, where now everyone was Comrade. It seemed the Bolsheviks were in control to stay, and abroad the price of the Czarist ruble dropped lower every day. *Émigrés* who had smuggled bills out somehow were selling now for any price in any currency. Dimitri had Swedish money. He bought rubles.

The war ended; the civil war in Russia warmed up. British money financed White armies which were sent against the Reds, and Allied troops were ashore in Murmansk and Vladivostok. If you cared very much, you could come to believe in a White victory that would make everything as it had been. The *émigrés* cared very much. They rushed to buy back rubles to spend when soon, very soon, they would return in glory to their homes. Dimitri sold them back their rubles—at a profit.

The civil war went on and a great White drive on Moscow began, mounted by the former Czarist General Anton Denikin. Dimitri had known Denikin for years and so he made his way back to Russia for the last time, to the general's headquarters where he was appointed finance minister of the army. The job mostly meant that Dimitri was in charge of the general's treasure chest, filled with British pound notes, during this last fling of the Russian aristocracy on their own soil. Top-heavy with officers wearing their old Imperial uniforms and talking about the traditions whereby regimental officers led the first wave of attack, Denikin's army went to its destruction before Moscow. After that, of course, there was no hope left for the *émigrés* and in Sweden and hundreds of other places the rubles became worthless. But in Denikin's treasure chest were good pounds of sterling that had suddenly become Dimitri's. The White army was gone and Denikin and his officers scattered away, but Dimitri had the chest and the British money. He returned to Sweden, gathered up his family and went south.

They went to Vienna. It was 1920. The Great War was two years ended and with it the Austro-Hungarian Empire, gone to become a multitude of little countries spread over central Europe. The government employees who had administered those countries came flooding back to the Austrian capital, the great metropolitan head now without a body to go with it. They came back from Prague, Cracow, and Budapest and milled about the halls of the enormous government buildings along the Ringstrasse, great buildings with immense statuary, the Ministry of War, of Justice, of This, of That. There were no jobs in the government for them any more and no work to be done in the great buildings even more impressive than those of London. Lost along with the jobs were the vast markets of the Austro-Hungarian Empire and with those the business opportunities that once had been. The ancient, almost perennial Emperor Franz Josef was dead and his successor fled, and the Austro-Hungarian war bonds with double-headed eagles were all as valueless as if once a nation and its investors had not thought them as secure as surely the Hapsburg monarchy would always be. Austria was going down hill. The hundred-year-old business based upon Austrian patronage and Austrian money slowly started to retrench as it needs must do to exist in the tiny land which now it served, and its employees in turn cut their own expenditures, and soon everything was falling down and everyone was trying to make a penny by doing any old thing, selling, buying, scrabbling, digging, and cheating with gypsy orchestras in the background. Austria, which meant Vienna, was hungry, but for four years the city had been dim and without the great balls and now the people wanted to dance, to live, to do, to see, to be reminded that if the youth of the country had gone to its death in the trenches then at least not everyone was finished with life. The old world of Austria was not with them any more but their new one had not quite arrived and so it became a time of the most elaborate of moments with the greatest of masquerade balls at which the girls wore beautiful gowns and covered their faces and the gentlemen wore frock coats. It was a time for doing sudden foolish things to prove you were gay in spite of all. Crazy Rose sold flowers in the Ring and a man without a job might suddenly take it upon himself to buy all her roses and put her and them into a carriage to send to a girl. In the night clubs it was chic at midnight to fling glasses into the mirrors on the walls, to pay with a laugh for the shattered glass.

Vienna was hungry and getting hungrier. Every day in those first years after the war there were new business failures and new, reluctant extensions of credit. On every corner where there was a coffee shop there suddenly appeared a bank which lent too much, went too far, failed and disappeared. The next week the coffee shop would be back. Vienna in its sudden need, so different from what had been, began to sell what it had: the silver service, the fur coat, the antiques. Then came furniture and engagement ring, although when you went with your new sad money past the great marble entrance halls of the large department stores you found only the shoddiest goods for sale. Bearing the names of Austria's most distinguished manufacturers, they yet were produced by men who had to cut costs or die. In the great restaurants built once to serve the finest of Viennese specialties, the food was barely edible.

There were no jobs. The lawyer's coat slowly turned shabby; the doctor's white jacket grew raveled at the sleeves and collar. In the coffee house the waiter whose pockets were once filled with bills found instead that his old honored patrons preferred to pay in IOU's. With it all, with splitting an egg— half for the soup, half for the dough—came the devaluation of money, inflation, deflation, bank crashes, trade barriers and more trade barriers until the one hundred Swiss francs which in 1919 would bring 567 Austrian kronen brought 360,000 in 1922.

Finally Vienna was starving, her streets filled with beggars and undernourished children. Borrowing became a way of life for everyone, imposed upon anyone with any money left, catered to by special societies set up to advise those "in financial difficulties through no fault of their own." Not paying your bills was no longer considered unusual—no one paid bills. A song of the times asked how do people live, how do people live? and the answer was by selling, by selling. A man might be down to one suit and that a shabby one but somehow he found something to sell: alleged influence, his wife's body, a car he did not own—anything. And what did he sell for? Not for the Austrian kronen or the German mark. He sold for real money, for blooded money, for thoroughbred money—for valuta. And what was valuta? It was the American dollar, steady, unwavering, dependable, God to the black market's King. Or it was the British pound.

Dimitri Rubinstein had supplies of the latter. And with

31

pounds you could buy dollars in Trieste or Lisbon and you could come to Vienna and buy whatever you wanted. Everything was rationed but for valuta everything could be arranged. The night clubs might close early to save on coal and electricity but afterward on the sidewalks outside you would find people asking you to their homes, there to do what you could with whom you might. Everything was ridiculously cheap to him who had such money; nothing was beyond his reach in business or pleasure. And so Dimitri, perfectly equipped by training and profession, became what was called a *faiseur,* a *macher,* a *schieber.* This was a class of men born in the aftermath of the war when all values and institutions in middle Europe were coming apart and governments were corrupt and everything was for sale. The type of man had existed before, operating through illicit commissions and bribery and dealing in foreign exchanges through his knowledge of inside information about government moves. But before such men had represented solid companies, usually armament concerns. If in the Balkans (and elsewhere) army orders were placed only after the proper persons had been "seen" and "royalties" paid, still the armament salesmen were representing great corporations. An agent might say to a Turkish official that he understood Bulgaria was placing an order for 100,000 rifles and it would be true. He had understood it because he himself had sold Bulgaria the rifles, just as he would now sell Turkey a like amount. Or such a man might learn through his contacts in the army intelligence services of various nations that Greece was buying three submarines, and immediately fly to the Italian Navy with the news. At least the man sold and delivered and worked for Krupp or Vickers—that was something solid. But suddenly in the capitals of the defeated monarchies, Berlin and Vienna, appeared men who represented only themselves. Somehow they had gotten access to valuta and with this that was so fantastically valuable as opposed to German or Austrian money, such men became masters of great enterprises not founded upon solid foundations. During the war it was impossible because there existed after all a wave of patriotism, a discipline and some controls. But afterward all that was swept away along with traditional art forms, music, architecture, social strata—along with many things, along with all that which in time would be called in Europe the good old days of before 1914. The men with valuta functioned for a very short time, until in the middle 1920s financial stability of a kind arrived and the great inflations ended. The Dawes and Young plans were put into effect and regulatory agencies created which enforced more stringent currency restrictions and so made it logical that the traditional business leaders would again take control. By the late '20s the debtor countries were no longer fertile for such men; many in fact had been selling short and holding options and building upon so precarious a base that the re-establishment of normal business practices wiped them out.

But during their few years of tremendous success their way of life rivaled that of the vanished Hapsburgs and Hohenzollerns. The way they lived—they had palaces, but only historic palaces. There was a mistress, but who was the mistress? A Countess, a Duchess. There were chamberlains for them, and stock loans, footmen and bought ministers of state, liveried servants and planted newspaper stories about impending wonders; there was money smuggled across borders and jewels smuggled the other way, stock sales, secrets, rumors, a special way of life born of their knowledge that theirs was a kind of Caribbean situation with the people in power not knowing how long they would be there. In a place and at a time when normal business life meant to lose all, when doctors ran, or tried to run, employment agencies, and dentists sold land, the great man of valuta was supreme.

Dimitri moved his family into a palace, Villa Chaire, which he rented from an Austrian Count. It had been built for the lover of a Hapsburg ruler and stood in a park bordering the grounds of the Imperial summer residence of Schoenbrunn. It had magnificent gardens and beautiful gates. Dimitri was a great *faiseur;* in the street he stopped old friends and cried, "I have deposited a billion! To buy a bank!" and went each day to his Commerce and Discount Bank on Wipplingerstrasse where for him all was hustle and bustle and lending and borrowing and special leased wires to the floor of the stock exchange and shares shooting up on inflation money. He was often away from home—Stella took up with a friend to see her to the opera and the shops; the man would still be with her thirty years later—and he became known in Claridge's (where he arranged with the headwaiter once to be seated next to the table of the Prince of Wales), and in Berlin and the Balkans, buying, selling, bringing people together on deals. He bought an abandoned channel outside of Vienna and announced via willing newspapers (for valuta who was not willing for what?) that he was rejuvenating the channel and would build giant hydroelectric power stations while he was at it. The shares of the company shot up and then collapsed, as shares did in Vienna in those days. His bank closed, as banks did, and he opened another in Berlin. In time it too collapsed. Away from Russia his touch was gone and although for the short period of Austria's frenzy he lived in the greatest style, he would die with very little.

Meanwhile, his sons were growing up. Serge was twelve when the family went to Vienna and he was enrolled in the Goethe Realschule. On his first day there he was driven to school in a chauffeur-driven limousine and when he got out the other boys saw he had very long hair with curls and was wearing, in the Russian fashion, a blue sailor suit. During the recess between classes the new boy was made the general laughingstock. In a day or so both long hair and nautical outfit disappeared but the memory of the class hooting stayed on so that decades later the grown man was able to say that the boys never did accept him and that his school days were miserable. (In the crowd, however—very quiet, for he was always quiet—was one boy, Theodore Schulz, later to be important in his life.)

The school was a technical high school but Serge, totally uninterested in technical subjects—afternoons Teddy Schulz would tutor him in physics, geometry, and chemistry—went to it because to go to a regular high school for a degree meant an extra year's matriculation. He did very well in French and history and he played tennis a lot. But economics was his pet subject and at fourteen and fifteen he would give Teddy long lectures about how things should be done in the world. At home, Dimitri was fond of telling his two sons that they were all on alien ground and that to make their way up in the world would be terribly difficult but they must try. The boys did try, in competition with each other. They used to buy old iron and sell the parts, and somehow Serge always did better than André. But in Dimitri's eyes the older son was the more promising—or at least that was the way Serge saw it. "My father," he said later, "pronounced my brother a financial genius at the age of eleven. I could never see what he saw in André." Already, perhaps, there were the beginnings of that great hatred which would later exist between them, which André would say stemmed from Serge's greed and which Serge would attribute to a fall on his head that André took from a Shetland pony when he was a boy.

Serge was getting his weekly allowance in British money and going out a great deal to night clubs and theaters where the possession of valuta insured a joyous welcome, but he was often quarrelsome and frequently fell into moods of depression. And his school work was not getting any better. It worried his mother and she decided to send him to a psychiatrist. To treat her son she selected Dr. Alfred Adler, founder of an entire school of psychology and inventor of the concept of the inferiority complex. Aged fifteen, Serge went to see Adler.

In later years those who heard the story got the impression that Serge and Adler met as absolute equals and that Serge found no use for Adler in his life. Adler might have seen it differently, but as Serge told it, Adler spoke with him for four hours straight—actually Adler never conferred with a patient for more than one hour at a sitting—and then told him he was a neurotic who could be cured at a price, and that the price would be that he forfeit his opportunity to be a great man in the world. "As you are now," Serge quoted Adler as saying, "you will be driven by ambitions and desires all your life, forever reaching out for bigger things and grabbing them whenever you find them. This is your way of compensating for your inferiority complex.

"But," Adler went on—according to the later Serge Rubinstein telling the story—"if I cure you of the consuming complex that's pushing and pulling you, you'll be an ordinary person. Which do you prefer? Do you want to be a healthy person but an average man? Or do you want to keep your inferiority complex, stay neurotic for the rest of your life and ride the high horse of your ambitions and desires?"

Serge's reply, as he related it, was that there should be no cure—greatness was better. But then he began to study psychology and became very much at home in its terms and schools. (That he should later tell the Adler story in so unsubtle a manner—for the psychiatrist would hardly have spoken in such a soap opera fashion—indicated Serge's desire to simplify the incident for unsophisticated listeners. But no lack of sophistication could prevent a hearer from grasping the implied point that from the session emerged a man marked for, nay, stricken with greatness.)

He was going out more and more. He had a romance with the daughter of an inflation-ruined Count in Bratislava, across the Czech border, and, armed with his valuta, looking older than he was, a rather good-looking teen-ager despite his moon face and tendency toward plumpness, he went several times a week to the night clubs of Vienna where in chorus lines danced little girls in whom, as in all Austria, the remembrances of the great past lived on. For such as they, the hazy dream was of the Archduke who comes to woo the dancer at the Imperial ballet. They were not ballerinas and Serge Rubinstein was no Archduke, but then, the days of Archdukes were over and without a title he yet had something much more valuable in the Vienna of the '20s. His plans for the future were not really formed, it seems, but he talked a lot about how as a dictator elite was slated to one day rule the world, he intended to be of the group. Sitting in the gardens of his parents' home he was able to talk with adults on their level about this dictator elite which would exist all over the world, above law as the Grand Dukes had been above law in Russia. The future would belong to it; there could be no doubt.

Meanwhile all around Villa Chaire Vienna refused to answer its telephone—it could only be the creditors calling yet again—and then the telephone was taken out for nonpayment and Vienna walked most carefully wherever it went, for standing before half a dozen coffee houses were the waiters told yesterday that today, without fail, the bill would be paid. Middle-class Vienna, or what had been middle-class Vienna, took to staying indoors while the one white shirt was being washed, and the founding of businesses based upon the hope that after the inevitable failure there would be something coming from the Law of Settlement became endemic, and those on unemployment relief became a great power, for there were so many of them. At Villa Chaire, Dimitri and Stella spoke longingly of their great days in Russia, giving out that they lived in the fashion of the Russian overlords for whom the divine right of kings applied. It was always Russia, Russia, where everything was different and better. (The famous cradle copied from the Czar was made of imported wood inlaid with gold and above it was a canopy of Venetian lace; the caviar served at table was only of the rarest; where could you ever find railroad cars to compare with those wonderful ones made in Riga and used in the night train from Petersburg to Moscow?)

Allen Gordon Foster came into Serge's life. A handsome man—all through those years, his friends later said, he had been known as one of the handsomest men in Europe—he was Scottish. His father had died when he was very young, leaving an income not quite large enough to allow the boy to live as what was called a gentleman in Great Britain at the turn of the century. Foster was sent to Paris where he had access to what he would call "the greatest houses" and schooled in art under the direction of a French clergyman made his guardian. He lived in a studio where one day the clergyman found him in bed with a model. The clergyman suggested a tour of the Continent; a horse cab took him to the station and he went to Italy where for a few pence he purchased the drawings of those somber students seen sketching the doorways of every great chathedral. The sketches went back to Paris to enchant the clergyman with his ward's progress. Time passed and Foster came back to Paris. He had not got, in the British phrase, enough to live without work, so he looked around for the right job. He found it in the household of a retired Russian general living in the French capital. The officer needed a man to run his place; Foster was the man. The general's table served food only worthy of royalty; they had the rarest fish sent from Russia—it was so delicate, he would remember; the Americans have nothing like it—they had everything.

The general died; he was very old. It was just before the First World War. There were no relatives at hand and Foster took charge of taking the body back to Russia. There was a special train with guards of honor from each country taking their positions as the train passed the frontiers. The general possessed the highest decorations of each country; it was his right to have such guards standing by his coffin rolling back to the motherland. At the funeral in Petersburg, Foster walked beside the German military attaché there, a giant of a man wearing his helmet with the Hohenzollern eagle rearing its head toward the sky, and then went to hear the reading of the will. The late general had not forgotten him and left him vast timber lands along the Finnish frontier. It was forbidden for a foreigner to own lands on the border but a special dispensation was made by the Czar and Foster stayed in Petersburg to marry a Russian Princess, to be active in theater work, to go to the opera where one night a Grand Duchess invited him to her box and then to her home and her bedroom with walls of red brocade and great white bearskins covering every inch of the floor. Afternoons in his home he used to have Russian ladies in to eat of his English plumcake.

He had "dozens of Khrushchevs" on his estates and years later he would tell the mild Teddy Schulz that he owned three villages of Jews, but he never learned to speak Russian because in Petersburg it was only necessary to speak French at home and at the parties he attended—some of which were given by Dimitri Rubinstein. The war came and he planned to join Russia's Wild Brigade but didn't; he was still thinking about it when the revolution was upon them all. He took his wife and son and his wife's mother and went to Yalta where he sat with other helpless refugees soon to become *émigrés* or, for the most part, corpses, and saw out in the harbor a warship lying at anchor flying the Union Jack. Somehow he got hold of a jacket that looked something like that worn by British naval officers and had himself rowed out to the ship. His gentleman's accent and vague nautical look impressed the ratings standing by the rail and he was taken to a large salon where the captain sat upon a raised stage playing Chopin on a concert piano. Foster stood in respectful silence until the captain finished with a crash and, noticing him for the first time, asked, "What did you think of it?" Foster said it was magnificent. The captain was very happy and said Foster and his party might sail with him to Constantinople. The city was filled with loot and murder; Russians there who had gotten out money or jewels went about saying fearfully to one

37

another that they'd be murdered here. Foster went into the business of smuggling things across Europe to Paris, and so it was that on a layover in Vienna he got word that Dimitri was ensconced in a great palace with parties and free-running liquor.

After that Foster always stopped by on his trips through the city packed with Russian *émigrés* and new-made swindlers—and gentlemen such as himself. One night he went to Villa Chaire to find Dimitri and Stella were just going out. "Serge will take you to dinner," Dimitri said, and Foster and the sixteen-year-old went to the Bristol, Vienna's finest hotel, where Serge asked about how a gentleman should dress and how one should act in company and about the manners of a man of the world. Foster lectured him at length about what hat to wear on what occasions, about the way of a gentleman, and while he was at it, also let him in on a little deal he was promoting which had to do with some cultured pearls an *émigré* had brought back from England, the first, according to Foster, seen on the Continent. The *émigré* had bought them from a Japanese who had just brought them out from the Orient, and Foster had gotten them from the *émigré* and now he was going to give them over to Serge with the advice that the innocent-looking youth take them to pawn at the Vienna pearl center which was similar to the New York diamond center, with the resultant profits to be split down the line. Foster had paid the *émigré* perhaps $100 for the cultured pearls and he reckoned Serge could pawn them for perhaps $5000. He went on his way saying he would pick up his share of the $5000 at another time, but before he left he told Serge, "You've got to get away." He said that everything was wrong on the Continent and the place to go was England. Many years later Serge was to say to Foster that he had told him the first things in life, and many years later Foster was to be one of that succession of handsome and distinguished-looking men who could be rather well used by Serge Rubinstein, but upon Foster's next visit to Vienna when he called at Villa Chaire to collect his share of the $5000 he found that Serge was gone from the city and that neither Stella nor Dimitri knew anything about any $5000 nor cared to know. When Foster inquired where Serge had gone he found the youth had taken his advice in addition to his share of the $5000. He had gone to England, to Trinity Hall of Cambridge University.

Chapter Five

Paris

He was not a Cambridge type and never would be. Later on something of Cambridge and the British could be heard in his speech; he might say "I expect" rather than "I suppose," and perhaps there could be seen in his thinking the Cambridge method of reasoning step by step instead of swooping down upon a decision, but of more obvious signs there were none. Cambridge was all what the English call county types coming from small estates with long histories; their women wore tweeds and their men hunted and perhaps 25 per cent of the student body would cut dead any Jew met in class or seen on the street. In the afternoons there were no classes and traditionally the students reserved that time for punting on the River Cam or other sports, but Serge was not very much interested in that although he did play a little soccer. He had to master Latin before he began classes and did so by locking himself into a London boardinghouse room for a month or two of declining verbs and reading Caesar's Commentaries, but after that he did not pay too much attention to his studies although Cambridge's leisurely way and the servants bringing breakfast in bed appealed to him. Later on his stories of his life at Cambridge deviated extravagantly from the facts; he had it that he was a star boxer there and that the high level of his grades was never again reached by any succeeding student, but it was not so. In fact, although he passed his final examinations with top Second Class honors, a better than average mark but below First Class honors, he never took his Bachelor of Arts formally, paid the final fees or went to the degree-giving ceremonies. He left behind him an impression that was distasteful to the British gentlemen; their picture was that of a more self-reliant sort of young man than most people like to see, who, more adult than the other students, indicated a little too often his belief that he had solved the problems of this world. Actually he was out of place and unhappy there but determined to stick it out.

He was twenty-one when he finished—one cannot say graduated because he did not officially receive his degree—and ready to go to work. Probably Dimitri could have found a place for him in the distillery owned in Poland or the asphalt works in Czechoslovakia, but he did not want to work for his father. All during the period when he was known not as Serge Rubinstein but as Dimitri Rubinstein's son Serge he was anxious to let people know he was not associated with his father in business in any way and never had been. He was not then at twenty-one the graduate of a technical institute with a recognized trade and he seems to have wavered somewhat about what to do. For a time while he was at Cambridge, very much impressed by two of his professors, the famous economist John Maynard Keynes, who created many of the philosophies used by the future American New Deal, and the equally eminent Arthur Cecil Pigou whose field was political economy, he let it be known that he would be a teacher, but then he changed his mind and perhaps still uncertain went about London and Paris, where his parents were temporarily living, and looked for a job. In Paris he approached the relative of a school friend engaged in investment work and after an interview the man asked him to step outside so that the partners could discuss the question. When he was called back in he was told a nephew of one of the partners, himself a new employee, had argued against taking Serge in; the firm was very sorry. He never forgot the incident. Many years later a woman married to one of the partners met him in New York and the talk turned to the nephew. "I helped demolish him," he told the woman. "A German once came to see me and wanted to invest in a business; I didn't like him and so I sent him to your nephew. I told him your nephew was always short and that he tried to act the playboy but needed his sleep and so must not be seen in the early morning. The German went and got your nephew's business and got your nephew out into the street." But that he would help destroy, or say he helped destroy the nephew many years later did not get the recent student ahead in the world in 1928. He did no work for a time and then he and his brother André decided to open a theater-night club. They financed the place, which they called The Broadway, via a loan from their mother. She owned an enormous sapphire, almost egg-sized, and they persuaded her to pawn it for the equivalent of $50,000 which they put into their venture. It was a strange business for the two of them: it lacked class, it was something like being in trade. But there seems to have been an idea in their minds that it could lead to better things. Serge used to say of it that "where there is theater there are beautiful women; where there are beautiful women there are rich, foolish men; where there are rich, foolish men, Rubinstein can make a fortune." It was a brave thought, but neither Rubinstein made any fortune on The Broadway.

The place was, however, imaginatively run. It is thought to have been the first club to introduce an innovation later very popular in German night spots. Each table in it was equipped with a telephone and, on a pole sticking high into the air, an illuminated number. If you sat at Table 9 and someone at Table 29 seemed your style, you dialed 29 on your phone. Across the room 29's rang and when it was answered you announced your table number—or perhaps did not; it was great fun to watch 29's occupant looking around the room to determine who the other party to the conversation was—and then you went on from there. The Broadway also aimed at engaging the services of the former singing waiter Ivan Zoubkoff, who had married the rather aged sister of ex-Kaiser Wilhelm of Germany, but lost out when the French police refused him an entry permit to the country.

Even with the Kaiser's brother-in-law singing on its stage, however, The Broadway probably would have failed. The place never did make any money and it was only a few months before Stella's $50,000 was gone and the last telephone was hung up. Stella never forgave her sons for the loss of her great sapphire and they in turn emerged with a certain amount of mutual ill feelings toward one another, but the place was never really important in Serge's life. It had after all something about it that was akin to the iron salvage work he and André had done in Vienna; it was schoolboy stuff, done on Mother's money—fun, perhaps, but not really appropriate work for the son of Dimitri Rubinstein.

Fun was not what the twenty-one-year-old Serge Rubinstein wanted. (He never did have much fun in his life, for all the parties for three hundred persons he gave, for all the skiing and bobsledding weekends and many nights spent with many women.) He used to say, "My first ambition was to be a Grand Duke. As a boy I noticed they had the longest, blackest limousines and the blondest women. Both, I find, are disappointing," and the statement was mostly nonsense, for he never in his life drove any car, black limousine or Model T Ford, and in time his greatest happiness, so he said, came from nights spent with three blondes in bed with him all at once. But part of what he said was completely true. He wanted to be a Grand Duke, a Prince, a Count. Such a nobleman is a magnificent person who gives gifts when he wants to (Tolstoy's Count Vronsky builds the most modern of hospitals for his peasants but refuses to lower their rent when they ask him to), has no moral responsibilities (the Prince who slew Rasputin lived on without punishment), can do no wrong because the laws do not exist for him, has every right to do just as he wants, is a member of what the fifteen-year-old Serge Rubinstein sitting in his father's Vienna gardens called the dictator elite. Dimitri Rubinstein had created such a life, within limitations.

41

Dimitri had power—he had a great palace, servants, men of rank around him, the ability to get out of jail—and his power stemmed from his banks, his insurance companies, his investments, his money. There is a German saying which holds that business is business and schnapps is schnapps. Dimitri had precious little time for schnapps and Dimitri's son was going to be the same way. Dimitri's son wanted money; had to have money; was going to have money. What was Czarist Russia but a place where either you had power or you did not live? And what was power if not what postwar Vienna called valuta, valuta? Serge Rubinstein was a paradox of a man but certain goals stayed with him always: power, glory, position—money.

He went back to England and to Professor Keynes, who admired his ex-student's mind despite the mediocre grades and had told him, "You will be one of the world's top financial figures." He said to the professor that he wanted to do postgraduate work in economics—research on the dormant bank accounts of wealthy Russians killed by the revolution and what came afterward. Much of this money was scattered around the world but a great deal of it was sitting in banks of Switzerland, that traditionally neutral Switzerland of stable currency where even today accounts can be anonymously maintained with only a number used for the designation of the depositor. Professor Keynes thought the project a worthy one and gave him a letter certifying him as a student-researcher carrying on economically important and significant work.

It was June 1929. Serge went to Switzerland and found out that the banks which had benefited by the deaths of so many depositors were not at all happy to see him. But he gained entrance to one in Lausanne and determined that a wealthy merchant ten years dead, Nicholas Chakhov, had maintained a large account unknown to his eleven heirs and one mistress. The young student-researcher sought out the heirs and mistress and gave them happy news indeed. In the middle of 1930 the bank parted with the money and handed it over to the twelve who now had considerable reason to bless the memory of the departed Chakhov. Serge Rubinstein could also feel affection for the merchant. The relatives presented him with 300,000 French francs and the mistress gave him 120,000 more—the total equaling the equivalent of $17,000.

Everybody was happy except the bank, which thereafter was not terribly co-operative with student-researchers. Serge went back to Paris, aged twenty-two, and took a large apartment. It faced the wide and beautiful Avenue Henri-Martin with its fine chestnut trees and had originally been occupied by the founder of the Nobel prize. The probability that Swiss banks would welcome its new occupant was not great, but there were other wells to be tapped and he looked around until he happened across word of an estate in Scotland owned by the estate of some obscure relatives of an eminent Russian family that had, like himself, fled the motherland for France. Unhappily the matter of laying claim to the Scottish lands was difficult for the eminent Russians because of their lack of proper papers. But the proper papers could be rather easily come by in the Europe of those days where forgery was a going business. The war and the unsettled conditions had caused the loss or destruction of lots of papers and it was not difficult to find artists capable of reproducing what was missing. Rubinstein went to see a Russian Princess of the eminent family and put forward his suggestion that he be entrusted with the arrangement of all details in exchange for a commission. The Princess had been brought up amid race horses and ballet performances as the daughter of a Czarist Prime Minister and she had not adjusted to the new Europe as well as had her young caller. She disdained the opportunity to become the owner of the Scottish lands and suggested to the young man that he leave her home. As he did so the Princess' young daughter came into the room and there for the first time saw the man who would play a most important role in her life once a few years had passed. They did not speak; the little girl was still only a child and there was no need for her mother to introduce her to a conniver presenting a matter based on forgery. It was perhaps unfortunate for the Princess that she felt the way she did, for the young man would go on to someone else with fewer scruples—or more sense of reality, depending on how you looked at it—and with the other person put across the profitable deal while she herself would go from genteel poverty to poverty not genteel at all and finally to the pauper's ward of the city hospital at Nice where she would find her deathbed. Her little girl who for a moment saw Serge Rubinstein heading for the door would grow up to blame him for many things in life, including that lonely death.

But all that was still to come. The deal went through, there was a good commission and thus a little more capital. He used it to go into the banking business. His later conversation about that banking business—"When I owned several banks in Paris"—made the two institutions involved sound only slightly smaller than the Bank of England and the Chase Manhattan, but the actuality was less glamorous. Still, they were banks, he was a bank owner, and he was making money.

He began by making friends with Alfred Massenet, a young nephew of the composer of *Manon* who despite playboy tendencies was well connected in French financial circles. He was vice chairman of the Banque Française de l'Afrique, the largest in French Africa, and had entrée in many places, partly through his own name and partly through that of his wife, a well-known Russian singer. Massenet was associated with Paul Dormann, a Russian *émigré* who had constructed a financial empire which was starting to fall apart in those first Depression days, but Rubinstein suggested to him that he free himself from the sinking Dormann ship and that then the two of them should move in on one of the Dormann-controlled properties, the Banque Franco-Asiatique. This bank, which had been appointed by the Paris courts as a corporate receiver for thirty years to the Banque Russo-Asiatique, which before the revolution had been the world's sixth largest bank, had branches in Harbin, Mukden, and Constantinople, and through an agency in Shanghai was fiscal agent for the Chinese government. Its shares were listed on the exclusive section of the Paris stock exchange and the main office was near the Place de l'Opéra. Despite all of this, however, the bank was a vest-pocket operation typical of dozens of little European banks of the period between the end of the Great War and the beginning of the Depression. It was located in a corner building which bore its name on one side only. On the other side of the building appeared the name of the Banque Mandchou. Both signs told the truth and both banks were serviced by a very few employees. But the Banque Franco-Asiatique did have money-making possibilities which were to be nobly realized after Rubinstein and Massenet took it over. This they did by the careful use of the name of one and the brains of the other.

First they went to Dormann who consented to part with the company that controlled the bank, the Société Financière Industrielle et Commerciale, if the two buyers would in turn assume an $80,000 debt Dormann had previously contracted. They agreed to it—Massenet had good banking connections—and got the $80,000 credit from the Banque les Fils Henri DuPont. Then they formed a company called the Syndicat Privé Fiduciaire, which was given the former Dormann company, of which they had both been named directors. Both companies—the one they had formed and the older one—then applied to other banks for loans which enabled them personally to buy large amounts of Franco-Asiatique stock in the open market. The total transaction had cost them, in cash, a total of $500 apiece—the money they subscribed when they formed their new outfit. Massenet became managing director of the Banque Franco-Asiatique and the Banque Mandchou and Rubinstein became assistant manager at an official salary of $200 a month with $80 a month for expenses.

Now he was a banker, given to sitting in a café near his place of business drinking tea and acting in a fashion calculated to make anyone who came near feel very small indeed. He walked in a way that made one man seeing him at that time think to himself that the Emperor Napoleon must have looked so when he strode these same Parisian streets: This is all mine, here for me. He was gaining weight rapidly in those early banking years and wore his brown hair fairly long and slicked back in pompadour style from his high forehead under which his green-gray eyes looked down his nose at those with whom he chose to speak. His appearance and manner were not to be described as modest —arrogant was the word most people used—and his associates at the bank, the directors and those who held that part of the interest which he and Massenet did not own might have had questions in their minds about him, about his youth and attitude. But they were not going to have much time to mull over their doubts. Serge got rid of them.

It was not hard. Part of his work at the bank was to be officer in charge of selling collateral given in exchange for loans. Some of the associates at the bank were as a matter of course holding loans granted against the collateral of their stock in the bank. (It was against the law for them to pledge their stock for a loan from their own bank, but European banking has known greater crimes.) Rubinstein as officer in charge of selling collateral had access to their certificates which were kept in the vaults along with the collateral of other borrowers, and when there came a day upon which the shares of the bank dipped sharply on the stock exchange, it became his duty to say to them, as to any other borrower, that as the shares were now worth less than the value of the loans, more security must be put up to insure the loans and that if this were not done, the bank would be forced to sell the certificates. When, however, the day arrived and he legally had the right to sell the stock, he did so at once with no notice—to a broker who had previously given him a commitment to sell him personally just exactly as many shares of stock as the associates had. It all took place during a weekend. When the associates came to work on Monday morning they found they no longer owned stock in the Banque Franco-Asiatique and that a new board of directors was in the process of being selected.

The new board was composed for the most part of distinguished names. On it sat General Henri Patey, Grand Officer of the Legion of Honor; Gustav Fort, Officer of the Legion of Honor and former treasurer of the French Republic; a former French Minister Plenipotentiary in Sofia; an official banker to the French Foreign Office and, perhaps not unexpectedly, Serge Rubinstein.

The last named had grown friendly with the distinguished board members and many other important gentlemen by virtue of his constant attendance at the frequent soirées held in the salon of the Marquise Marie Louise Crussol of Paris, a lady whose romantic attachments generally, but not always, centered upon important French politicians including Edouard Daladier and Pierre Laval, both of whom served as Premier of their country. It may be asked what the young and not very distinguished Serge Rubinstein was doing at the elegant salon of the Marquise, and the answer is that he was supporting it. The Marquise lacked operating funds and these the young banker supplied in exchange for entrée to her salon in addition to any news she might pick up that could be of interest to a man commanding a certain amount of speculative capital looking for investment opportunities.

One such opportunity, not necessarily indicated by the Marquise, was Rubinstein's establishment of a company financed by the Banque Franco-Asiatique with himself as controlling stockholder to operate the Hotel Baltimore on the Avenue Kléber in Paris. For a time he lived there with various business acquaintances. Another venture was his $500 purchase from an English bank of a large claim the Britishers held against a Russian nobleman in Paris. Rubinstein attached all the nobleman's accounts and arranged a settlement with him for $12,000, with a net personal profit to himself of around $10,000.

He made many times that amount a while later when the bank in its capacity of fiscal agent for the Chinese government was asked to act as French paying agent for some $1,000,000 of interest payments on an issue of a government bond that had been floated in Europe. The arrangements were made via the Shanghai office for the transfer of money from China to Paris but during the negotiations the young banker purchased for himself some 65 per cent of the total issue of a 1913 Chinese bond which in the fine tradition of unstable government had long since been defaulted upon. Such bonds from many countries were always available in Paris for anyone willing to pay their holders a few cents on the dollar. (Even today bonds of Czar Nicholas' government can be bought in the hope that one day the present Russian government will redeem them.)

When the $1,000,000 transfer was arranged, the Banque

46

Franco-Asiatique decided the interest payments should be made not on the bonds the Chiang Kai-shek government had selected, but upon the bonds of the 1913 issue. It was a matter of Rubinstein transferring money to himself without even leaving his office. There was some protest from the Chinese, but things there could be arranged by a little distribution of a little money. The young banker's profit in the transaction amounted to several hundred thousand dollars.

He was attracting attention in many Parisian circles by then. He had a romance with the Spanish opera singer Conchita Supervia, a very beautiful girl whose Carmen received glowing notices in Europe, South America, and the United States. She was the daughter of a Barcelona bullring impresario and had been taken to Buenos Aires at the age of fourteen allegedly because a famous toreador and a dashing Spanish Army officer simply would not leave her alone. She began her singing career there in the Argentine, and then returned to Europe where she appeared in *Il Trovatore* and *Der Rosenkavalier* to the accompaniment of raves only slightly less enthusiastic than those which greeted her Carmen. She loved swimming, tennis, and horseback riding—which were always Rubinstein's sports also—and she moved in high government circles both in Spain and France. She had titian hair, which was usual for a Rubinstein girl friend, for then and always he liked them light, but she was petite, which was rare, for he preferred his women tall, even taller than his 5-foot-7. It was perhaps through Señorita Supervia that he met a Spanish Duke who in 1935 was arrested at the home of the Infanta Eulalia, sister of the ex-King of Spain, and charged with passing a rubber check for $300 in French money. Tall and slim, with a tiny mustache and what the French newspapers called the Bourbon chin, the Duke said he did not know what a check was. "I was not versed in the legal implications of the document when I signed it," he explained. Rubinstein made good the amount for him; he was one of those wandering blue bloods somewhat lost in the non-royalist twentieth century who could always be sure of a welcome from the son of Dimitri Rubinstein but at a price, the price being that when that son loaned or gave you money he was thereafter always certain in his mind that you were his, as indeed you generally were.

It was 1934 and the Hitler regime was in power in Germany and the first streams of refugees were coming across the border. Among them was the former Chancellor of Germany, Joseph Wirth, who arrived penniless, but still well known because of his former position, to be completely at ease among the fashionable circles of Paris where perhaps not completely by chance he met the rising young banker Serge Rubinstein and was offered a job with the Banque Franco-Asiatique until he could get on his feet. Dr. Wirth accepted this hospitality in the same manner in which somewhat later several United States senators and congressmen, among others, would accept similar commissions. Through Wirth, Rubinstein met Eduard Benes of Czechoslovakia who later would be one of the others joining the American legislators.

He was ready now to begin his last French deal, save for his market speculations—some of which were performed with the money of the depositors of the bank. The deal was not a pretty one. Rubinstein in those Paris days used to talk a great deal about how the life of the Russian *émigré* was a terrible struggle for survival. His moneymaking activities could be interpreted as the response of a young man to that struggle, the doings of an uprooted person trying to get started in the world. He had to get started somehow; this was the place and the way. He was not a Rover Boy; he was a European working in a grown-up atmosphere with men twice or thrice his age. But his final French deal, which involved the Compagnie Anonyme des Etablissements Duval, had about it something disturbing. It was not part of the putting of one stone upon another in the building of an empire. We like to think of young men as builders but Rubinstein at twenty-six was not building with the Duval organization. What he was doing was bleeding and squeezing a going concern. When he spoke of it he did so in terms we do not like to hear from a rising young man. "My technique in finance is to figure out how much a company is worth dead, not living," he said. "I don't pay much attention to figures on a company's earning power. I'm most interested in finding out if the liquidation price of a company's assets are worth more than the price of the shares. Of course if you don't control you can't liquidate, but a wide awake man with 20 per cent control can run a company."

So thinking, he moved into the Duval organization. It was composed of a group of restaurants scattered throughout Paris and serving rather simple food at inexpensive prices. The assets of the chain were worth about $450,000 and to buy control under Rubinstein's 20 per cent rule would have meant purchasing $90,000 worth of the company's stock, which was for sale in the open market. He managed it for $60,000. He became vice-chairman of Duval and started dipping into the till. Siphoning off the assets meant that the various restaurants of the chain would start to run down hill; it meant there could be no more expansion and that the quality of the food served would decline, which in turn would mean fewer customers and fewer restaurants until finally there would be the prospect of bankruptcy and an end to the jobs which the chain had offered its employees. It also meant, however, that Serge Rubinstein would have nearly half a million dollars to play around with.

After a while the other stockholders caught on that the young banker was not primarily interested in turning out a better meal for less, and a great battle was undertaken to get rid of him. He did not fight too hard to stay, for he had what he wanted and finally he resigned as vice-chairman and unloaded his shares. They were sold at only a slight profit but what had gone before their sale made him if not rich in the sense of having a great vested fortune, then at least rich for a young man a few years out of school. He had, when he was finished with Duval and very near finished with France, something in the neighborhood of $1,000,000 which was put to work first to enable him to speculate in the stock market and second to get him around in Paris society. "I know the changing moods of politicians' mistresses as minutely as the exchange fluctuations," he said, nicely summing up the two interests all at once.

He also played matchmaker for a wedding which, largely inspired by his money position, would aid his society position. The two people he sought to bring together were his brother André and the grown-up daughter of the Russian Princess who years before had spurned Serge's offer to help her claim the Scottish lands. The daughter's name was Valerie and as her mother was a Princess she was a Princess also. She was seventeen and attending her first ball in May of 1935 at the moment when André came into her life. She was pretty and rather petite and graceful, and although she was engaged to a youth of Russian *émigré* family, she was being trailed around the ballroom by a group of young men anxious to talk with her. She ignored all the young men as she had not been introduced to them until one of them slipped away and went up to talk to her mother, who then introduced him to the daughter. The young man was André. He had green-gray eyes and dark hair, the same as Serge, and he was a little stout but better-looking than his brother—or at least Princess Valerie thought so—and that same night he proposed marriage to her.

Her mother was leaving the ball early in company with Valerie's ten-year-old sister who was along to sit in a corner and watch the dancing, and the family's original plan had been for Valerie to leave early also. But André asked the mother if Valerie could not stay a little longer if he would promise to see her safely home. The mother consented.

After the ball André took Valerie for hot chocolate and sitting there across the table from her asked her to marry him. She told him she was engaged to someone else and that it was impossible but he persisted and the next day sent her flowers and candy. Then he called upon her and her mother with more flowers and with tickets to the opera for all three. The mother remembered the incident with André's brother and at first was opposed to his cause, but times were very hard for her and she had very little money and André's brother was very prosperous and spoken of as a coming young man and the aura of his success touched André in her eyes. A few days after the ball Serge himself came to call upon mother and daughter and when he stepped inside the door Valerie remembered him and the way he had looked the last time he was in that house.

This time he said to the older woman that he was sure she wanted to see her daughter secure and that his brother André had fine prospects, that the two of them were to be in business together and were certain to make a fortune. Serge owed André some $20,000 payable in the fall and he was supposed to be very wise and the mother thought that as someone else had gone along with the Scottish forgery and gotten rich from it then surely it was so that Serge was quite something and would make André rich also. The mother had not had things easy since the Russian revolution's outbreak had sent her fleeing with the infant Valerie in her arms to join a troop of ragged people making their way to the border by horse cart. They were gypsies and the mother sang with them and they liked her and the baby and so she came to safety. The mother's father, Valerie's grandfather, had been a Prime Minister of Czarist Russia and the mother's uncle had been the officer who crushed the 1905 rebellion in St. Petersburg. Leon Trotsky had written of the uncle as a "police thug" but if anything that aided the family's position in the White Russian colony of Paris in the '30s where they had a great name, the former Prime Minister being a leader of the Russian Monarchist movement and head of the Paris branch of Imperial Military School graduates despite the fact that he was penniless as was his daughter and her children.

The mother was quite ill in 1935 with a heart condition, quite afraid of the uncertainties of a world that had reduced her to such low estate from one so high, and inclined to think that perhaps the best thing to do was get her oldest daughter married off to André Rubinstein, who seemed to guarantee a secure future. André had a little bank in Holland—which was shortly to fail—but aside from that André had this brother of whom everyone said it was

50

certain that he would be a rich, rich man. So the elder Princess did everything she could to break up the engagement of the younger to the other man. Meanwhile André was very gallant, coming with bouquets of flowers and taking the mother with Valerie and himself wherever they went. He paid the older Princess much attention, spoke of how happy they would be, and pressed for an early wedding. Brother Serge was often on the scene speaking of the great money André would make through him. Away from the scene Serge would repeat his statements about how rich he would make André, but he would add comments about his own visits to the home of so eminent a woman as Valerie's mother, where he had complete entrée, and of her daughter whom his brother was courting. It did not hurt his standing with the Russian *émigré* groups or with French society that he was able to allude truthfully and rather often to his own role in the romance. "I arrange things with the Princess Valerie and my brother; when I speak the old Princess listens!"

Valerie found it hard to go against her mother's wishes and there seemed at the time no alternative but even as she stood up at the altar of the American Church in Brussels in July 1935—less than three months after the ball—there came into her mind the thought that perhaps the other marriage would have been more suitable. After the wedding the couple traveled through Europe on a brief honeymoon and then returned to Ostend to vacation for a while in a hotel by the water where Serge and a blond ex-high fashion model joined them. Conchita Supervia was gone by then and this was her replacement. The blonde was a Countess. She had gained her title through marriage with an impoverished Hungarian nobleman but that had broken up in short order and she and Serge were very close. She dressed very well and with each costume change wore a different set of jewelry: rubies with her red dresses, emeralds with her blue. The jewels had been paid for by Serge but they were not exactly gifts, for to friends he pointed them out as investments which might in times of inflation grow in value and then be converted into cash. As it turned out one day they were so converted, not by their buyer but by their wearer, who because of the act became more than a minor figure in the life of Serge Rubinstein, being noteworthy as one of the two women who ever took him for anything of value.

Valerie could not help but admire the jewelry of the Countess even though she found it and her a little gaudy. Noticing that, Serge told André to buy his wife a nice gift and send him the bill—it would be his wedding present. André bought a diamond brooch for his bride but when the bill came in

Serge refused to pay, saying he could not afford such extravagances. Valerie was terribly angry and argued the matter with André, but André said to her that, after all, Serge was a brother and that she shouldn't pay attention to what had happened. It was the first breach between Valerie and André on one side and Serge on the other, but apart from that the two couples got along well enough in their hotel by the sea where at table Serge did perhaps 80 per cent of the talking in his vibrant way, going on about his financial ideas and the famous people he knew. Yet Valerie felt strained in his presence and ill at ease and later she thought to herself that she was right to feel that way, for it had been a presentiment of what was to come.

August was in its first week when the two couples parted, André and Valerie to go back to André's Dutch bank and Serge with his Countess to Paris. But he was not to stay there long. On August 11, 1935, after a meeting of the French cabinet, an executive decree was signed ordering Rubinstein out of France forever. It was an ex parte order—one entered without notice nor right of appeal—and it was served upon him by two policemen as he walked to a plane which with propellers turning was about to take off for London. The ostensible reason for expelling him was that he had been speculating against the franc, selling it short and thus pulling down its international price for no reason based on any economics but his desire to make money for himself. Actually there was another reason for the order. True, it was against the law to speculate as he had done but many people did so and few got punished and in any event he was not so powerful a financial figure that his speculations could appreciably damage the currency value of a major world power like France. The actual cause could be understood by looking on the signature on the order of expulsion, which was that of Pierre Laval. Laval had decided that the sponsor of the Marquise Crussol's salon had moved beyond a business arrangement into a more intimate one. "Laval was convinced," Rubinstein said, "that I of all people was her lover. Imagine." It was the end of his French career but it didn't really matter to him. He had better things going in London.

Chapter Six

Chosen

Martin Coles Harmon was a rugged-looking English financier from Cornwall who made some money and with it purchased a small flat island in the Bristol Channel. It was known as

Lundy Island, was inhabited by less than a dozen families who lived in small cottages and fished for a livelihood, and had always been considered a small but undoubted part of the British Empire. Harmon decided to change that. He held a coronation ceremony for himself and from it emerged His Royal Highness the King of Lundy Island. As such he announced that he wanted to remain on friendly terms with the subjects of his fellow King, George the Fifth of England, but that as a sovereign in his own right he had an obligation to coin money and issue stamps for his citizens. This he did. His money and stamps were based not on the penny, shilling, and pound, but on the puffin and half-puffin, the puffin being a sea bird native to his realm. His copper coins featured his profile on one side and an image of the large-billed puffin on the other; the stamps simply had him on them.

The government of King George, however, took issue with the coining of money by the King of Lundy Island. A prosecution was begun and successfully concluded. Martin Coles Harmon ceased to be a King. But unhappily for him this was not to be the only prosecution against him by his majesty's government, for one year later a more serious indictment was handed down. It was not against him in his regal capacity, but for his activities as head of the Chosen Corporation, Ltd.

The Chosen Corporation began life in 1923 as the Chosen Syndicate, its name being changed in 1929. It was a holding company owning three Japanese subsidiaries mining 87 square miles of Korean land rich in gold. Its shares were sold on the London Stock Exchange and it had some 7000 shareholders whose occupations as listed in the company records included Merchant, Banker, Spinster, Knight, and Gentleman. The stock was not doing too well in 1933, when Harmon's troubles began, and could be bought for a little less than two shillings a share.

In 1933, of course, a great many other companies were not doing too well either, and among them were several which, as with Chosen, were controlled by the ex-King of Lundy Island. Chosen at least had some assets, but the other companies were on the very edge of bankruptcy and just about to go over that edge when Harmon decided to spread Chosen's wealth around so that it might bail out what was left of his other companies. He had these other companies buy Chosen shares on the open market for the trading price of two shillings a share. When they had accumulated many tens of thousands, he had the shares privately sold to Chosen's three subsidiaries. But the Chosen subsidiaries did not pay two shillings per share for the stock. They paid at a pound a share, ten times the value of the stock. Some

$750,000 of Chosen money was thus transferred to the other companies by the Chosen subsidiaries.

The matter was found out and Harmon and several other Chosen directors were indicted on charges of fraud and conspiracy to defraud. Harmon was a very likable man and a clever one—at his subsequent trial he conducted his own defense and was complimented by the Lord Chief Justice of England—but he knew that what he had done was a business that was not going to sit well with the Chosen stockholders. He decided to get out of Chosen before their impending suits tied up everything he owned. In April 1933, a month after the indictment was handed down, he sold out. For his private buyer he chose the head of the bank which through its Harbin office had handled financial matters for the three Japanese subsidiaries. The bank was the Banque Franco-Asiatique and the buyer was Serge Rubinstein.

The arrangements included a provision that Rubinstein and two associates should be put on the Chosen board of directors without the formality of an election. This was done, Rubinstein being listed as an Austrian who had never held any other citizenship and whose occupation was Director. The new Director also purchased 50,000 Chosen shares on the open market to go along with Harmon's 100,000. He held, then, a substantial interest in a company whose board was pretty much under his thumb, his two associates being under his control. With their votes backing him up, the new Chosen board voted to sell Rubinstein an additional 150,000 Chosen shares for a down payment of one-fifth of their market value.

That was the situation in November of 1933, when Harmon went off to the prison of Wormwood Scrubs. Rubinstein, based in Paris but commuting to England three times weekly, was very much in command of Chosen. But there were still the shares that the Japanese subsidiaries had purchased at Harmon's inflated price. Rubinstein did not let them sit around very long, for he set up a new Japanese company which he called Godo, or the Chosen Union of Mines, and negotiated a trade between Godo and the three subsidiaries. The subsidiaries gave Godo their stock in Chosen, worth two shillings a share, and Godo in return gave the subsidiaries a good dosage of Godo stock, which was worth absolutely nothing but was made to look like something via a careful juggling of Banque Franco-Asiatique figures. It had all happened so fast—Rubinstein had after all only been in the Chosen picture for a matter of months—that the other stockholders, Spinsters, Knights, Gentlemen, and so on, who had not yet recovered from Harmon, barely knew what was going on. Shortly thereafter, in the wake of Britain's departure from the gold standard, there was a sharp rise in gold securities. Rubinstein held more than enough stock to control Chosen and could afford to let some shares go. He did so, selling 150,000 shares for a profit of some half a million dollars over the average price he had paid. It was a complicated business. (The later Chosen minority shareholders' suit, which was to drag on for many years, described it as the creation by Rubinstein of "a series of subsidiaries, sub-subsidiaries and affiliates of the subsidiaries and sub-subsidiaries and a series of financial maneuvers in the process of which secret profits, commissions and bonuses were garnered by Rubinstein and his dummy nominees.")

In August 1935, ousted by Laval, Rubinstein arrived in London to stay. His take-over of Chosen had attracted attention to him in the London financial world located in what the British call the City, and his dramatic departure from France was extensively covered in the press. He was now the "Golden Giant of 27" whose "magic touch makes fortunes." He was no longer simply the rival of Laval for the favors of the Marquise but "the man a whole nation fears," the "man without a country waging a grim battle in obscurity," the "mystery genius of finance." To those who interviewed him he "radiated dynamic energy, his keen eyes flashing, restless and alert."

Shortly after he arrived the Countess followed. They set up housekeeping in a suite at the May Fair Hotel on Berkeley Street, one of London's finest, where reporters found him "living like a Prince." With the Countess as hostess, he began to throw frequent large parties. Soon he threw one of the biggest of the year. It was held the same day the Duke of Kent was married in Buckingham Palace and the guest list appeared side by side with the Court Circular listing those present at the Palace affair. Rubinstein called it the pinnacle of his English stay—"My guests listed alongside those of the King!"—but there were Englishmen who thought he was going a bit out of his class and that instead of glory the two lists had brought home the fact that none of his guests were important enough to be invited to the Royal nuptials.

It hardly mattered. He was riding very high. Almost as soon as he took over Chosen the price of its shares started to climb on the stock exchange. Wild dividends were paid, amounting in the years 1933–37 to a total of ten and a half shillings for a stock which was purchasable in the Harmon days for two shillings. Chosen went up and up, eventually reaching a high of forty shillings.

And yet not everybody in the City was enthusiastic about Chosen and its new head man. "Mr. Rubinstein is a young man of about 27," wrote one financial expert in a British paper. "He is associated with a bank in Paris and distinguished himself in economics there . . . In spite of this the shares should be sold rather than bought." Another writer in the late 1935 said, "Probably because of his inexperience in British corporate arrangements Mr. Rubinstein does not take shareholders into his confidence as fully as some of them expect." The writer, S. W. Alexander, of the *Sunday Express* added, "I am anxious to help Mr. Rubinstein. I am even more anxious to help the small stockholders."

A theme had been sounded and soon a spate of suspicious stories appeared indicating the writers' belief that the corporation's condition was not so good as the dividends made it seem. Matters were not helped when a team of independent consulting engineers sent to Korea reported back that things were bad and could only be improved by time and money. The engineers also said in a printed circular they sent to all shareholders that they had reported the necessities involved to the management but had been ignored. They added that unless something were done the mines would soon lose much of their productivity. When the report came out the Duval organization was remembered at once and it began to be said that Rubinstein was out to milk Chosen as he had milked the restaurant chain. He had his own thoughts on that when a reporter called upon him. "The City rumors regarding the Chosen Corporation are entirely fantastic, outrageous in fact," he said. "Believe me, I am a large shareholder and would never, never sell because I have complete faith in the company." He was very elegant in the traditional black jacket and striped trousers of the City and he wore a red carnation and carried an umbrella but in the self-contained financial community in which he moved it was said of him that he wanted watching quite carefully. His were not the people the City wanted to mix with. He himself did not trust many of the Europeans surrounding him. "If only I had the people around me that you have," he told Harmon just before the latter went to Wormwood Scrubs. "I have to buy loyalty. I'm all right as long as I pay but when I stop . . ." Meanwhile rumors were flying that Chosen was to be sold out, that the giant dividends were coming straight out of assets that should have been plowed back into expansion projects, and that the whole aim of the management was to drive the market price to an artificial height at which they would sell out leaving the corporation's shell to crash to earth. Rubinstein loftily had it that he was above all such arguments. "Directors are not supposed to be interested in market fluctuations," he said. "And I am one who is not."

Then one December day in 1935 a number of persons having luncheon appointments with him went to his office and found he had vanished. He was gone without notice. The

May Fair was telephoned and reported that Rubinstein and the Countess were gone for an indefinite period. The statement was not one to calm those in the City with money invested in Chosen and there was immediate total panic among them. It was openly said that Rubinstein had run off somewhere with the firm's money. Somehow the financial writer Alexander found out that Rubinstein was en route to Southampton and managed to catch him there for a brief moment. The interview was not very fruitful. "I suggested that before he left he should leave in my hands a few more of the inner secrets of the Chosen Corporation," Alexander wrote, "but he would have none of it." The writer added his discovery that Rubinstein "goes about secretly and makes up his mind quickly." When the words were read Rubinstein was gone, en route to New York on the *Mauretania* with the Countess and a business associate or two. He refused all transatlantic calls to the ship. The City boiled.

But if the dramatic departure was not really called for, the trip itself was. For in Japanese-controlled Korea the subsidiaries were in danger of being expropriated by the Japanese government, an act which would have ended the life of a corporation owning nothing of value but the subsidiaries. Even a cancellation of concessions, an increased tax, or an order barring remittances to England would have been disastrous. All were very likely possibilities.

The *Mauretania* made port in New York and the Countess and Rubinstein entrained to California where they booked passage for the Far East on the *President Coolidge*. When the ship's officials found out they were not married, however, they were refused occupancy of the same stateroom. They settled for adjoining ones and set sail.

On January 9, 1936, they reached Japan. But foreigners were not at all welcome in the Tokyo of those days and some sort of good-will gesture was needed to give entrée to those places where the interests of the Chosen Corporation and Serge Rubinstein could be advanced. Rubinstein made off for Korea armed with money for two public donations. His first consisted of 100,000 yen (about $25,000) given to the Japanese Army and Navy relief fund along with a statement praising their "fighting discipline and valor" in the war in China and expressing the hope that their country would become the "stabilizing force in the Far East." The other public donation was 140,000 yen given the Japanese governor of Korea to be used for health purposes and bonuses for laborers. Rubinstein was operating in alien and hostile territory at a time when all Occidentals were regarded with the highest suspicion and trailed everywhere they went, but he had approached the problem with the right formula. Back in

Tokyo he was granted entrance to government circles. Governments all over were pretty much the same, he had long since decided; he knew what to do with governments. He found his way to Prince Fumimaro Konoye, Japan's last pre-war Premier, and invited the Prince to an evening of chess. The Prince loved chess. They played for high stakes and each time the Prince won. There was no bribe. It was all very Oriental. A story exists, but perhaps it was a Rubinstein invention, that he met with the Emperor Hirohito himself. According to the tale, the Emperor suffered from insomnia and learned through Prince Konoye that the white devil Rubinstein could cure the affliction. Rubinstein was brought to the Emperor and the two lay down in a cool room, side by side on two beds. Rubinstein soothingly whispered instructions on how to breathe deeply, breathe deeply, and after a while Hirohito dropped off to dreamland. At least that was the story Rubinstein told later. He summed up his activities with other Japanese more tersely by pointing out that with them as with every other government man he ever knew "bribery is the best investment." It was a slogan he often used.

The question was, what could be done for him by the Japanese officials? They could not easily exempt Chosen from all anti-foreign moves the government might make in the future. But they could sit as board members on a Japanese corporation that would buy the mines from Chosen. This they consented to do. Rubinstein set it up with Viscount Tadashiro Innouye heading the new company and 51 per cent of its stock held by Japanese citizens. The mines were safe from expropriation.

Rubinstein and the Countess left Japan and went to China where there were certain arrangements to be made concerning his disposal of the $1,000,000 which the Chinese government had sent the Banque Franco-Asiatique for bond issue interest payments. The Chinese were still unhappy that Rubinstein had not paid on the designated issue, but he made it up to them by negotiating the sale of a railroad to them by Russia. He took no commission and having thus smoothed down the ruffled Oriental feathers he departed the East and went back to England and the Chosen stockholders who were all in a flurry about the sale of the mines to the new company. A continuous rush of circulars sent out by various groups of holders to the other holders kept things churned up, one announcing Rubinstein would shortly be back to explain everything, another saying he was delayed in Japan and wanted to return by air but found it impractical. The newspapers contributed their bit to the unrest, one pointing out in remarkable understatement that the shareholders were "looking forward with interest to the return of Mr. Rubinstein." Some of those waiting with such interest wanted to form a committee to work with the directors. Others wanted the corporation liquidated.

Finally he appeared and a giant stockholders meeting was convened on July 15, 1936. The first speaker was a little smiling Japanese, very charming, whose topic was good Anglo-Japanese relations. He was cheered loudly but the holders were sitting on the edges of their chairs waiting for Mr. Rubinstein. He stepped to the rostrum as the little Japanese bowed his way out. "Are there any questions?" he asked. There were. A stockholder sitting at the rear of the group asked a question about one of the mines and in response Rubinstein displayed a large and complicated chart with lines running off it in all directions. He lectured for some time, pointing now and again to the chart, and speaking what sounded terribly much like double talk. "I think that answers your question," he ended.

"I am still confused," said the stockholder. "Perhaps your explanation did not reach as far as me, or maybe I was unable to follow it."

"I will repeat it," said Rubinstein but shouts and cries of others with new questions drowned him out. John Wilmot, a former Member of Parliament, took the floor and began shouting a question which Rubinstein interrupted. "Are you a shareholder?" he asked Wilmot. "You are not. Your stock was transferred to Mr. Gough and Mr. Gough has not dared to come to this meeting."

Friends of the absent Mr. Gough jumped up. "For shame, for shame," they cried. "He has been in a motor accident." A man with a loud voice leaped up and pointed to Rubinstein. "Do we want him or not?" bellowed the man. There were shouts of "Yes, yes," and "No, no," which were overcome by a chant of "We want Wilmot, we want Wilmot" which carried the meeting.

Wilmot demanded silence. "I note there were no interruptions in the speech of the gentleman who was brought here to talk about Japanese imperialism," he said. A chorus of boos and cheers mixed together rose from the crowd. "The shareholders want to know something about the management of this corporation!" Wilmot roared. Yells of "No, no," were heard. "Then I will say a considerable number of shareholders want to know!" People were jumping up and down, shaking their fists and banging on their chairs. It was a most un-English kind of performance. Rubinstein declared it ended. But the board of directors voted him a bonus for his good work in the Far East.

The following year, 1937, Rubinstein returned to Japan.

For months there had been rumors that the Orientals were going to double-cross Chosen and take over the mines despite their ownership by the ostensibly Japanese-controlled company. This time, he traveled alone, for the Countess had gone. The couple had been asked to leave their suite at the May Fair and had moved to separate apartments but one night they had a raging argument over the telephone which ended with Rubinstein shouting that he wanted his jewels back. She told him she didn't want his blasted jewels and he could come over the next day to pick them up. When he arrived at her apartment in the morning he was told that she had left London and taken the night boat-train on her way to France—where he was still barred. His rage was monumental. All day he went about hoarsely shouting out his anger and frustration. "After all I did for her she stole those things," he told everyone he met. "How could she do this to me? Thief! Bandit! How could she do such a thing?" After that he took up with a very attractive girl friend of the blonde Countess, a dark-haired girl who was her complete opposite. She was an actress of sorts and the former common-law wife or mistress of a famed Russian movie actor whose star set with the advent of the talkies. The girl, anxious to go to Hollywood, was stranded in London when Serge took her in, but there were never any lavish presents for her, nor would there be any ever for anybody, save those he gave to the girl he married.

So he sailed alone for Japan. The situation was not good and he was hardly performing from a position of strength. The Japanese government could, if it wanted to, simply take over the mines without compensation or apology. But he managed to get a Japanese concern, the Nippon Mining Company, to buy the mines for 15,000,000 yen or $3,500,000. The dummy Japanese company he had set up the previous year went along with what he said and that was the end of Chosen's mining in Korea. The sale was effected on May 9, 1937, some three weeks short of his twenty-ninth birthday, with the day of final settlement September 10. But before the sale and settlement the Sino-Japanese War heated up and the government banned the removal of any of its currency out of the country. Rubinstein pulled all possible strings and got the government to relent a little; half of the money, in British pounds sterling, could be sent to England. Taxes and expenses cost Chosen and Rubinstein about $1,000,000. That left some 5,000,000 yen, or approximately $1,500,000 sitting in a Japanese bank completely beyond the reach of any foreign company or foreign citizen who wanted to take it beyond Japan's shores. For a while Rubinstein stayed in Japan trying to figure out how the Yokohama Specie Bank and the money could be parted so that the latter could be taken off to happier climes. His brooding over the impounded money was not unknown to the Japanese; detectives followed him everywhere and officials of the bank were told to allow no withdrawals beyond those necessary for Rubinstein to live in Japan. Customs inspectors were supplied with his photograph and warned to search all his baggage when he left the country. There seemed no way out and he departed for England.

By then Harmon was out of jail and leading a group calling for the compulsory wind-up of Chosen's affairs. The minority stockholders felt Rubinstein was eating up too much money in expense accounts and commissions, and besides he had become notorious in the City because of a wise crack he had made at a board of directors meeting. A director not of his coterie had suggested the election to the board of another man, a retired Admiral of the British Navy. "What are his qualifications?" asked Rubinstein.

"He has only one," the director pointedly said. "He is honest."

"Oh?" asked Rubinstein. "Perhaps we could find a place for him as night watchman."

The remark was repeated and repeated. No one found it funny. But there was not much the minority holders could do. They were continually calling for the Board of Trade—the British equivalent of the American Securities and Exchange Commission—to investigate Chosen, but for such an investigation to be made it was necessary for a resolution to be passed by a vote of shares. Rubinstein controlled too many shares to allow passage, so the investigation could not be begun.

In France, meanwhile, Laval had fallen from power, and so Rubinstein was allowed back. Officially he had been barred forever, but after Laval left office, no one seemed to care if he returned. His mother was living in Paris as a widow by then, for Dimitri had died in 1936 in Zagreb, Yugoslavia, an embittered old man with almost all of his money lost in the failure of the Czech asphalt firm he owned. He was getting by on perhaps $500 a month when André and the Princess Valerie visited him shortly before his death. Valerie found him a difficult person, bad-tempered and sharp-tongued, and she did not get on too well with Stella. After Dimitri's death the young couple took Stella for a trip to the French Riviera in a car belonging to Serge, but whenever Valerie went out in it by herself Stella was always after her to replace the gas in the tank. In addition Stella never forgave Valerie for the fact that many years previously her grandfather, then Russian Prime Minister, refused to receive Dimitri when the latter wanted an audience. "Your grandfather thought he was too good for my husband," she would say. "I was only one year old at the time," Valerie would reply, but the answer did not satisfy her mother-in-law. Valerie also felt coolly toward Serge, and when he returned to Paris she took the lead in pressing him for a return of the $20,000 he owed André. He replied that he was not yet in a position to pay, but he did offer André a job with him as a kind of roving deal-finder. André accepted. The agreement was to lead to years and years of unsolved legal bickering, but at the time it did not seem that way.

Once back in France, Serge was reminded of his Countess and he decided to call upon her. He had not forgotten the jewels but he telephoned her and asked if he might come to see her. She consented and the next day he took a taxi to her apartment house. But Stella had been listening in the next room when he telephoned and when he stepped out of the cab before the building he found his mother standing in the lobby with arms outstretched to block his way. "Don't go in," she said to him. "That woman is not for you." He did as she said; they left in a cab together. It was the end of the Countess in his life.

The money still in the vaults of the Yokohama Specie Bank preyed on his mind all during this period, and he discussed it endlessly. How to get it out? More than a million dollars all tied up and out of reach! For a time it was thought that André might go to Japan and get it out but then another, better, candidate was found. His name was Konrad Sztykgold.

One day, years later, in the summer of 1940, a man who had left Paris as the German Army arrived found himself accosted in the middle of Fifth Avenue. He had not been in America three days when there in the street appeared the fellow who had been his first client years before when he was starting in the law business. In the man's family the first son had always been a lawyer, the second a doctor and the third not worth talking about, and here was his first client of long ago buttonholing him and, without mentioning that they had not met in ten years, asking if he was free for lunch. The man who stopped the lawyer was Konrad Sztykgold. Sztykgold said to the man, "Didn't you once tell me you wanted to be in the oil business?" and the man thought to himself that it was quite remarkable indeed for he had said it to Sztykgold twenty years earlier. But that was Sztykgold; he had an enormous IQ and a photographic mind and the kind of intelligence that does not memorize anything but is selective.

"*I* am in the oil business," Sztykgold said.

"What kind of oil business?" asked the lawyer. "The castor oil business or the palm oil business?"

"The crude oil business," Sztykgold said. "I'm distilling it. I work with Serge Rubinstein."

The man recoiled. He had first heard the name in Paris many years earlier when a friend came to him speaking of this Rubinstein as a great genius. "How do you tell one genius from another?" asked the lawyer and the friend said, "I can tell from the way other men listen to him." That had struck the lawyer as an approach somewhat Oriental in philosophy and he had forgotten the name Rubinstein after reflecting briefly that such a name must have originally belonged to a jeweler. For when Frederick the Great issued his edict that the Jews must have new names—how could you run an orderly Prussian state when half the Jews had the same or similar name?—it was generally Frederick's men who decided the name and hence a jeweler could very likely be called ruby stone—Rubinstein. But then in the early '30s the lawyer had gotten to hear quite a bit about this Rubinstein and he could find nothing of the beauty of the ruby in him. Now here in the summer of 1940 in New York was Konrad Sztykgold saying he worked with Serge Rubinstein.

"I heard he was a fiend," said the man.

"Did you?" asked Sztykgold. "Where did you hear it and what do you mean by it?"

"I heard it," said the lawyer, "not in the salons of Paris where one can hear such things, not quite there but perhaps in the stables of Paris or better still in the offices. And what I mean by fiend is that he is the earthly configuration of the devil. That is what I heard they said, beneath the salons. How can you work with Serge Rubinstein?"

"Anyone can work with Rubinstein who knows the Russian soul," said Sztykgold, "and knows how to take his ways and happens to own facets of brilliancy that Serge likes to have. And these are very few and I own them."

"I see," said the man. They went to lunch, he and Konrad Sztykgold who came from what in the Jewish quarter of Warsaw was considered the nobility of that city. Such nobility was meant to be how close you were to a given rabbi. It was a nobility of learning, not that of a reigning family sitting three hundred years on the same farmland, and Sztykgold was very high up in it. He had between the wars been European representative of an investment bankers' firm and had owned his own bank in Danzig and had worked at getting money out of Nazi Germany. He had lived in an up-and-down way, now pawning his wife's jewels, now on a pink cloud, going broke or half broke and then becoming rich as people did in those years. He had met Serge Rubinstein through an employee of the Banque Franco-Asiatique and he was in a down period, having very little money, when in 1938 Rubinstein went to him to ask if he, Sztykgold, could undertake to get out of Japan an ungodly amount of frozen yen.

Without batting an eye Sztykgold said yes, possessing little knowledge about yen frozen or unfrozen but having his mind and nerve and the ability to wrap anyone around his little finger. And so he set out for Japan and the Yokohama Specie Bank, in whose vaults lay that great sum of money which the Japanese government was determined that neither Serge Rubinstein nor anyone else was going to have. Sztykgold took with him a supply of bandages and various salves, for he suffered from a skin disease of the hands which forced him to wrap them each night before going to bed. He also took with him a plan, but that was hardly visible for it was in his head and what was there did not show anywhere, neither in his face nor in his actions.

He arrived in Japan and sat in his Japanese hotel room and there wrote many hundreds of letters to the many manufacturers of the Japanese obi, which is a long scarflike piece of apparel worn about the waists of Japanese women. He said to the manufacturers that it was his belief that nothing brings out the charm of a woman's midriff better than the obi, and that the obi is unknown where the white devils live but that he was willing to bear back supplies of samples and make an obi exhibit such as the West had never seen. The manufacturers began appearing in his room. One would point out that the obi could be made as cheaply in America and there seemed therefore little market here, only to be told that the subtle and authentic Japanese obi alone would catch the American eye. Another saying that the obi would possibly not appeal to the housewives would be told it could also be hung on the wall as a fine and true example of Japanese art and craftsmanship.

Soon the hotel room was filled with obis, one of each kind, each more brilliant and beautiful than the other, and each carefully wrapped around a cardboard tube which was hollow in the middle. When there was barely room for the newly made obi importer to move around his room he went out and made his way to Viscount Innoye, the former Minister of Communications, to Diet member Juji Kasia, to Barons Nomurai and Okura and to Prince Ito, and announced to them that he was authorized to deposit 300,000 yen in any American bank account they would designate if they in return would be so kind as to make possible the withdrawal of the Chosen Corporation's frozen funds.

And so one night when day was done and shadows fell across Yokohama, a bank official stole into Sztykgold's hotel bearing many, many packages that had lately lain in the vaults of the Specie Bank. When the official stole away, Sztykgold sat surrounded not only by obis but by three million of the five million yen, (the other two million could not be un-banked) all in one-hundred-yen denomination bills.

Now, Japanese hotel rooms have no privacy. It is nothing for a Japanese maid to come in when you are standing stark naked shaving before the mirror. The walls do not go up to the ceiling and the doors do not lock. But Sztykgold could not have a maid coming in to change the towels or dust. So he went to a doctor who gave him a prescription which made his face swell up like a football. His eyes were varely visible and he fed himself with a spoon. He did not exactly say the unfortunate illness was contagious but the hotel em-ployees appeared to wonder if it were not and few seemed anxious to find out. That took care of the privacy of his room. But it would have disturbed his work to have anyone in the next room, so he announced that any vibrations caused him horrible agony and that therefore no one must be al-lowed next door. He also let it be known that in the United States such an illness was treated by the application of steam. All day and all night, therefore, the hot water tap in his room had to be open, its rushing water pouring noisily down.

Then alone he sat up and carefully unrolled each and every obi and into the hollow cardboard tube which had the previ-ous year caught Serge Rubinstein's eye, he carefully stuffed thirty rolled-up one-hundred yen notes. From each tube he snipped off sufficient cardboard so that the shipment of obis would not be suspiciously heavy. Then he rewound the obi.

It took several days. There were 29,300 notes. When the job was finished he had himself carried to a train which made for the *Empress of Japan* lying at dock in Kobe. His swollen face had returned to something like its normal size, but he plastered it with white salve that left him looking not at all well. He and his shipment arrived at the pier where they found waiting a small crew of customs officials proud to know that so specific an item as the obi would soon carry the mes-sage of Japanese culture and good taste to the waiting West. Sztykgold was carried aboard in a stretcher after the ship-ment had been weighed and found just exactly as it should have been. Somehow he managed to have his shipment put in his stateroom and there, still a sick man in the eyes of all on board, he whiled away the time during the trip to Hawaii by plucking the obis from the cardboard tubes.

A day out of Honolulu he wired for an armored car and sixteen guards to meet him at the pier. It was showmanship not for show but for Konrad Sztykgold, but it alerted the East to his feat. The Honolulu papers soon got the story and the exact amount of yen smuggled out, which perceptibly reduced the market for them, everyone knowing just how many were now for sale. The disclosure also shook the world value of Japanese currency. In the normal course of affairs very little foreign currency leaves a country. Such a shipment from Japan, perhaps the largest ever taken from there, was a blow to the yen from which it would take years to recover. It also caused passage in Japan of a law known as the Sztykgold Law, making it slightly more difficult to roll yen notes into obi cardboards.

Sztykgold telephoned Rubinstein in New York and reported success. His original agreed-upon compensation was rather measly, considering that he might have been incarcerated or relieved of things such as his tongue or fingernails—this having been reportedly done to several of the Kobe customs officials—and he said to Rubinstein that instead of merely two per cent it might be more equitable if he were given fifteen.

"Well," said Rubinstein, "I'm very glad you said that because you could have gotten away with it all, couldn't you?" But that was not Sztykgold's way, to cheat a friend and business associate, and he took the shipment to New York. Before he arrived, and before the whole world knew about the performance, Rubinstein went to a New York bank and announced that he would shortly be depositing some 2,500,-000 yen and wanted a commitment as to what rate of exchange the bank would give him. The bank offered the prevailing market rate for money credits. That rate was a good deal higher than the rate for actual physical notes, which are always sold at a discount away from their own country, as anyone returning from an overseas visit will find out when he goes to cash any foreign money he has brought back.

Rubinstein received a written confirmation of the proposed deal from the bank, which upon Sztykgold's arrival was most surprised to find itself stuck with actual physical bills to the number of about 25,000, rather than the check that was expected. The bank was sufficiently upset to go to the trouble of sending out a letter warning other banks against this sharp dealer, but that was not the sort of thing that worried the young Serge Rubinstein. He now had a good fraction of a million dollars of Chosen's money in his own name secured far away from the Chosen stockholders and the British law which might protect them, safe and sound in the country to which he would shortly come to live, to eat and dance and sleep with many women, to make much money and, finally, to die.

Chapter Seven

America

If you are a schoolteacher or office clerk or store owner and you walk into a brokerage office or bank to open an account for one or five or ten thousand dollars, nothing much more than your name and address will be asked of you. No one will have any additional questions; no one much cares about such an investor or depositor as you are. But when a man comes in with a one hundred thousand dollar account the door does not close behind him before questions are being asked. Who is the man? Where does the money come from? The attitude of the bank or brokerage house toward such a man is that we're going to guard ourselves against you; you won't be putting anything over on us. If you've got a deal which can make us money we'll go with you. But we'll let you know that we know about you. Depend on it.

What the bank or brokerage house comes to know is part and parcel of the bargain they will make with the man, if deal there is to be. Not all houses will deal, of course. Once a man opened an immense account at a very conservative Wall Street brokerage house. But the house found out he had about six wives scattered through his past, that he was a kind of junior Tommy Manville. The house asked the man to withdraw his account, thinking to itself that suppose when he dies the wives descend upon us? The publicity wouldn't be nice. A front man for Frank Costello had similar problems. But when the man with the wives took his money out of the conservative house he had no trouble placing it elsewhere. The Costello man also found an outlet for the money he had been given. It used to be that a man who had gone bankrupt or been in prison was suspect forever more in any business dealings, but that time is past. Today you can walk out of Sing Sing and step up with a plausible deal and be listened to by most people in Wall Street. Wall Street is not forever looking for the dirty deal but it is not going to worry too much about sin. A dollar is a dollar. There are men in Wall Street who will say that for some types money is not enough, that from these types money can be made but that for such types gold as collateral is not enough. But the men who say that are quite few in number. More will say, as a very famous financier often does, that as long as I can make $10,000 commission on a man, what do I care who the man is? What is that to me? Wall Street will say that, but Wall Street wants to know about you.

To find out about you and your money there exist in Wall Street several firms which, operating like detective agencies, seek out information on men in whom clients are interested. One such firm is Bishop's Service, Inc., which in the late fall of 1938 was suddenly swamped with some thirty or forty requests for advices about a man who was opening dozens of accounts for tremendous sums of money, $85,000 here, $125,000 there, $160,000 someplace else.

The man's name was Senhor Sergio Manuel Rubinstein de Rovello, a Portuguese citizen. He had entered the United States as an immigrant at Buffalo, New York, on April 2, 1938 thereafter leaving with a re-entry permit. He came back, using the permit, in September 1938, on the day Chamberlain went to meet Hitler at Munich.

Senhor de Rovello, Portuguese, had gained his name and nationality in 1935 when as Serge Rubinstein, Gentleman and Director of the Chosen Corporation, he made his first trip to Japan. When he left England for the Far East he traveled on a League of Nations passport which that group regularly issued to Russian *émigrés* such as himself. But certain nations did not accept the League of Nations passport, and Japan was one of those nations. A new passport was needed; he had to get to Japan. It was a business detail. So he got a new passport—a Portuguese one. How did he do it? In the same way that thousands of newly rootless Europeans got theirs. By paying for it. In those years after the break-up of Imperial regimes in many countries the sale of passports all through Europe was a commonplace thing. In Leipzig the Costa Rican government ran two offices side by side. In one they sold land in their far-off country. In the other they issued passports to anyone owning land in Costa Rica. Purchase of land and establishment of citizenship took an hour, two hours. In Milan the Turkish Consul sold passports making any applicant an honored citizen of Turkey. It was arranged by slipping the document into a diplomatic pouch going back to the homeland to be quickly stamped and recorded by an official who was a realist about such matters and who enjoyed the bit of extra income the act brought him. Portugal made it a little more difficult, but not much. En route to Japan, Rubinstein paused at Shanghai and went to the office of the Portuguese Consul with a forged certificate of baptism allegedly issued at Hankow, China, in 1908. He told the Consul he had been adopted by a Portuguese family named de Rovello, and that, with a few specimens of valuta, got him a passport. A few years later, when the passport had to be renewed, he changed the story. He swore he was the il-

68

legitimate son of his mother and an unknown Portuguese lover. He had four Portuguese citizens back up the statement that he was in truth the bastard son of one Stella de Rovello, a spinster. On a later renewal the story was again changed so that now Estella de Rovelo (with one "l") was his mother, with his father listed as her "lover of Russian citizenship."

Bishop's was interested in this, the story of how Rubinstein got his new name and nationality—all information about a man can be valuable to those who do business with him. But primarily the question was where all the money came from, all the hundreds of thousands of dollars which allowed him, ideas and propositions and deals pouring out of him, to burst upon the American financial world.

The answer was that some of the money was that which Konrad Sztykgold took out of Japan in the obi cardboards. But that was only part. The rest was the money the Japanese had legally allowed Chosen to send to England at the time the mines were sold. That latter portion, which amounted to more than $1,000,000, lay in the Westminster Bank of London during all the months while Rubinstein worried about what was in the Yokohama Specie Bank and Sztykgold worked at getting it out. When Sztykgold arrived in America, Rubinstein went back to London taking with him a small fraction of the smuggled-out money. This was a sop to those in England who were starting to say that as the mines had been sold anyway, the thing to do was liquidate Chosen and distribute the assets to all shareholders. This money, the sop, which Rubinstein brought with him from America to England, was placed with the greater sum in the Westminster Bank. And then one day the whole account was gone without warning and Rubinstein along with it. Stockholders calling Rubinstein's office at Cross Keys House in Moorgate in the City were told Senhor de Rovello was gone. No explanation was offered and at first in the rush and heat of the Munich crisis the sudden disappearing act did not get the publicity it otherwise might have. But anyone who later cared to inquire could find out that the Chosen Corporation assets had been removed from the Westminster Bank and taken to a very far-off place, to be exact a small bank in downtown New York. Those stockholders who did inquire, very bitter, incensed that their money had been made off with, started a campaign to get the matter wound up and Chosen liquidated.

To calm them down, if only for a while, Rubinstein sent word from America that as war seemed imminent, he had only acted in the best interests of Chosen by taking the assets to America where they could be carefully safeguarded under his stewardship. He also pointed out that the American dollars into which the pounds sterling had been converted would almost certainly increase in value on the world market, with consequent advantages to Chosen. The City did not see it that way; in the City's eyes Rubinstein was a bloody sneak thief who had simply run off with the firm's money. "The history of this company is the history of a racket probably without precedent," cried one stockholder. "There can be no doubt that the disposal of our property was conceived in iniquity and born in sin." Another groped for words to describe what had happened. He finally came up with resounding definitions: "Financial jugglery, jiggery-pokery." They all went to court about it, hiring American lawyers to try and get their money back to England.

But it was not so easy a thing to do. For as soon as the money was safe in America, Rubinstein placed it into a newly created "investment trust," British-American Equities, Inc. And British-American Equities immediately traded its stock with another newborn firm, Norfolk Equities, Inc. Norfolk Equities at once shifted assets and stock to Norfolk International, a corporation chartered in Cuba, outside American jurisdiction. At the same time, along with the Norfolks, Rubinstein formed a dozen other corporations, each with a hold on the other, many of them issuing shares out of a name on the door of a lawyer's office. These shares would be traded to a different Rubinstein corporation in another state's jurisdiction, or they would be sent on to one of the foreign outfits. Corporations would suddenly go out of business and new ones would as suddenly come into being. In a short time, a matter of months, Chosen's money was held by Rubinstein corporations all over the map.

The companies all had the most tangled relationships one to another. Each was siphoning from the other; some actually owned assets of value and some were pure dummies. Some were private holding companies accountable to no one but their principal, who was Rubinstein or a Rubinstein dupe anxious to get a little cream off the top of the pitcher. Chosen's money was sifting down, vaguely seen here, buried there, so that to really trace it was impossible. The American lawyer hired by Chosen's minority shareholders to make claim to their money was constantly on the move in tracking it down, flying to Rio, Vancouver, Toronto, Ottawa, France, all over the United States. "A gigantic jigsaw," he said.

A typical set-up was that of Stock and Shares Realization, Inc. Rubinstein originally set it up in Delaware via correspondence. It was first named Chosen Corporation 1934, Inc., the name later being changed. Its assets were worth almost nothing but Rubinstein worked a trade by which 75,000 shares of its stock were exchanged for 75,000 shares of Chosen's stock, which at the time of the transaction was selling for six dollars a share. Then Stock and Shares Realization, Inc. folded up, paying a liquidation price of twenty cents a share. The total liquidation of what had once been close to half a million dollars amounted to $15,000.

The investigations inaugurated by the frustrated Chosen holders were conducted in the United States, South America, and Europe. The whole business took years. Thousands of pages of testimony were recorded. Great files of briefs and correspondence were created. But during the time that all this was going on, Rubinstein had Chosen's money at his disposal. He used it. One of his corporations bought real estate. Another went oil prospecting in Louisiana. Others plunged heavily in the stock market, particularly British-American Equities.

That was what brought him to the attention of Bishop's, the investigation agency. They wrote a report to be sent to any clients requesting information on the firm and its head.

"It is thought," the report read, "that while he may not be intentionally dishonest he believes that others are always trying to do him injury and for that reason has no care or thought for what he may cause. It is believed advisable that a clear and concise agreement (preferably on paper) be made prior to any business agreement being entered into."

The report was notably accurate. Rubinstein was forever saying people were out to make a patsy of him. He often used the word "sucker," not in reference to others, but to himself. "Who's going to try and make a sucker out of me here?" he would say when going into any deal. On the ship coming over to America the first time, he met a business acquaintance from London who told him of the purchase of a ticket in the ship's pool for the day, ticket number 555. "You've got a partner," said Rubinstein. "I've got a partner if he gives me half the twelve shillings the ticket cost me," said the man. Rubinstein gave him that sum and asked to hold the ticket—he would bring it luck. That night 555 was announced as winner of the ship's pool, which ran to several hundred dollars. Rubinstein cashed the ticket and when the man went to him for his half of the money, Rubinstein refused to give it to him. "That was my ticket," Rubinstein said. "Are you trying to make a patsy out of me?"

The Bishop's report went on:

"He is very positive of his own opinions and has little regard for any other opinions."

This was accurate as few statements are. For by 1938 the thirty-year-old Serge Rubinstein had advanced beyond his earlier belief that a dictator elite was destined to rule the world. He had arrived at the point where he believed that he,

71

Rubinstein, would do it alone. Or at least he said so in just so many words. The twin sister of the girl he shortly would marry has vivid memories of him, still so very young, saying it. "I'm going to run the world," he would say. "You'll see. I'm going to own Wall Street and the City both. You'll see."

It was always believe me, wait, you'll see, I'll show you. He had it in his mind not like those who sit in madhouses saying they are Napoleon, but with a good appreciation of reality. Those in the lunatic wards also dream great dreams. But Rubinstein in 1938 was a young man with the ability to put his dreams into action. And with the ability went a great and terrible drive to do, to be. His was the urge of the painter to put down on canvas what he sees in his mind; his was the need of the writer to express. He had to live out his great dreams of conquering the world; those who got in his way and got hurt—the Duval people, the Chosen investors, the others—that was their lot. It was not being against people, but being for power.

No one who knew Serge Rubinstein in those his great days ever thought that anything less than three-quarters of a genius was being dealt with. He read everything and he remembered everything. Spencer Samuels, an art dealer whose family then owned the famed New York firm of French & Company, met him for the first time at dinner one night and never forgot an argument that arose at table. One of the guests was the leader of an Indian religious sect and halfway through the meal the man and Rubinstein became involved in discussing what had happened two thousand years ago when a group of Indian mystics invaded Persia. It was the most esoteric kind of thing. Rubinstein was very definite in what he was saying in opposition to the Indian gentleman. Rubinstein did not say, "I may be wrong but I think . . ." He said, "I tell you I'm right; there's no doubt about it. Why do you argue with me?" In the end he turned to a servant. "Go bring an encyclopedia," he said in his brusque way. The book was brought and it was found that Rubinstein was right and the Indian wrong. Persian skirmishes of Christ's time could not make Rubinstein money, but he was the same way in financial matters. He was in the financial world as a tiger among pussycats; all those who knew him there felt that. He could drop down to an accountant's office and pick up a piece of advice and take it at once beyond the scope of his advisers. They would tell him the law and picking it up at once he would say, "If that's so then I can . . ." and he would say what he could do. The accountant would ask himself, Well, can he? And the accountant's thinking would be pushed well past where it had begun, to end at the conclusion that yes, Rubinstein could do that. A well-known, capable, highly paid accountant was once engaged to prepare a tax statement for him, and having gotten into the matter found a perfectly incredible tangle of corporate affairs, all interlocking, all writhing together. There seemed no end to it. Knowing vaguely that the man's reputation was not good, the accountant determined that everything would be absolutely correct. He was not going to be put in the position of making factual representations which could be pulled out from under him by a government examiner. He resolved to check everything all the way down. Not a fact would be allowed to go by on an oral basis. There would have to be written proof for everything. But when he would call Rubinstein to say that there was an apparent discrepancy, a contradiction, Rubinstein always knew—immediately —what was in the accountant's mind. And he would want to know why it was there and what was the exact materiality of the question and just how it could advance Serge Rubinstein's standing with the tax collection agency of the United States government. Satisfied that there was a reason for the question, Rubinstein would explain it with total recall. "What happened was that this time I was at the Roney Plaza in Florida in my suite and I had been up late the night before, but that morning I got on the phone early . . ." and the accountant would go back to the records, to the immense series of memorandums and files of documents sent from British-American to Norfolk Equities to Norfolk International to American Overseas Mining Investment Co. to Techeland Oil Corp. to Midway Victory Oil Corp. to Jackson Heights Properties to Mercantile Engineering and Repair Co. to Mid City Properties to Caroline Properties to 137–139 East 28th St. Corp. to all the others, and find that like a figure eight it all wound back to what Rubinstein had recalled from memory. There would always be a rational explanation which would, however, introduce a mass of new material. The accountant would fit it in again and find ten more of what seemed to be discrepancies. But they were never discrepancies. Rubinstein would have the answers to all ten. The accountant never caught his client in a mistake. In every other case he saw in his thirty-year career, the man involved would tell what happened in this way today and in another way next month. But not Rubinstein. There were never any mistakes. It was always what does it bear on, how is it material, what statute is involved, and then Rubinstein was hours ahead of the accountant in his thinking. The accountant—and all the other accountants and lawyers Rubinstein dealt with—never found out everything about any segment of Rubinstein's affairs. They had pockets of information but that was all. Nothing was ever done with just one purpose in mind, nothing was simple. Sometimes it seemed a large expenditure of effort was put into things that did not seem worth it, but the ramifications did not confuse the man who had created them. On the contrary, it kept him in his own mind safe that nobody knew more than a few things about him. There was a high correlation between self-sufficiency and success in his thinking. You never expose yourself. Someone will use it against you.

It was this underground, twisting approach that drove them crazy in London. Later, a British paper carried an article about him signed by A Former Business Associate. The Former Business Associate was of the City with its wonderful old buildings and pubs, of English gentlemen saying they lived by the standards of their public schools and Oxford, of those keeping Old Boys Day at Harrow in their schedules each year. "He was the meanest man I ever knew," wrote the Associate. "He had a twisted mind that went around corners. He could not even leave a room in a straight line." They noticed that in America too, that he could not walk down from Broadway to the New York Stock Exchange building without crossing the Street from north to south or south to north at least once.

The Former Business Associate had been used, of course, (and the marks were still on him) in the way that Serge Rubinstein used people. Men's mistresses were used to get to them, secretaries were used to calm angry girl friends, distinguished European *émigrés* were used to bring respectability to his suite . . . it had always been his way. And in that way there was something akin to the child playing with the Tinker Toy, erecting bridges and buildings, controlling his little world, playing God. A boy with an Erector set builds, masters, destroys. A man with many Associates, all subservient to him, with many names, with interlocking directorates, with front men used as new faces for himself, is playing with toys in adult form. It is the little boy in man's estate reveling in the complexity of all that he has, all that he does. He is at the top of the heap, horse laughing at the world and running the world. He is the master. He is God.

"I can break mountains!" Rubinstein used to cry in those days, clenching his fists and shaking them in the air. He named one of his companies that to prove it—Mountbreak Corporation.

The Bishop's report went on:
"Although he is known to many individuals, there are those who are dubious about being seen in his company or having business dealings with him. He is said to make many acquaintances but has few friends. Various unflattering

statements about Rubinstein, his lack of ethics and so forth, have been made. There seems to be little doubt that anyone entering into business dealings with him would have to proceed carefully and keep in close touch with the situation.

"While British-American Equities is in itself a domestic corporation, in numerous quarters the opinion is held that there is more to its intentions than meets the eye, that its creation foreshadows singular events. Adequate reservations are expressed in customarily informed circles to prevent our even attempting to charter its future programs of operation in advance."

Before the report was sent out to inquiring clients, however, a copy of it was submitted to its subject. He was told that he might if he wished prepare a statement that would be added to it.

Immediately after receiving it, the subject telephoned a lawyer who joined him as he rushed to Bishop's. There the two men were shown into the office of the president of the firm. "You're trying to ruin me," Rubinstein shouted at the Bishop's official. "I am an honest man, a misunderstood man, and you're taking advantage of me. Why? Why are you against me? Why do you want to destroy me?" The president denied any destructive tendencies. Rubinstein yelled louder, only lowering his voice to ask if perhaps there was not something he could do for the president, some little favor to make them friends. The meeting lasted three hours and ended with Rubinstein's promise to provide character references and a statement which could be included in the report.

The Bishop's investigator who had led the field investigation, William Malloy, had lived through many such scenes. It was in his eyes the typical act of a quick wonder boy popping up on the Street with a bagful of money from hazy or questionable sources. It was to his thinking of the pattern of the manipulator from nowhere who hits today for a bundle and who tomorrow is broke. The lower echelons of such men, their offices in their hats, used to congregate in those days before the war in the American Telephone and Telegraph building lobby, their pockets full of nickels and dimes for calls to be made from the line of public phone booths there. The same thing happens today. The talk is always in terms of millions of dollars but at the end of the conversation the man doing the talking is fully capable of asking for a five-dollar loan until the weekend. And yet—funny—the man borrowing the five may next week pyramid things up and ride high with it and come out with fifty, one hundred, four hundred thousand dollars. His Bibles are the books listing companies and directors in which he looks for a company going to seed and not paying dividends. He goes to the old and tired management of such a company and gets from them an offer to sell an interest. He sells it for some stock plus a finder's fee, spins off the stock and with the proceeds works in someplace else. Or for a promise of 20 per cent he will sign to distribute the stock which is sold—it will say on the prospectus he gets out—with an eye to expansion. Handling the whole thing, he will be on the phone day and night spreading the word that the thing has terrific potential; it's a good deal, a big deal; it's going to merge; it has a big Navy contract in the works. A line of his friends join him at the phones calling strangers and buying and selling the stock from each other—the Street calls it "washing" a stock —so that the resultant activity catches everyone's eye. It is gotten out that now Super Duper Goldmines has acquired the Hotsy Totsy strike and word spreads that with this immense lode the stock cannot miss. The activity and the soaring goes on while the man who last week wanted five dollars starts quietly to unload. Or he approaches the owners of Zoom Zoom Corp. which is for sale and buys it by giving stock in Super Duper. Now he has Zoom Zoom to absorb or liquidate—usually to liquidate, for absorbing and expanding is a bird in the bush while liquidating is one in the hand. People say my, they're branching out, they just merged, let's buy. The underwriting is always for exactly $299,000, which is what is called a short form and does not require full disclosures to the Securities and Exchanges Commission, and so all kinds of interesting things can be done. And from such beginnings . . .

Or a lease is obtained on a hole in the ground with a glowing geologist's report to go with it and that becomes in the quickly printed prospectus a booming oil territory that must produce thousands of barrels to make rich anyone buying in. It is not impossible to reach some who write for financial advisory services and publications, so soon there are recommendations saying this is the steal of the year. And again from such beginnings . . .

But Rubinstein was a little more substantial than all that. He was able to give Bishop's the thoughts of all sorts of Wall Streeters on Serge Rubinstein which went along with Serge Rubinstein's thoughts on America.

"Due to the unsettled political conditions in Europe," he wrote, "I feel that America is the only place where capital and ability can find some proper reward." It was a concept that appealed to him; at the same time he told someone else he thought that America "best exemplifies the Darwinian theory of natural selection. When people are born in France

76

or Russia, they're just born. But when they're here, there's a reason for it."

The recommendations he submitted came on the letterheads of banks and brokerage houses. ". . . Some of his transactions run into several hundred thousand dollars," wrote an officer of the Manhattan Trust Company. (The men in the AT&T lobby couldn't get *that* kind of endorsement so easily.) "It is a pleasure for us to commend Mr. Rubinstein and his companies to you as deserving of every consideration."

The Sterling National Bank and Trust Company agreed. "He impresses us," wrote one of their officers, "as an individual worthy of your consideration and one who will live up to his commitments." A host of brokerage houses had similar thoughts.

Bishop's took into account these offerings and submitted to their clients an estimate of their subject which somewhat hedged their earlier thoughts. "All unflattering remarks are unable to be traced to a definite source or action," they wrote. But they added that Rubinstein's discussion of his work was "done without presenting us with the character of substantial intelligence about his companies with which a true measurement could be made." With an eye on the anguished British stockholders, it was pointed out that "there is a question of whether the money can be retained or whether the funds and assets will be attached and possibly returned to England."

They added, "There is evidence of envy of the success of one so young as Rubinstein. His success as a foreigner in times of none too good business in this country has not added to his popularity with some."

The report went out to be read and talked about. Rubinstein again called at Bishop's to threaten gigantic suits for libel and slander. "You're trying to crucify me," he shouted. "Why? Why?" But he calmed down enough to present the head of the firm with a page he had cut from *The Tatler,* a British magazine. It showed photographs taken at El Morocco, which was described as a "magnet for notables who want to see the city at its gayest, a great gathering place for international celebrities." There were pictures of Alfred Duff Cooper, Alexander Kerensky, William K. Vanderbilt, and, sitting at a table in evening dress, Rubinstein, the Austrian Archduke Franz Josef von Hapsburg and his wife, and Lady Kerr-Clark-Kerr, (sic) the Chilean wife of the British Ambassador to China. Rubinstein wrote across it, "With best regards from one who finds himself called a 'celebrity' by the English in spite of efforts to the contrary by certain quarters over here."

El Morocco was not the only night club that knew him in those days. He went out every night—every night without exception—to where people went just before the war. The Stork saw him, and the Pierre, and "21." He did not go alone. There were always women along and promoters looking for a deal and European refugees on the make. Wherever he went there was noise and uproar and a sudden rush to the best table, always the best table. Those were the good old days of night-clubbing and of no suburbia and no television; those were the days when the Copa had a third show starting at 2 A.M. and the after-hours spots were hopping. Those were the days when in the summer café society people went on weekends out to the beach clubs on Long Island where one day the eyes of Teddy Howard, who handled the publicity for a couple of such places, popped out to see a chubby man go dashing across the sand with six—six!—models racing along with him. The group of them, the one man and six models, went roaring down to the waters off Sands Point, splashing sand into sun-bathers' eyes and, as perhaps is not to be wondered at, taking the place by storm. "Who in hell is that guy?" Howard asked, and someone told him Serge Rubinstein, a new Wall Street man. "Six girls?" asked Howard incredulously. But then he got used to it; every weekend after that there was always a gang of girls with Rubinstein. One night Gordon Foster—who had not seen or heard from Rubinstein since the fake pearls episode of ten years before —found himself being pounded on the back as he stood at a night-club bar. It was the boy who had asked him about what to wear on what occasions when they had dined together in Vienna's Bristol Hotel. "Gordon, Gordon!" boomed out the boy, who now was a man. "How are you?" he shouted —he always boomed and shouted, then. "I'm having a party in my suite. Come on!" Foster had drifted to America to become an interior decorator and this was opening night at a club he had done, and Morton Downey was singing, but Rubinstein insisted he come along to the Savoy Plaza Hotel where he was living in a big suite. They went up together and Foster found the party consisted of himself, Rubinstein, two other men and exactly (for he counted them) twenty-two girls. Foster was a little dazed. He found Rubinstein much heavier than he had been, he thought him a big overgrown boy weighing 200 pounds, fat in Foster's eyes, a fat boy wearing a tuxedo. (Every night he wore a tuxedo. Now there were no questions about what to wear.) The girls, all twenty-two of them, were circulating around the expensive suite, digging into the catered dinner brought up by uniformed waiters and busboys who in the tradition of good hotels were looking for a chance to light their cigarettes.

The girls were all shifting around, bare shoulders and arms smooth and perfumed and catching the eye as they sought to get a little closer to their host. A dinner, a suite like this, drinks flowing galore, a young and eligible bachelor . . . Rubinstein was laughing, shouting, talking and talking, cracking jokes and running his hands through this head of hair, over that gowned rear end. "Astounding, Gordon!" he cried out, flinging up his hands. "Look at them clamoring around me!" He ate prodigiously and constantly gobbled chocolates —it was a vice—but he did not drink. Perhaps there would be a highball in his hand but he never touched his lips to it. There was never a cigarette, pipe, or cigar in his mouth.

After a while he vanished into his bedroom with one girl; they were out a little later, half an hour later, and he was back telling the hotel people to get some more hot duck up here and be quick about it, hop to it. It was two in the morning, three in the morning, four in the morning, and he was dancing in the middle of the room with one of the girls and then another of the girls. They were all Sweetheart, Honey, Darling, and then he was gone again, vanished again into the bedroom with another girl, a different one from the first, and by then the party was starting to break up. "I have to be up early," he said. A big man was coming to see him, a very big man. He had a deal cooking, that was why he had to be up early. It was a really tremendous deal, millions were involved, millions. But soon he would have another party: Sweetheart and Honey and Darling would have to come, they would have the greatest time of their lives. But now good night. And out. The girls were gone. "Gordon," he said, "I've got a dozen companies; you should see; I'm going into every business you ever heard of. And I'll make you a director of a few of my companies, you'll see. Call me and I'll take you in and give you . . ." I'll make you, I'll take you, I'll give you. Foster called and did in fact become a director, an officer, a trustee. His salary was $75 a week.

Meanwhile the Chosen Corporation matter dragged on and on. It was always there, the stockholders with their briefs, the government agencies with their pronouncements, the accountant-investigator Sir Harry Peat charging concealment of assets and nonco-operation in divulging information, the British financial writers calling for a compulsory liquidation of the corporation. Rubinstein fought back, retaining the firm of Goldwater & Flynn as his lawyers and writing back about Boss Ed Flynn to an English friend, saying that "there is nothing to worry about as I have engaged as consul the most powerful political figure in the United States." Frederick Miller, an English engineer with a good amount of Chosen

79

stock came over to Rubinstein's camp and was with him in New York, a tall and distinguished-looking older Englishman whose appearance was such that the Americans decided he should be called "Judge" although he possessed no juridical qualifications. Others called him "Pop" Miller and he accepted both titles with a grave manner which gave confidence to American businessmen meeting him as officer of several of Rubinstein's new corporations. Chosen and the British could say and do as they liked but meanwhile Rubinstein had the money and could do with it very much as *he* liked. Using it he became an incredible master of arbitrage, which is the selling of a country's currency in terms of the rate of exchange in another country or countries and for which there is needed the greatest knowledge of political and economic trends and the undercurrents therein, but in the practice of which there is the greatest danger. For if the British pound rises in value one fraction of a penny in terms of the American dollar, or if the German mark goes down the smallest part of a pfennig in terms of the French franc, then at the moment it happens the arbitragist who has guessed wrong loses all. Rubinstein's arbitrage transactions were terrifying to anyone who watched them; one man privy to his doings never forgot how once for forty-eight hours it became a matter of the loss of half of Rubinstein's money if the British pound went up half a penny. It did not go up that half a penny and Rubinstein was home free. Ever after the man let it be known that this bastard was a genius and nothing less. (To the man Rubinstein was a genius because of the arbitrage work; a bastard because of the business of ticket 555 in the ship's pool, which the man had originally bought.)

On Wall Street it was a regular thing by then for Rubinstein to be called a Boy Wonder of finance, which is a term the Street periodically digs up to bestow upon a nonshopworn shooting star. Rubinstein accepted the title and made himself very accessible to anyone seeking to put through any kind of a deal. He was, he let it be known, a stranger in the country but one anxious to become affiliated with men of stature and means seeking new expansions of business ventures. The important financial and banking community of the Street is a tightly knit crowd and there was something about an alien Jew coming to their homes which did not appeal to them, so when they took Rubinstein up on his offers (which they did) the meetings were at luncheon in the Stock Exchange Club or in private dining rooms in downtown restaurants. Uptown, later in the evenings, with a few chorus girls or models sitting at the night-club table, things could also be worked out. And still later at night after coming out of the bedrooms of mid-town hotels, alone now among their own sex, the three or four older gentlemen along for the party could see even better why they should deal with the young European who was their host. "I gave the chickens"—chickens, that was a word the American bankers and brokers used—"I gave the chickens two hundred bucks apiece," the young European would say—which was a total lie for he never, or almost never, paid for sex in his life—and the Wall Street gentlemen would nod over their cigars and brandy . . . Now here's something you might want, there's a fellow downtown hold-ing a commitment on an order of goods from the West, a perfectly good order, perfect collateral all insured, and he wa. s to assign it to someone with a little loose money look-ing to be lent out . . .

At Eastertime, of 1939, he decided to get away from it all for a bit and took a model with him for a Caribbean cruise aboard the *Kungsholm*. The model had a girl friend she wanted to bring along and that suited him fine so the trio sailed off and when they came back the model went to live with him at the Savoy Plaza. But no one held his interest very long and he and the girl took to having loud arguments. One day the manager of the hotel was called to the Rubinstein suite where he found the model screaming in rage. "You've ruined my soul and reputation and now you're trying to throw me out!" she was crying over and over. There was a complaint to the police and a few threats of legal action but it got smoothed over. Still the Savoy Plaza felt a bit upset over it and Mr. Rubinstein was asked to move. He got himself an apartment at 1016 Fifth Avenue —Gordon Foster did the decorating—and then had the model move back in with him.

But the business with her was a nasty affair and word of it got around. The Chosen matter still hanging fire was a constant irritant. Financial writer Burton Crane of the New York *Times*, who had done newspaper work in the Far East, was very much up on Chosen's doings and was frequently writing less than complimentary articles about the Boy Won-der. That worthy announced he didn't care what Crane or anyone else said—in early '39 he had sent a defiant message to Crane saying that he "didn't give a God damn" what the man wrote or didn't write—but there was no getting away from it, there were too many questions about him in people's minds and he didn't know why it was so. Unable to comprehend why all the fuss was being made—he'd never done anything wrong, had he?—he decided to consult the lawyer Max Steuer, at that time perhaps the most eminent attorney in New York. An emissary went to Steuer to explain that Mr. Rubinstein sought guidance as to what path of conduct he might advantageously follow in the New World. Steuer opined that such a question would have to be discussed at great length and suggested a meeting in his apartment.

So with a friend Rubinstein went to see the lawyer. After dinner they went to a quiet room where Steuer sank into a chair and asked his new client to tell him all about it. Rubinstein began to walk up and down the room talking steadily about himself, his parents, his life in Russia, Vienna, England, and France, about how his enemies were trying to do him in because he was so brilliant and a foreigner. At length he arrived at his business affairs and went on for three hours about them. All during the long speech Steuer sat and asked not a single question. At the end the lawyer got up, tapped Rubinstein on the shoulder very briskly—one, two—and said, "Don't let it happen again." Then he showed his visitors to the door. His bill came the next day. Five thousand dollars.

The bill was paid. But the man who paid it would not have been Serge Rubinstein had he followed the advice.

Chapter Eight

America (II)

One winter night at the Hotel Savoy Plaza an American businessman attending a party given by the new Wall Street wonder, Serge Rubinstein, learned to his astonishment that a fellow guest was a high diplomat of the German Embassy. It was 1939 and every day the diplomat's government was thundering out diatribes against the Jews. New York was filled with refugees from that government living in little apartments in Washington Heights and Kew Gardens and studying to pass the State exams that would enable them to take up in New York the professions they had practiced in Berlin and Munich. It simply flabbergasted the American to see an officer of the German Government quietly sipping cocktails as an invited and honored guest at a party given and paid for by anyone named Rubinstein. He communicated his amazement to another guest, a Hungarian baron.

"Unbelievable," he said to the baron.

"What is unbelievable about it?" replied the baron. "Here is a man with twenty or thirty millions. When you have that, you have no race, no color, no religion. It is the same as munitions sales: it cannot be comprehended on a legal, ethical basis. There are places such as Hong Kong or Macao or Curaçao where high level declarations of governments, spheres of influence, war situations mean nothing. You reach across them. It is that way with Rubinstein. He is an international person. In that world such classifications as Jew or Nazi are for children. Or Americans."

Children and Americans did not dominate the parties of the international person picking up the tab at the Savoy Plaza. Representatives of both these groups would be there —the children generally being around seventeen or eighteen and just getting started in the world of movies or modeling or something a good deal worse—but for the most part the guests were Europeans. But they were not the Europeans counting their pennies in upper Manhattan and Queens; they were rather the representatives of an older Europe that crumbled before the advent of Adolf Hitler. They were aristocrats, but aristocrats of two groups. The first group was composed of real aristocrats, or what had been the real aristocrats of that older Europe. The second group had been God only knows what. They said now that they were aristocrats. That was good enough for the Americans. The aristocrats of both groups became in the New York of those days what were called promoters, or simply worked this way: they got in with a rich American woman who told her broker that Lord So-and-so now handles four hundred thousand dollars of my speculative money. There then was no need for His Lordship to do anything beyond receive his monthly check from the broker, who figured that half a commission is better than none.

Rubinstein knew many such His Lordships. But the highest adornment of his home was a real Archduke of the family of Hapsburg, Royal of Hungary and Imperial of Austria. The name of the Archduke was a fortunate one. He was Franz Josef von Hapsburg, owning the same wonderfully resounding name borne by that ancient man who ruled Austria-Hungary for nearly seventy years. But where the earlier Franz Josef had been an Emperor, Rubinstein's Franz Josef was a promoter.

And Rubinstein could use promoters. Promoters had always surrounded him, each with a little deal and angle. The time has to be remembered: this was New York before America went to war. In Beverly Hills there used to be a genuine Imperial Highness of the Romanovs who delivered liquor for a living and was happy to get half a dollar for a tip. The aristocrats said that was typical of California, where they talked movies. In New York they talked about Danzig and whether the Maginot line would hold forever. It was the right time to have a name and a little promotion going for you.

The Archduke's wife, who was called Princess Marta de Bourbon despite her totally non-noble Austrian origin, worked out one very attractive promotion. It stemmed from the British attempt to make it socially nonacceptable for an American to be anything but wildly pro-British. Marta and an English Lady arranged production of a big bag with a beautiful British lion embroidered on it, its mouth open to presumably roar out defiance óf the Teutonic foe. The bag was filled with pins and needles and knitting yarn. The idea was that you were knitting a sweater for the British Tommies, or socks for them or something like that—Bundles for Britain. The bag sold for $500 and cost about $15 to make. At a party a woman could carry it in, take out the needles and the yarn and then put them aside until the end of the evening when they would be stuffed back into await another inevitable emergence at the next party. It all went to prove the woman was pro-British. Had the war lasted ten years not one sock would have been made and anyway you could go around the corner to Third Avenue and there buy a pair of socks for the British for 69 cents. Negligible results if any went to England, but so what? Marta did quite well with the promotion. She also branched out into the buying and selling of artistic objects. Once Marta came into the Hungarian baron's home for a party and wandered into his bedroom. She came out hurriedly, broke into a conversation he was having and said she could get him $1500 for his bed. "Seven fifty for me; seven fifty for you!" The baron disdained the offer.

Marta and the Archduke also raised pedigreed cats which they carefully trained to make use of the plumbing in the bathroom. It was not an easy trait for a cat to acquire and the animals were generally in good demand as in addition to their unusual abilities they were very beautiful. The girl friend of a Rubinstein lawyer, hearing of them, made the mistake one day of expressing her admiration for such remarkable felines. The next day a toilet-trained cat was delivered to her apartment, courtesy of the Archduke Franz Josef and the Princess Marta. As Rubinstein had introduced the woman to the regal couple, he was thus a kind of indirect party to the transaction.

Unfortunately the lawyer's friend found to her sorrow that capable as the cat was in the bathroom, it lacked savoir faire in the living room, where it tore to pieces a lovely set of curtains the lawyer's money had purchased. The cat was put out on the market and at a Rubinstein party was handed off to a Russian beauty a good deal past her prime who was very fond of animals. (The cat was originally offered to Rubinstein but he did not accept it.

Although he liked dogs, cats with their independence and haughtiness did not appeal to him.)

The incident pleased Rubinstein, who liked to see his guests mix in each other's lives. You never could tell what kind of new thing might come your way as a result of widening your operation and letting in air, meeting new people and making them your people. Of course the aristocrats circulating around the new Wall Street wonder sometimes got in one another's way. One such time Gordon Foster was thrown into a rage. Foster had bought two Louis XVI commodes for Rubinstein, not real old things, but very nice Meissen urns. After they were put in a room of the apartment, they caught the eye of the Archduke. He suggested to Rubinstein that they could be improved by the addition of illumination from below. Rubinstein told him to go ahead and do it, so the Archduke had holes bored into the urns for electric wires leading to bulbs inside. The next time Foster was in the apartment, he found great glaring searchlight beams probing the air above the urns. He rushed to Rubinstein. "Who did that?" he demanded. "Oh, God, I'll bet it was that God damned Archduke!" Rubinstein told him he was correct, but to let it go, it didn't matter. Foster went wailing off, crying out that the Archduke was impossible.

Franz Josef meant no harm; it was a chance to pick up a couple of dollars. He was a harmless type despite a few habits that were somewhat unexpected in a Hapsburg. One was collecting old rags. Doting on cleanliness, he would circulate at a Rubinstein party asking the guests if they had any rags to give him, explaining that he collected them so as always to have a plentiful supply to dust with. One Rubinstein girl friend found herself absolutely beyond words when one day the Archduke suggested that he would be happy to come to her apartment and clean the windows. He told her he loved to see shiny clean windows and that he could clean them better than anyone else in New York. Another girl friend fell afoul of the Archduke but gained stature in Rubinstein's eyes by the way it happened. She was sitting in the corner of a room during a party when a man walked into the room. She was a new girl friend and had never seen the man, but it was the Archduke making his entrance for the night. All around her the old people creaked and groaned their way to their feet. The girl sat where she was, one hand occupied with a drink and the other with an ashtray. The man glared at her and walked out. Then he came back and spoke with Rubinstein. Rubinstein walked to the girl and identified the irate newcomer. "The Archduke says he is highly insulted," Rubinstein said. "He demands you stand up when he enters the room." The girl was flabbergasted but she had spunk and brains—one of the few Rubinsteins girls who had either of those qualities. "I will *not* stand up!" she said. "Here I have something in each hand and all and anyway, why should I get up for him?" All around her the Europeans were saying please, please, it's the Archduke, stand up, stand up. "No!" said the girl. Rubinstein took it all in, the pleading *émigrés*, the blazing Archduke, the seated girl, and staggered off to cling to a fireplace mantel while he bent double with laughter. His cackling took utter possession of him and half an hour later he was still gasping away, weakly hanging on to the mantelpiece. The girl had never seen him so happy before and was never to see him so again, ever. She remembered it always, through marriage to another man and childbirth and all of that: the only time she ever saw Serge really, really happy.

There were those, such as Igor Cassini (who under the pen name Cholly Knickerbocker writes a society column for the New York *Journal-American*), who found the spectacle of European nobility in this new setting an unappealing sight. Such as he thought it was time for Europeans in America to be done with all of that and to settle down to earning a living the way other people did. He thought the Counts and Dukes elbowing each other to get at Rubinstein's food and liquor would have done better to finish with Yesterday; he resented seeing them used as window dressing. It was not in his eyes a savory business nor one done with any great finesse by the host at all those soirées. But it seemed the aristocrats saw it another way. They found people through Rubinstein. And there was always the free food and drink and the being catered to, or thinking you were, the being seated well at table and the rather dynamic experiences you might find there. Perhaps it would have been better that rather than being seated well a commission had been paid in cash, but Serge Rubinstein did not easily give such commissions. Quite the contrary. He gave orders. It was the most common thing for him to pick up a phone in front of a few people and announce that he would now call his friend and confidant the Archduke Franz Josef von Hapsburg. How the name rang out! "Hello, is that Your Imperial Highness? Come over at once! I am having a party! Good-by!" The American businessman who had read a somewhat adverse report on Mr. Rubinstein and his companies might still have doubts about his host, but he would enjoy addressing the summoned Archduke as Your Grace or Your Imperial Highness. There was a way that the disinherited of Europe lived in New York in those days, a way that allowed those brought up to expect only the best in life

86

to exist on someone else's money. The others who perhaps had not been brought up that way retained the memories of the comfortable post by the wall of the coffee house in Vienna, or the respectful "Herr Doktor" of the peasants and the custom-made suits so inexpensive to anyone of even the middle class in Europe. Someone else's money . . . and yet if Rubinstein would not give that, he was at least willing to supply dinners, champagne, night-club parties, a chance to wear the swallow-tails and the made-over gown. And a chance also to meet the American businessman who would listen, between the recitation of Yesterday's past glories and titillating scandals, to a little deal: Would not the gentleman be kind enough to accompany the Prince to the home of a friend in rather unfortunate circumstances which have necessitated the sale of some old family silver held for hundreds of years and only to be parted with for a sympathetic, understanding buyer?

And for the businessman at the parties there were always women. Rubinstein was generous with having women around. Some were rather eminent actresses or society women and others were bug-eyed little models charmed to meet the hand-kissing aristocrats with the beautiful manners. Promoters tended to have girls around and they brought their girls to Rubinstein's. And among the promoters were women with resounding titles and all the charming abilities of Old Europe at their command to entrance the Wall Streeter who moved in displaying affluence enough to insure a welcome from the lady. It was not a situation where you said here's a hundred dollars; let's go in the bedroom. Such an approach would produce a slap in the face or a gracefully performed faint and besides, that could be done with the garden variety American girls living in this apartment and that hotel on the East Side and giving out their telephone numbers to gentlemen met through mutual acquaintances at night-club tables. No, a woman with a title and the most charming accent is not approached that way and anyway, what was one hundred dollars to a big Wall Street man? Something more subtle and costly was needed, but men in any event tend to desire that which is most expensive. The game would be worth the candle, though . . . There was the Princess whose attire for the bedroom consisted solely of high black stockings and long, long strands of pearls which hung around her neck but reached almost to her knees. There was the Countess who had a gigantic bed. At the moment she and the gentleman of the evening would fall upon it she would push a button that would summon her four maids to the completely lighted room. They would group themselves about the bed and express their thoughts: "Countess, how I envy you!" "Countess, tell me, is this man as good as the man last week?" The Countess herself would not be silent: "Magnolia, how is the movement of this man? What do you think?" "Ah, Countess, how I wish I had as good a time in Harlem last night!" It was the most embarrassing thing in the world for the man, but he would be anxious to admit to his friends drinking at the club that at Rubinstein's parties you found things you were not likely to find on the 5:49 to Scarsdale.

The parties grew bigger and bigger. It was nothing for Rubinstein to give a party for three hundred, four hundred persons, or to take twenty-five couples to the theater and a night club afterward. There was never a quicker check-grabber than he was in those days and never a more charming surprise party-giver. He was great on getting together two hundred people to celebrate the birthday of a pleased and flattered guest of honor who had not expected any such festivities. Two or three times a week he had dinner parties for twelve or twenty or twenty-four guests.

It all was done in a vast, Russian, European way, the host moving among his guests in his lordly way to constantly inquire if they had gotten all they wanted; would they not have a little more champagne or Benedictine? He had a magnificent memory; he would remember your grandmother's first name and ask after her health. He was the perfect host elegantly garbed in evening clothes and making sure to greet each guest with a shout of joy, anxious to introduce you to this one and that one, ruler and ringmaster of this Court. There were always titles to meet, names, positions. He was through Mountbreak Corporation the American financial representative of his former employee in the Banque Franco-Asiatique, the one-time German Chancellor Dr. Joseph Wirth, of Emilio Portes Gil, the former President of Mexico, and, after the German occupation of Czechoslovakia, the fiscal agent for the Czech National Committee in America. He carried with him a photostat of Eduard Benes' telegram: IN NEW YORK YOU ALONE ARE ENTRUSTED BY US TO NEGOTIATE FINANCING.

Something of a find by the smarter, more moneyed New York crowd seen at opening nights and in the night spots, he was in those days himself being cultivated as a guest. "I didn't know a doorman when I came here," he would say, "and look at me now!" Everywhere he went there were people who knew him and he loved that, loved also to read his name in the papers and know that the society columnists found his parties "fabulous," "splendiferous," "out of this world." At charity dinners and balls he always took at least a couple of tables and was always ready to pledge

88

a large sum. At one such affair he promised to give—and gave—some money to a favorite charity of Mrs. Eleanor Roosevelt, and that got him an invitation to dinner at the White House. Ever after in New York and Washington there were stories that he was very close to the President and the First Lady. "You know what this White House is?" he would ask. "I can go in or out of there whenever I please." He was seen with a couple of the Roosevelt sons and the stories about his complete entrée at 1600 Pennsylvania Avenue were strengthened. Invited again to a White House affair, he was given a special plaque for his car which said or it that the auto was to be admitted via the East Gate. The plaque was not removed from the car, a chauffeur-driven Lincoln, for many months. Boss Ed Flynn was a Democrat and so was Senator Brien McMahon of Connecticut, another Rubinstein lawyer, and at their suggestion he began to contribute heavily to the Democratic party. (During the 1940 Presidential campaign he gave $10,000 for a pro-Roosevelt broadcast by the writer Dorothy Thompson.) In those Roosevelt years there were, of course, a great many people who were invited to the White House as a sign of recognition for contributions for one cause or another, but in the Washington gossip of those days it was said that there was more to Rubinstein's relationship with the family than that of a some-time contributor and that there was in fact a feeling of coziness between him and the Roosevelts. It was to evaporate a few years later after Eleanor Roosevelt bawled him out at the Washington airport for using some letters of hers as character references. "I don't want to speak to you ever again!" she snapped at him. But for a few years it was said in Washington that he was really quite close with the Presidential family. Certainly he was friendly with several United States Senators including McMahon, Claude Pepper, Burton K. Wheeler, "Happy" Chandler, and Robert F. Wagner.

Aside from political contributions his gifts to charity had a European tinge and were given in a great and open way—checks to the Russian Children in Exile, to the Society to Aid Russian War Invalids (of World War I), to the Literary Fund of the *Novoye Russkoye Slovo,* the Russian language paper in New York. There were those, it is true, who pointed out that when you got into the Rubinstein class a gift of $20,000 to the United Jewish Appeal to aid Nazi victims became a tax proposition and not an act of charity, but when they said that they did not know, perhaps, of his other charities. For he was the easiest kind of touch any European could find. There used to be an old Austrian gentlewoman who had come to roost in a tiny apartment on the West Side near those little hotels which catered to such as she and where day in and day out you could see sitting in the lobbies the aging gentry of Europe staring out into nothing, or, if not nothing, then West End Avenue or West 76th Street. The woman's husband had been a Deputy in the Austrian Parliament but by the late '30s, very fragile, she dressed in the old black elegance of God knows when and reminded those who saw her of the late stage actress Maria Ouspenskaya. You could see that she had once been quite beautiful and you could also know by looking at her that it was impossible for her to get a job or hold one. Rubinstein barely knew her and did not see her for years on end but each month he sent her a check for $100. It was all she had to live on and it came month after month, for years, until she finally died. There was no reason for him to do it, but he did. He could be that way. Sitting in a restaurant he might see an old man—likely with a beard and an ancient fur-collared coat—and he would leave his party and rush up and kiss the man in the Russian way. They might talk a few minutes in agitated French or Russian and then he would hand over a check for one hundred or two hundred dollars. George Shiskin was such a man, a Russian of gypsy blood and dark gypsy eyes and hair who had once been very wealthy and known all through St. Petersburg as a lover of the arts and the theater. The revolution cost him everything and had Rubinstein not given him money he surely must have died of hunger in New York, for he was a very old man and no job would have been offered to him. But Rubinstein supported him. There were a great many others like the old Austrian lady and George Shiskin flitting in and out of his life, quite helpless and quite useless to him (for by now they were too tarnished and obsequious to shine at a party) but he rather quietly took care of them, a hundred dollars here, a hundred dollars there.

But he did it only if he were in the right mood and the petitioners asked in the right way, which was to approach him somewhat after the fashion that one imagines a humble family retainer approaching the Czar of All the Russias. Once a German actor, a very serious man, came to Rubinstein as he sat with an Austrian intellectual whom Rubinstein called "Herr Professor." The German said in essence, I am here, I have nothing, can you do something for me? But his bearing and resonant actor's voice did not please Rubinstein, who replied by saying, "What can *you* do for me?"

The actor fumbled—really, what could he do for Rubinstein? "There is something," Rubinstein said. The actor asked

what that might be. "Procure me women," said Rubinstein.
The actor was shocked. "This is a joke?" he asked.

"No, it's not a joke!" Rubinstein said very forcefully. "That is the only thing you can do for me. If you do it, you can have money or whatever you want. Good-by!"

It all depended on his mood, and if they came to him in the right way.

There was one element in New York that did not accept him with open arms then or ever. They were those Jews of the conservative financial community downtown, almost all of uniformly German ancestry, who found this Rubinstein from Russia impossible—too loud, too gaudy, too showy, too quick. With that group, which was more sophisticated in the ways of Europe than perhaps any other in America, Rubinstein's reputation was always below zero. In that group's eyes it was wise for him to do business more with Americans than Europeans, for his type as they saw it could do better with the former than the latter. In that group in those days, and later, they used to say that it was fantastic what recent *émigrés* were able to palm off on the American public. To the Americans any Russian or Hungarian was a nobleman or great intellectual who could tell great stories of past glories and be taken on faith with no questions asked . . . a big story, the great past, his father the richest Jew in Russia and friend to Rasputin; who can prove that? With all of these there is the same rootless story and the Americans believe it. Hypnosis. It is not possible in London, Paris, Vienna—only in New York. It is not possible in Sydney. This kind of man would never be accepted in Europe. Von Hindenburg would not have accepted such a man if he had had one hundred million marks. . . . Such was what the Jewish old money of America said in its somber tones and quiet voice and conservative way, pointing out that in England things are more solid, in Germany in the old days such a man would have been totally impossible and that it was only from *"hinter Berlin"*—from the other side of Berlin—that such Jews came. There was a cruel saying among the German Jews that if you put a tuxedo on a Polack he was still a Polack, and the thought also applied to the Russians. Rubinstein to the old American Jewish community was of a piece with the poor and fly-by-night peddlers of violently anti-Semitic Poland coming to German business offices before Hitler, with the cattle dealers and shysters and talking-with-the-hands *hinter Berlin*. And they suspected the stories of his twenty or thirty millions, saying to one another that there is one thing we have learned throughout our lives and that is that only the good deals are talked about and that such as Mr. Serge Rubinstein do not talk about the bad ones. To those who were of a special wide-awake segment of the American old rich, Rubinstein was a bluffer. . . . Ninety-nine per cent of all people are overestimated anyway, one knows that. All New Yorkers spend more than they earn, but then, where could you spend it in Waterbury? With the same salaries in Kansas City you spend twenty per cent of what you spend on the East Side where every summer and every Christmas the rent is late by a month for half the people in the big apartment houses because of the bills for the children at camp in the first instance and the Christmas gifts in the second. In Iowa you see a lawyer walking around and you think, well, the man makes a living. Actually he has millions. But where can he spend it? They have no The Colony or Le Pavilion in Iowa. They go on a picnic. But here in New York, in this atmosphere, here everyone can find in his life whatever he wants, or thinks he does. Call it business. The little girl from Illinois comes here—Illinois, Pittsburgh, God knows where they come from—and they think they can make big money. They can't, of course. They think they can. . . .

. . . . And the little girl from Illinois or Pittsburgh or God knows where ended up going to the parties of Serge Rubinstein where she met and mixed with many, many different types, and had her hand kissed by the elegant host and perhaps was sent home in his gleaming Lincoln. And the other types got his ear with deals and little jobs and oil-field investments and stock kiting and loans on jewelry at high rates to those temporarily in embarrassed circumstances and juggling of foreign credits and small matters involving the smuggling out of bonds from Nazi Germany or Fascist Italy—Konrad Sztykgold had a whole set of special false-bottom luggage for that—and on and on. The parties grew larger and larger, the host ever more open-handed and grand and regal in dispensing largesse to the courtiers.

"Friends?" said Gordon Foster. "He had no friends. There were people he knew."

Chapter Nine

Laurette

Stella came over from Europe. Dimitri was dead and the Germans were in Paris and Stella took an apartment in the Hotel Navarro on Central Park South where she lived in considerable splendor with her Swedish maid who had been with her for twenty-five years. Aunt Genia came over too and put up at the Hotel Park Plaza on West 77th Street and found new teachers to help her get ahead with her voice studies. Serge paid for both their accommodations and for everything they did, and the two aging sisters interested themselves in charity work and in the doings of the little *émigré* groups in New York. A kind of apart life filled with people talking Russian, French, and German was theirs, but while for Genia it began and ended with the opera and singing and charities, Stella was more ambitious in the New World seeing her son Serge as a younger Dimitri moving up to the kind of heights his father had known in Petersburg. She was filled with plans for him to advance himself—"Serge, you must take a table for twenty, for thirty, at the British War Relief Ball; you must be seen there"—but she was uneasy, too. She would never say it to his face, but to too many people she said he was no Dimitri; Dimitri was smoother and more brilliant, Dimitri did not grate on people as Serge did. Once a hanger-on said to her, "Ah, Madame Rubinstein"— that was what she was always called: Madame Rubinstein— "now you have had two great gentlemen in the family, yes." Stella looked at the man with the green-gray eyes so like Serge's and said, "No. There was only one." The gentleman who had made the remark went away confused but with a bit of good gossip to give out over the buffet where the cold chicken and roast beef was being handed out along with the white wine and the red.

Brother André and his wife the Princess Valerie also came over. They did not come in friendship, but to press against Serge their claim that he owed them a great amount of money. They bore with them a note signed by both brothers and by Konrad Sztykgold which said that as André had introduced Sztykgold to Serge, he, André, would thereafter be entitled to one-third of all moneys Sztykgold made through Serge, "of all commissions, awards, emoluments or remunerations of any kind and nature." The note had been signed in London on October 21, 1936, following a conference at the Park Lane Hotel in the West End at which time, according to André and Valerie, it had been agreed that as Sztykgold was older and had more connections, he rather than André would act as an agent for Serge. All through the business of smuggling the Japanese yen out of the Yokohama Specie Bank and all through the dealings with the Chosen Corporation André and Valerie had waited for payments, but Serge from America only wrote asking for extensions and more extensions. And he had never paid back the $20,000 he had borrowed from André many years before. There were letters and letters, all unanswered, and the war was on, so the couple came to New York and put up in a hotel and tried to get hold of Serge. But he had vanished.

Only after several days did he turn up and then he was a little sheepish but gave assurances that everything would be all right, he would take care of everything. André and Valerie were down to some few thousand dollars and they wanted the $20,000 and the other moneys they felt were due them so that they could settle down and find some little business to invest in, some little factory perhaps, some real estate. Serge was always saying he would pay but there was no money forthcoming and there started to form that hard situation where they would sue each other back and forth and fight an unforgiving battle that would end only with André literally driven to his death and Valerie to poverty and an all-consuming hatred against the man she felt had killed her husband and ruined her life.

But before the final estrangement André and Valerie were uneasy guests at the great parties where more and more Madame Rubinstein acted Dowager Empress to Serge's Prince. The guests were always brought to her to say good evening and to kiss her hand. She wore a great ring and around her sat or stood her own little group among whom she shone by virtue of her son who could pay bills for real imported Russian caviar and French champagne. Teddy Schulz was also occasionally there, that same Teddy—whom Serge always called "Theo"—who long ago at the Goethe Realschule in Vienna had tutored his now-resplendent host in courses at which he did not shine. When Serge left Vienna for Cambridge he all but dropped out of Teddy's life, Teddy who went to work in an office and was very impressed upon those two occasions when Serge came back to Vienna as the owner of a bank, with a business secretary doubling as glamour girl during after-business hours. But when in 1938 the German Army arrived in Vienna Rubinstein wrote to Schulz saying that if the latter wanted money to get out of Austria, he would provide it. Actually he deposited it in a Cuban bank for Schulz and so Schulz went to Havana and from there to Philadelphia and another office job the routine of which was now and then interrupted by an invitation to attend one of his ex-schoolmate's exciting parties. Teddy was only one of hundreds of guests and a rather unimportant one at that, being always a shy and retiring sort. There were other far more striking guests both male and female. Many of the latter type had had relationships of some warmth with the host but those women were never asked to act as hostess. That was reserved for Madame. Then came Laurette.

Afterward, it became the fashion in the group around Serge Rubinstein to say that in his European fashion he had married an ornament, a flower, a piece of fluff that looked good all shellacked and blonde and gleaming at the dinner table.

There was something to that, but with the thought went an assumption that simply was not so, and that was that Laurette Kilborn was stupid, a dumb model picked up to be dangled and turned to catch the light like a piece of jewelry.

She was not stupid. But she was very young when she met Serge Rubinstein. She was eighteen and one of two identical twins, the other being Betty, who were modeling furs at Russek's and doing a little picture work for John Robert Powers. She had grown up in a wandering kind of way produced by the Depression and her mother's pursuit of a legal claim that never came to fruition. The mother was from upstate New York but the twins were born in San Francisco. Their father worked on the railroads there. When the mother's father, the girls' grandfather, died in Potsdam, New York, in the late 1920s, the family, which included a younger sister, returned there to settle the estate. The girls' mother felt it was going to be a considerable one. Instead it turned out to be nothing, and the mother decided she had been jobbed out of a great sum of money by certain men in Potsdam. She accused them of stealing the estate. An energetic woman with a great deal of drive, Mrs. Kilborn set out to rectify the wrong she felt had been done. She bombarded Governor Franklin D. Roosevelt with letters asking for his aid; she went to every important lawyer in the East; she wrote letters to the newspapers; she ranged up and down Potsdam and all upstate New York crying to Heaven that she had been robbed. Her efforts led to nothing save the slow eating away of the family's resources, but she continued. Finally they were dispossessed from the family home in Potsdam, she and her husband and the twins Laurette and Betty and the younger Janice. It was 1931 and they drifted south in their old car, to the back yard of a deserted homestead in Tappan, New York. They slept on blankets on the ground and then in the back of a roadside gas station. Then they moved on to a little shack big enough for the parents to occupy, with the children sleeping nights in the car parked close to the thin wall so the parents could hear them if anything went wrong. People gave them berries and vegetables from home gardens. They moved on, not the only family patrolling the roads at that time, and went to a siding of the Saw Mill River highway at Ardsley, the parents sleeping in the front of the car with the three girls in the back. Some construction workmen gave them a tarpaulin and they made a small shelter there by the side of the road. The workers brought cooking utensils for them and they camped out for several weeks. They had a fireplace in the ground with an old milk can for a chimney and they brought water from a quarter of a mile away.

The winter of 1931 came on and they arranged to live in

a deserted auto camp in the Bronx, surrounded by ground littered with broken furniture and old bedsprings. The children did not go to school; Mrs. Kilborn taught them herself and a Welfare Department investigator came to give them ill-fitting secondhand clothing. At length the worst was over and they came to roost in a home near Mount Vernon. The twins went to Evander Childs High School in the Bronx, terribly pretty now and impossible for strangers to tell apart. They were sixteen and wearing identical striped dresses when they posed for a picture for the school's science magazine to illustrate chromosome development in twins. The picture came to the attention of John Robert Powers and he called their mother with a modeling offer.

So they became models, very young ones but still stunning girls. They had big blue eyes and faultless complexions but they were children. They did not have serious boy friends but there was always a crowd of young kids around the house, and stickball and hopscotch in the street. They moved to Flushing minus the father, who had separated from his wife, and every day the twins went off on the subway to work in Manhattan. Their mother gave them a dollar a day spending money.

They were eighteen and it was 1939 and one day Laurette met a German boy at a tennis club and the German boy asked her to go to a party with him. She went and thought it a very strange affair, very fancy and swish, but funny with all the people with accents and all the kissing of her hand. She was only vaguely aware of the thirty-two-year-old host but the next morning a great bouquet of flowers was delivered to the house. The day after that there were yet more flowers and a week later there was an elegantly worded invitation for Miss Kilborn to come to another party and to bring with her the twin sister of whom she had spoken. A car would call for them.

Laurette accepted and Betty did also and so one night a long dark Lincoln with a chauffeur pulled up to their modest Flushing home. Inside the car, regally leaning back against the plush cushions sat Gordon Foster, very elegant and handsome and quite horrified at the, to him, squalid surroundings. There was a dog and a cat and the three daughters and the mother and some unwashed pots and pans. The twins were arguing about who should wear what of their mutually owned clothing when Foster arrived to make gallant small talk with the mother while he cast a fishy eye down his nose at the apartment and the bourgeoise American way in which the Kilborns lived. The trio finally departed in the Lincoln, the two girls thinking Mr. Foster was certainly a dashing sort of older man with his fine gray hair and British accent and ways, and Mr. Foster thinking they were nice healthy good-looking American girls but simple, very simple.

They went to the Rubinstein apartment on Fifth Avenue, to be effervescently greeted by their host, who made a great thing of their remarkable resemblance and showed them around, pointing to his life-size statue of Flora and to the gigantic paintings of heroic scenes which adorned his walls. Foster asked him, "Well, which one do you like the better?" and he replied, "Laurette; the other one's too sharp, too smart."

The analysis was a kind of half-truth. Betty was indeed the sharper of the two, the more verbal, the dashing one, the spunkier and the quicker, but Laurette was far from being a dullard despite her quietness. It was that she preferred to be silent; it was her way. She was the kind of girl who is not going to get involved in anything, not going to mar her make-up by taking a position: the glamour girl on a leash. Rubinstein always wanted the game and the victory and Laurette was something he could not have, not really, because she was the kind of distant person never fully committed. It was likely that which caught him. But that is not to say she did not have her interests; she had a certain amount of artistic talent and could paint and sculpt quite well. She was also sophisticated, or came to be, in art matters. She could lecture very well on certain painters, could point out the signs of Van Gogh's mental deterioration as seen in his paintings. It was not Laurette who set her cap for Serge; it was the other way around. Perhaps it was not only her classic beauty which struck him so much as her utter coldness and the great unapproachableness she had, the unconquered and unconquerable woman she was and remained.

Whatever the reason he laid siege to her with the inspired fervor that could be his. There were flowers, dinner invitations, candy for the mother, tickets to the theater, parties and more parties. Mrs. Kilborn was treated with a Continental respect as a *grande dame*; never had she seen such gallantry and never was her hand kissed so much. He came to Thanksgiving dinner and the first and perhaps only visit of his life to a middle-class kind of American home and announced himself astonished at the fineness of the fare and the selection of fruits and sweets. Only the very rich ate like that in Russia, he said. And so slowly his life became theirs and he moved in on them and they on him. He was in charge of them, their days and their nights. (In time he would set up Mrs. Kilborn in a Riverside Drive apartment which had once been occupied by Mayor James J. Walker's mistress—Gordon Foster would do the decorating job—and in time he would put younger sister Janice through New York University and pay for Betty's acting classes at Stella Adler's.) He started match-making for Betty at a wild pace and when the war came she knew not one soul in the American forces; almost all her boy friends were Europeans from Serge's crowd and eventually she would marry the son of one of Rubinstein's business associates.

Of course there were discordancies about him. Betty and Laurette never could get over all the nutty foreigners mooching around. The Archduke particularly amused them. Once they heard someone refer to him by the German word *"Spatzie,"* meaning sparrow, and hearing it they did notice that in fact Franz Josef had a long birdlike nose and was tall and thin with hair falling back from his temples in a winglike fashion. After that he was always Spatzie to them. They knew nothing of foreign wars and history and Rubinstein used to tell them tall tales improvising as he went along. He held them enthralled with a description of how in 1918 at the Russian border his poor father was shot to death before his horrified eyes. Years passed before Betty ever learned that in fact Dimitri lived nearly two decades past the time of the revolution. But that was Serge. He had his ways. Some of them were abhorrent to them, though. Neither girl ever forgot the time when the trio finished a horseback ride out on Long Island and went from the stables to a restaurant they had often frequented together. Rubinstein went in first, slamming down his heavy riding boots as he marched in like a Prussian Hussar until everyone looked up to see him open his mouth and roar, "Any calls for RUBINSTEIN?" The girls wanted to die, it was such a spectacle; the quiet diners interrupted in their eating to hear Serge's bellow. (All their lives as twins who were stared at they had sought anonymity but they weren't going to get much of that when Serge was around.) Even his riding had an impact on anyone who watched. He never learned, nor tried to learn, to post a horse, but would stand up in the stirrups like (in Gordon's Foster's eyes) a bloody Cossack charging the enemy, and he would gallop up and down hills where anyone else would have slowed his steed. He had no particular desire to keep to established riding trails but would roar off across the countryside, charging over other people's land or onto highways where a horse should not have been. He was far from a subtle rider but was all bounce and arms pumping and a shouted laugh floating back. There used to be a place in Pennsylvania where he maintained a summer home and near by there was a riding academy which learned to dread his frequent appearances. "Oh, God," would moan the woman who ran the place, "here he comes." She would throw a Western saddle over a particularly strong and rugged animal who could take two hours of galloping uninterrupted by any quiet walking periods.

He had a great many other traits which irritated Betty and Mrs. Kilborn and Laurette also, but the future marriage seemed somehow to be a force that was inevitable. Once the twins and he had been riding in Bayside, where in those days before the war there was a lot of space suitable for horses, and, when they returned to Flushing, Laurette had to leave to go keep a long-standing commitment. Rubinstein invited sister Betty instead to go to dinner and a movie, and his chauffeur drove them into Manhattan. They went to a little dark movie house to see a French comedy. Quite crowded, the movie house yet had two seats on the aisle for them. But those seats did not suit Rubinstein—he wanted to sit in the middle—and so they wandered up and down until he spotted two far into a row. They barged in stumbling over people and forcing them to get up but after fifteen minutes they decided the movie was inane. Rubinstein indicated his displeasure by cracking his knuckles. That was a key to his unhappiness. And he could really crack them; it used to drive people crazy to hear them going *whap! whap!* one by one until he finished all ten and then started again. Finally in the movie he said to Betty, "It's no good. Let's go," and they got up and everyone in the row had to rise again with a great untwisting of crossed legs and shifting of coats. They went out into the street and to dinner where Rubinstein made a slight pass at Betty under the table because she was, so to speak, the only thing to hand. It infuriated her—first the business of disturbing half the people in the movie and now this. That night she had a talk with Laurette and said to her that it would be a big mistake to marry Serge. Laurette was something of a fatalist; "I have to marry him," she said, and so the family learned that it was indeed going to happen that she would be Mrs. Rubinstein (Mrs., not Madame—Madame was Stella).

He loved Laurette, there was no doubt about it, but there were other reasons for him to have an American wife. First, a beautiful girl, Mrs. Rubinstein my wife—that looked very good. Second, Laurette was gentile, Protestant—High Anglican, no less—and that would help him to be above his Jewishness which on the surface never meant anything to him save for its occasional use in dealing with Jewish businessmen who might take more kindly to someone who flung in a couple of humorous phrases in Yiddish. But most important there was the question of his immigration status. For in the short time he had been in America he had come to the attention of the immigration people rather forcefully. The Chosen suit had singled him out with his most questionable certifications of Portuguese citizenship, and there was a certain subway matter.

The subway matter involved the unification of the various New York City subway systems which before 1940 were not all gathered under the aegis of a municipal Transit Authority but were privately owned. Rubinstein had become friendly with an official of the Brooklyn Manhattan Transport Company who was in personal financial trouble. With the presentation of a check for $250,000, Rubinstein had eliminated the troubles. The money was handed over at the end of a dinner. "Just tell me six months before it happens when the BMT is going to be unified with the other lines and just what price will be paid for its stock and bonds," Rubinstein asked the man. The idea came to him, he told his friends later, when one morning he was reading a paper as he sat in the back of his car being driven to his Wall Street office. The article pointed out that the unification of the various lines was inevitable and that stock- and bond-holders would have to be bought out before the act could take place.

The man who received the $250,000 agreed to co-operate. Within a short time he informed Rubinstein that 90 per cent of its own outstanding preferred stock would be bought up by the BMT, that percentage being needed to put through the merger. He added that the price was going to be $65 a share for the stock. But—and here was what Rubinstein had paid cash on the line for—if any holders refused to sell out at $65, then after a while the price would be raised to $116.50 in order to obtain the necessary shares. Armed with the information, Rubinstein corporations and front men started buying BMT stock on margin, accumulating more than one-third of the issue. In due time the $65 offer was made and accepted by almost all of the other holders. But the Rubinstein one-third was held and held until, as the official had said, an offer of $116.50 was made and, of course, accepted. Rubinstein also purchased a substantial number of BMT bonds and under the same arrangement reaped $1050 a bond where other holders had gotten $950.

News of this coup was common knowledge in the Street and a stockholder action charging a conspiracy on the part of Gerhard Dahl and other BMT directors was filed. It was, however, dismissed. The SEC also made an intensive investigation, as a result of which the Justice Department presented the case to a Grand Jury. But no action was taken. Shortly afterward, while campaigning for mayor, William O'Dwyer made something of a fuss about the matter, charging a leak in the La Guardia administration had led to the stock killing. In general the deal disturbed Wall Street; here was a foreigner walking into so native a product as the New York subway system and garnering almost a one-and-a-half-million dollar profit. There was an element of jealousy in what the Street said that was not missed by one Rubinstein acquaintance. He baited a group of staid types about it in their club one day. "For God's sake," he said, "the guy had the guts to put out the $250,000 and then he had the guts to sit on the stock till the price went up and now you complain! Why didn't you do it?" There was no answer that could readily be made to the question. But that Rubinstein had finagled his way into and out of a deal catching the attention of so many people, including the government's Securities and Exchange Commission, could not help his standing with the government's immigration officials making a study of his entrance into the United States and the legality of his remaining there.

That was where Laurette Kilborn, the girl he loved, could come in handy. A man with an old-line American wife and hopefully a couple of American children, could not very well be deported to some war-ravaged country of Europe. More and more, then, he worked toward a marriage. Madame was against it and said so to all her people, but then it is likely she would have been against any girl. Sister Betty was against it also, although Mrs. Kilborn found it very hard to oppose a suitor so open-handed and so well placed. Slowly Serge and Laurette drifted away from their respective families putting pressure on them to break off the affair and soon everyone else was on the outside and the two of them were together like any more or less young and more or less well-suited couple. There came a day in 1941 when they went to Washington together to look into some business matters and to attend a reception at the White House. It was understood by everyone who knew them that it was just a little weekend trip, but after they had gone Mrs. Kilborn got a wire from Laurette in Alexandria, Virginia, asking her permission for a marriage to Serge. Mrs. Kilborn said yes and Betty went down to go to the reception after what would have to be called the elopement. The reception was at Washington's Shoreham Hotel and you had to have a special card to get in. It was March 19, 1941. Society reporters counted no less than nine foreign Ambassadors to the United States in attendance, plus innumerable senators, congressmen, judges. Mrs. Roosevelt sent a telegram.

Chapter Ten

André

Brother André and his wife the Princess Valerie were in America a year before they went to court about the money they said Serge owed them. It had been a difficult year for the couple. One of Serge's corporations took André on as a deal finder and investigator, but the salary was very low and Valerie had to go to work to help make ends meet. She modeled dresses in New York's garment district and acted as hostess in a restaurant. Meanwhile Serge was living very high, planning new financial conquests, giving parties, sending Laurette shopping in the Lincoln to Bergdorf Goodman and Bonwit Teller to select dresses for a showing at home, where he would decide that this one goes back to the store, this one you keep. He talked almost incessantly about building an empire and becoming the most important man in America but André and Valerie were living in a tiny apartment in an unfashionable neighborhood and they decided to have done with their waiting.

A conference was held at Rubinstein's Wall Street office. Valerie rode down in a taxi with her brother-in-law. "Look," she said to him, "why don't you settle with us? We'll give you a release and all this trouble will be over."

"Oh, you," Rubinstein said. He was in an expansive mood. "Why don't you forget what is past and think of the future?"

"Why not think of the past and forget the future?" she replied.

He laughed. "Oh, you are very clever," he said. They reached his building and rode up to his office together, he with his hat on his head, and went into his room where he put his feet up on the desk. The conference came to nothing; he was parting with nothing. It was the last amicable meeting the three of them ever had. André and Valerie walked out and went to a lawyer and instituted suit.

Rubinstein contested the suit. His principal lawyers to defend him were Frank L. Miller and Edwin B. Wolchok, whom everyone addressed as "Sonny." They began a long, long series of delaying actions which carried on for years on end. There were any number of suits and countersuits and hearings and trials. The scope of the battle was widened so that the original causes were sometimes almost forgotten. André sued Serge for blackening their mother's name by proclaiming his allegedly illegitimate, Portuguese, birth; Serge countered by successfully obtaining judicial orders impounding the court records of any proceeding where the illegitimacy matter was mentioned. And when a newspaper article would criticize Serge's role in the continuing Chosen litigation, Serge would sue André, charging the latter had conspired to defame him with the author of the article. Several judgments were entered against André but he fought on, even instituting suit against Serge and Stella both, saying "the defendant Stella Rubinstein my mother has repeatedly informed me that she is absolutely at his mercy and unless she complied with his requests of any kind or nature, her income from him could be cut off as well as that of her sister whom he is supporting." Serge on the other hand charged that André and Valerie "maliciously and in bad faith and without probable cause tried to compel him through suit, through fear and duress of unfavorable publicity" to part with large sums of money.

They fought their way back to the question of Dimitri's estate, André claiming Serge had jobbed him out of his share of it, Serge being a man "who will not stop at anything to cheat me out of my rightful inheritance as he has on numerous occasions cheated me out of other moneys rightfully and legally due me." Serge's reply denounced André's "conduct and antics resulting in the institution of this and other unwarranted and unjustified law suits," and said this one was "but a part of a plan devised by his diabolical and perverted mind to mulct from the plaintiff Serge Rubinstein his brother, a man of means, large sums of money."

Out of court they also hacked away at each other, Serge circulating in the Russian colony of the city with stories that André was a blackmailer and André saying that when Dimitri their father was on his deathbed Serge bent over him and the dying man reached up and slapped his son's face, perhaps as a last reprimand for all the unthinkable things he had done, including as a child the stealing of the father's shoes from a sleeping car to sell when the train pulled into a station.

Serge went to the tax people with a story that André was cheating on taxes; André documented for the immigration people that Serge's Portuguese ancestry was pure fraud and that thus his entrance to the United States was illegal. Back and forth they went, delays following examinations before trial, applications piling on affidavits. André's health began to decline. He lost weight and his color was not good and the people around Serge all joined in urging him to settle the thing and have done. But there was something in the combat that appealed to Serge; one of his acquaintances likened it to the love of fighting of the Russian Cossack who when there was no war fought for fun with crude slashing swords, impervious to danger and pain. Another thought it was Serge's great inborn affinity for law—he was always ahead of his lawyers and always the first to spot a damaging remark or trend. He was asked by Konrad Sztykgold why he did not end the damned business and pay André off, but he replied that it would be a dull life, wouldn't it, without all those jousting sessions where he could show up the lawyers and have fun with them? And in fact he did love being examined, being the center of attention displaying himself, and in the process matching wits with his questioner.

André had no such great love for the complicated claims and counterclaims; his response was to become a sick and semi-hysterical man chasing a shadow, that shadow being his hope that one day he would yet win out over this younger brother who had everything, money, car, mansion, while he himself had nothing of a material nature and only his fiercely determined wife to stand with him. André did not have the entrée to the many circles where Serge's charity donations made him welcome, but the older brother could at least go to the editor of the Russian language paper in New York, *Novoye Russkoye Slovo*, and offer letters denouncing Serge. A few were printed but André wanted one to be run every day and he wrote more and more, each increasingly violent and unrestrained in its wording. The paper desisted after a while, the feeling being in its office that André was almost unhinged with envy and hatred of his brother.

Stella was caught in the middle. Serge ordered her to call the paper to speak with its editor, M. Weinbaum, and tell the man that Serge was willing to do things for André but that André would not be helped, that he was beyond any aid. She did it, reluctantly. George Shiskin, an old friend of Weinbaum's, was also sent to the paper to say that Serge was really good and kind, that he helped his mother and aunt and all the refugees and charities. In front of Serge it was forbidden for Stella to even mention André's name, but when Serge was not present she would speak feelingly of her older son, saying he was more "beautiful" than Serge, much "prettier." Called as a witness in one of the unending hearings, she presented a sad sight. "They were suing each other for such a long time," she said. "Since three years only suing and suing. I'd like them to come to an agreement and not to sue." Trying to stop it all, she asked the Austrian intellectual Serge called "Herr Professor" to come and see her. Herr Professor went and Stella said to him, "I see in the eyes of my son André a hunger. I want to end that hunger. Can you be a bridge to Serge for him?" Herr Professor went to Serge and said to him that he must think about the fundamentals of life. "One fundamental," he told Serge, "is the relationship you have with your family."

Serge understood him at once. "I did everything for my mother and father," he blazed back. "Who paid for my father's medical bills before he died? Who supports my mother? How can you say I do not understand the fundamentals?"

"And André?" asked Herr Professor.

"You have to keep away from him," replied Serge. "Keep ten feet away from him, with a pole. No one can do anything for him."

The older man persisted and jollied Serge into a better mood so that he would at least stop shouting. Then Serge allowed that André really didn't know what to do with money, anyway. "I will give him what it is right for him to have," he said. "I'll give him a handout after a while." He laughed about André, saying that really you had to consider his brother a comic character. Herr Professor told Stella he did not see what could be done.

But in fact there was nothing very funny about André, for he was in desperate ill-health, his clothes baggy on him, his nerves almost gone. The newspaper reporters in the press room of the New York State Supreme Court building came to consider him a strange bug indeed, forever hurrying in to tell them of a new motion or countersuit, almost incoherent as he whispered that this time, this time, he was going to get what was coming to him, and then rushing out on some errand connected with the never-ending fight against Serge.

They were down, André and Valerie, literally to living on bread and water. André was far too ill to work and his doctor told him he was in need of regular twice-weekly diathermy treatments. But they had no money at all, so Valerie went to Stella in the Hotel Navarro. She asked the mother for the necessary money for the treatments, six dollars a week. Stella was paying $260 a month for her apartment in the hotel and $60 a week for her maid's room—or rather, was having it paid for her—but she told Valerie she had no money to contribute for André's treatments. "You go pledge all your things, whatever you have," she said, "and I'll redeem them when I get some money. I'm expecting money from Sweden." Valerie had already pawned most of the mementos of happier times in Europe, but she went again with her lace and what little bits of jewelry she had left, and her mother's furs, and got what she could. She never saw them again, for Stella did not give over the promised money.

The couple hung on, André telling his wife that when Serge paid the money they would be secure and have a nice home and children. In Paris meanwhile Valerie's mother lost her home when Valerie was unable to send a little money to pay the rent. The mother sickened and went to Nice and was practically in the streets there until she was taken into a charity hospital where she died. Valerie blamed Serge. If there had been money, perhaps something might have been done for the old Princess.

But there were still appearances and appearances in court. Feverishly ill and disregarding the advice of his doctor who warned him that he was jeopardizing his life by going, André continued the fight. But in early 1943 he collapsed and was taken to a hospital. As André's mother was living in one of New York's best hotels, and as his brother was spending perhaps $20,000 a month, it was impossible for André to qualify as a charity patient. So Valerie went again to Stella to beg her to pay the bills, and Stella said she would do so.

Stella had reckoned without Serge. Serge went to the hospital and standing in the lobby picked up a house phone. He got André on it and as soon as his older brother came on the wire Serge began to shout at him. "Get out of this hospital at once," he raged. "Get up and get out. I'm not going to pay your bills! Do you understand? Now out you go!" André did get out and went home. A few days later, on March 16, 1943, his lawyer appeared before an Official Referee asking for a postponement on the grounds that André was too ill to be present.

Miller sneered at that. "You've been pulling that stuff since we started this exam," he snorted. It was an unwise remark, for by March 25 André had again been taken to the Beth David Hospital, where on that day he died.

Valerie was just outside his room when the end came. She waited a moment, talking with the doctor, and then went down into the lobby.

Serge was there with Stella.

"Fratricide!" Valerie screamed. "You have killed your brother!"

So the mother and son learned André was dead. Stella leaped in front of Serge, arms outstretched to block the way in case Valerie should spring at him. But Valerie went off weeping, back to her shabby apartment. Serge went to his home on Fifth Avenue and immediately got busy on the phone. He called a great many people, including Herr Professor. As soon as the older man came on the wire Serge said, "You know André died?"

"I know nothing," said Herr Professor. "What did he die of?"

"Uremia, uremia," said Serge very hurriedly and with impatience. "But you must do me a great favor. I will make the greatest funeral in the history of Temple Emanu-El. You

106

must come, there must be as many people as possible, there must be an overflow of people, there will be the most flowers in the Temple's history."

The conversation ended and Herr Professor sat for a moment thinking ah yes, I understand: Now that André is dead people must say that Serge can do anything, can make the greatest funeral ever. But he went.

Valerie did not see things Serge's way about the funeral. She told Stella she would not allow Serge to come. But Stella said she must, that if she did not there would be a scandal and that after all in spite of everything André had been Serge's brother. Valerie had no real guns to fire, so Serge came and sat apart from the rest of the family, at the back of the temple, alone. Aunt Genia was very much affected by the funeral, for André had always been her favorite, but Serge was quite dry-eyed although he was pleased at the fine turn-out he had produced. He and his sister-in-law did not speak.

But Valerie was not finished. She continued the pending suits as executrix for André, working nights so as to be able to appear days in court to face the hated Miller and the somewhat sinister-looking Sonny Wolchok, who had immensely bushy eyebrows that made some people call him the poor-man's Dean Acheson and others liken him to, and call him, Mephistopheles. He was, he often let it be known, destined to be a United States Supreme Court Justice—an ambition as yet unfulfilled. Rubinstein encouraged him in this belief. The two were often seen together socializing and it was generally thought that Rubinstein trusted implicitly in Wolchok, but this was hardly the case. He trusted in no lawyer and in between sessions with Miller and Wolchok and Daniel Katz of Barron, Rice & Rockmore, one of his first lawyers in the United States, he would go off to some other lawyer, generally Bernard Newman, to ask for an outside opinion on the way his affairs were being handled: Was Sonny approaching this in the right way; was Danny Katz correct on that question? The fees he paid to these his steady lawyers were not as large as might have been expected—instead he paid in allusions to the great roles they would play in the coming days when he became, as become he must, the most important man in the United States, when Sonny would be Supreme Court Justice Mr. Wolchok and Danny would get his. There were other favors for these specialized courtiers who yet did not have an easy time of it with this client who was always ahead of them and awfully happy to let them know it and whose duties for them always included playing Charlie McCarthy to his Edgar Bergen as front men and dummies of the Rubinstein corporations. One favor was residency in the large and fashionable apartment house at 19 E. 88th Street which one of the corporations purchased and which was converted into a kind of sorority-fraternity house for the people around its owner. Konrad Sztykgold's daughter was given an apartment, and Gordon Foster, and Ann Smith, Rubinstein's longtime secretary. (Twenty years later all the others were gone but Katz and Wolchok were still in the building hanging on to the rent-controlled apartments which were the last vestige of all the glory they were going to have.) Occasionally there would be flare-ups as when the exasperated Wolchok would have to beg Rubinstein not to make speeches in court but for the most part the lawyers stayed loyal if not to Rubinstein personally then to his money and the hope of getting more of it. It took a hardy man to argue with Rubinstein for he had little use for dissenting opinions and took the view that anyone who was not with him was against him. Most of his regular lawyers were a little frightened of him and perhaps more than a little frightened to let go of him . . . André had tried that and see what it got André!

There were, however, a few people who could argue with Rubinstein, and in fact say anything at all to him, provided it was done in just the right way. Gordon Foster was one, making anti-Semitic remarks that made Rubinstein laugh and Betty Kilborn wryly think that now the King is amused at the court jester baiting him to his face. "Ah, you son-of-a-bitching people with your Eastern Jew stuff," Foster would say, drinking imported champagne the buyer of which would throw back his head and roar with laughter. Actually Foster was a kindhearted fellow, happy to be allowed to do his interior decorating under Rubinstein's sponsorship and to be vice-president of this corporation and board member of that one. It disturbed him to see Valerie's plight and he spoke to Rubinstein about it. "Why don't you do something for her?" Foster asked. "Give her a little money and an apartment at Nineteen East. Make a gesture." Sometimes Rubinstein would say all right, he would fling her a bone, but he never did.

The great parties went on. His annual affairs celebrating the Russian New Year became really incredible affairs. His birthday and Madame's were always occasions for invitations to go out to five hundred guests. He missed no charity balls or refugee affairs, taking tables for thirty or forty persons at $25 or $50 a head. But his tips to the waiters were always terribly low—five dollars was a big tip for him. He hated to part with cash of any kind and it was much easier for him to write a check for $5000 than to break a fifty-dollar bill. "If I have to make a phone call from a booth and I don't have a nickel, I certainly won't put in a dime," he would say. "I'll just let the call go."

He loved costume parties and would go en masse with a group of his people all elaborately garbed in outfits he bought for them. The get-ups were always the same. Gordon Foster would be Napoleon's great fellow soldier, Marshal Ney. Madame was Napoleon's mother. Madame's friend of thirty years standing, Robert I. Wyner, a kind of tortured European intellectual who affected lipstick, red nail polish, open sandals and strong perfume the odor of which lingered in a room hours after he left it—he was dressed as the eunuch that often accompanied Napoleon on his campaigns. Laurette made a perfectly gorgeous Josephine, hair up, gown low. Rubinstein —as hardly needs saying—was the Emperor in a beautiful and authentic costume he often took with him on his travels. And if the Europeans clustering around this tableau might whisper to each other behind their hands that most definitely Stella Rubinstein did *not* look like a Bonaparte, it could not be denied that Serge did look terribly like the Emperor. His hand was thrust into his jacket in the familiar Napoleonic pose and his hair was carefully slicked down into the widow's peak the Emperor affected and he looked broodingly out from under his eyebrows set above the heavy lower face really very similar to Napoleon's. A great hat was set on his head and shiny epaulets draped his shoulders. A tiara gleamed in Josephine's hair and a jeweled necklace hung from her neck. The eunuch wore a kind of babushka above his powdered features almost lineless from many face-lifting operations. Marshal Ney wore pinned to his beautiful uniform coat the great gold star of the Legion of Honor (made of tin) which on one occasion had to be replaced after Foster, drunk, gave it to some street urchins hanging around the Astor Hotel to watch the guests emerge from an International Ball. "A present from Napoleon," Foster said, grandly handing off the Legion of Honor to a redheaded kid. The whole gang of them was still fighting over it as Marshal Ney lurched off down the street looking for a cab.

The marriage seemed to be going well enough, although Serge was terribly difficult for Laurette or anyone else to handle. In restaurants he often made scenes. Some came from arguments with waiters over the bill, or from fancied slights in the service, but others came from his overpowering manner and habits. Often he would sit and look at a menu and after announcing he had found nothing there that appealed to him he would get up and walk into the kitchen and go past the cooks and dishwashers straight to the restaurant's refrigerator room. He would fling open the door and march into the cold interior to see for himself just what was on hand.

The confused waiters and maître d'hôtel would hover about as he examined the wares, finally designating this particular rack of meat or that special trout as adequate for his gastronomic needs. Outside in the dining room there would be mild chaos as the staff raced about wondering what was going on, who was this man fingering all the food in the refrigerator? The people with Rubinstein would sit stiffly in their seats wishing he would get through with his tour of inspection and come back. When he would finally return Laurette and Betty and Mrs. Kilborn would jump on him with entreaties that he spare them this embarrassment, but he would shrug off their pleas with a flip of the hand: he had done nothing—please, the matter was not worth discussing.

He was quick and imperious with the genuinely distinguished refugees who, neither aristocrats nor fortune hunters, were flooding New York to escape Europe and the Germans. He invited to dinner an old acquaintance who was the owner of one of the principal newspapers of Paris and said to the man, who was all but penniless and adrift in a foreign land with German officers directing his paper back in Paris: "Do you remember how we would talk of who would go to the top? Remember I told you, 'I don't have to go, I am on top, I come from the top?' You remember? Now you see where I sit and where you sit." The man had no answer—what answer could he give? He ate Rubinstein's food and was happy to get a good meal. But for him and the others there were assignments serving to reimburse the host for his generosity: Take Laurette and Betty to dinner, arrange my mother's ticket to the theater, sign this paper, write this letter. Quickly, quickly, I have no time.

With other men, Americans who were not down and out, he was more gracious, greeting them in his home with vast ceremonial gestures elaborately done. He did not just point to a chair and say sit down, but ushered you to the chair with both hands or addressed you, again à la Napoleon, with a hand thrust inside an elegant velvet jacket. He stood in awe of no man—the word "awe" is as totally out of context in discussing the Rubinstein of those days as would be the word "kindhearted" applied to Attila the Hun. Once at a party Rubinstein met a very distinguished American statesman and with an upward fling of his hand told the man to come to his home on the morrow. "My friend, come to my house," he said. "I want you there." The man, whose name was daily spoken in every chancellery and Parliament of the world, and whose thoughts were of importance to every American, was confused. "But why?" he finally got out. "I want you there, I will do something for you," Rubinstein answered. The man did not come—as it happened he had a

110

conference in Washington with the President slated for the next day. Rubinstein was quite surprised and put out by the man. He had been asked to come, hadn't he? Why did he not show up?

He was the same way in his elaborate office at 63 Wall Street, where the entrance lobby alone was larger than the living room in nine out of ten New York apartments. His own personal office was a wood-paneled affair furnished in splashy elegance with a great desk behind which he sat in a way reminding at least one man of the fashion in which the Eastern Pashas held court in their throne rooms. On the desk was a large printed sign facing any petitioner who sat before it: NO SMOKING PLEASE. Even Konrad Sztykgold, who ate cigars, who went to bed at night with a cigar in his mouth, even he had to go in with nothing between his teeth. Rubinstein's talk was filled with the mention of important names . . . "J. Edgar Hoover sent a man to see me. The man told me Mr. Hoover wished I would not come to Washington; it is too costly for the FBI to wire my hotel room in order to catch the conversations of the foreign diplomats coming to talk with me. I told the man, 'Tell Mr. Hoover to go to the devil; I go where I like' " . . . "Mrs. George Washington Cavanaugh was saying to me the other day" . . . "Senator McMahon was trying all last night to get me on the telephone" . . . "Herbert Lehman is trying to get me to go into a deal with him but I don't like the set-up" . . . "Hope Hampton was after me the other day to go with her to the opera. I said no, I'm too busy" . . . "At my party last night Miriam Hopkins and Ilona Massey were telling me I must come make a movie in Hollywood. I think I'll do that."

He was forever saying that foreigners such as himself were better fitted to succeed in a country than were the natives, pointing to the examples of Catherine the Great, a German, in Russia, Stalin, a Georgian, in the same country, Napoleon the Corsican in France, and Hitler the Austrian in Germany. This last success story he often, astonishingly to many people, praised at length: There was a man who knew how to take charge of things and run a country, you have to give him that! One acquaintance hearing Rubinstein praise the German dictator mused to himself about what Rubinstein himself might do in Hitler's place and decided that he would not kill the Jews but more likely simply content himself with putting them out of business.

He was at the peak of his form. And his greatest success was in front of him. The most important money was yet to be made.

Chapter Eleven

Panhandle

Was he a conman, a robber, a crook? One lawyer who knew him somewhat, but was not of his clique, could never decide about that. "I know very well," the lawyer said of him, later —after he was dead and after all the papers called him thief and destroyer—"I know very well that he used every precaution to insure that a deal should be correct. Each transaction of his was entered into with the advice of counsel and expertly handled by good lawyers. The proper legal attention was given every detail. More than that, everything he did was rational and in order and could be perfectly explained. You could look at it his way and everything added up. But I remember something my father used to say to me when I was a kid. He would say, 'All right, I understand why you couldn't help being late to school. I understand why you got into an argument with your mother. I understand why it wasn't your fault that the window got broken when you were playing ball. I understand all of that. But tell me one thing. Why do these things always happen to you?'

"Maybe that's the way you could look at Rubinstein."

Another man, an accountant who handled a few of his matters, said the answer was yes and no. "On his level of business, in his circles, I'm not sure the word larceny applies. Who was he in against in most of his deals? Not foolish laymen but smart operators and big boys. Can you rob these people? Or is it just business—making a dollar?"

All his life Rubinstein used to wonder at the things people said about him. "Why do they say I'm a thief?" he would ask. "I made money in the stock market, sure—but everyone else had the same chance. During the time the BMT stock was being bought up a man came to me and asked my opinion about whether he should sell the stock. I told him to hang on, it'd go up. He didn't follow my advice. He sold. Then when it did go up, he went around saying I was a thief."

There were those of the stock market, it is true, who damned him from a higher viewpoint than the man who sold BMT too soon, pointing out that in America it is of the greatest importance that a free market be maintained for the selling and buying of stocks, and that the entire American economy can be seriously damaged by an unrestrained market running amuck and uncontrolled—as has been seen in the past. In Europe every day things take place that

America calls outright robbery. In Europe, where in most countries it is common for shopkeepers to ask one hundred francs, or lire, or pesetas for an item they fully intend to sell for twenty-five, the selling of securities is carried on almost without any restraint. Continental Europe does not know one-twentieth of the safeguards of the New York Stock Exchange. America was once that way, but since the great stock market crash of 1929 the American attitude has been let the seller beware, for those that he sells to are more and more small investors, unsophisticated people putting away twenty and fifty dollars a month for stock purchases. And such small investors have to be protected. European thinking is that the big man dabbling in the market can be depended upon to take care of himself—there are no little investors in Europe anyway.

But even operating with a European orientation, was Serge Rubinstein a crook? "What is a crook?" asked one of his friends. "Who makes a lot of money in Wall Street without making enemies? Once a banker said to me that Rubinstein was a terrible man. I asked why and the banker said that once he had an account with us and it was tied up by a lawsuit and that we didn't like that; we don't like our accounts tied up that way. So what? So the account was tied up! That made him a crook. But if you told that banker that Jesse James had come back from the dead complete with six-shooter and stolen horse, and that he had set himself up to run a corporation and that he was going to fix it so that the stock of the corporation was absolutely going up ten points without fail, don't you think the banker would run to buy? Sure he would! Who wouldn't? Wouldn't you?"

Romeo E. Muller was a stockbroker with the fixed idea that it is unwise to give advice to a client. If the stock went up, the client would never remember that the broker gave him the word. (A good stock is always the client's own personal idea.) But if the stock went down, the client would come around with a funny look in his eye, remembering all too well just exactly who gave him this dog. The best thing was to keep saying I guess so, you might be right, to whatever the client said.

But on the other hand, Muller felt a broker ought to know something about the companies in which his people invest. So in the late 1930s Muller made something of a study of the Panhandle Producing and Refining Company, which had attracted the interest and money of one of his clients. Panhandle had been incorporated in 1919 under the laws of the State of Delaware as a holding company to take over the stock of the Panhandle Refining Company of Texas, plus a couple of other oil companies and a boiler and machine shop. It had ended up as one of those firms that dawdle along giving out silver pins for twenty years of service, but no raises, and by no means was it the popularly imagined Texas oil company, with millions coming out of the Southwestern desert to be translated into Cadillacs and private planes. In Wichita Falls, where its headquarters were, it was the largest employer in town, and it had several hundred gas stations selling its Noxless Gasoline and Panolene and Pangold lubricating oils, and it sold crude oil to major oil companies, but it was not a company that was doing well. Its president received a very modest salary and its stock never seemed to go anywhere much. The owners of the stock were mostly small investors with a few shares they hung on to for no particular reason other than that to sell would bring little cash. Muller was probably the first person in years to take any real interest in Panhandle—or at least the first person with any financial backing—and his attention was gratefully received. In 1938 he became a Committee of One to reorganize the outfit, and thus became something of a power in Panhandle's sleepy affairs. Company actions were routinely detailed for him and he was often on the phone to the company board members—who were for the most part not oilmen but small-town Texas lawyers and bankers. One such company action, entered into just after the war began in Europe, displeased Muller. This was the purchase by Panhandle of some very high-grade oil pipe, tubing, and casing from an important oil operator named William Rhodes Davis, who had obtained the material from the German government then in the process of over-running Europe. Davis had sold the Germans some Mexican oil, and as they were reluctant to part with money, he had accepted the oil equipment as payment. (The dispatch of the pipe, tubing, and casing out of Europe via Italy was the source of some satisfaction to the Germans, who said the shipment proved that the British blockade was overrated. But Davis's participation in the deal aroused the ire of Walter Winchell, who thereafter often referred to him as "an American Americans can do without." Davis, countering the question of his usefulness to his country, always insisted his buying and selling to and from the European oil market was done with the encouragement of President Roosevelt, who desired that someone, namely Davis, keep close to the foreign oil situation, which was a key factor in determining the outcome of the war.)

In any event, the equipment found its way to Panhandle, purchased for a sufficiently large amount of money to considerably irritate Muller. "Why in hell did you have to buy that kind of stuff?" he demanded of the Panhandle president. "Second-grade stuff would have been perfectly good enough."

114

The president was sorry, but the deal had been made and Davis now wanted his money—which Panhandle was hard put to find. It was decided to pay Davis off with stock in the company instead of money, and this was arranged. Davis became the owner of some 150,000 shares of stock and the major Panhandle stockowner. As such he was elected to the Board of Directors, to be shortly joined there by Muller himself, who was now taking a more and more active role in the company's doings.

Davis was a different sort of person than Panhandle was used to. He had begun life as a candy butcher, selling sweets up and down the aisles of trains crossing the Southwest. He had gone from that into the oil business and by the time of his entrance into Panhandle's life he had become a hard sort of man who in the tradition of Texas oil operators had made and lost several fortunes. He rarely ate anything other than sandwiches and he constantly drank Coca-Cola, hardly ever going anywhere without a bottle of it in his pocket. He was not really very interested in Panhandle—which was how most people felt about the outfit, always excepting Muller, who had arrived at the point where he felt Panhandle was his baby. So when Muller suggested to Davis that the latter become president of the company, Davis balked. He told Muller he was involved in world-wide oil dealings and couldn't see getting himself tied down to any company, particularly a company of the likes of Panhandle. This slur angered Muller. "You're a barnacle on my ship of progress," Muller cried. "Pitch or get out of the game. Either take an active interest or scram." Such language evidently impressed Davis, for he consented to become president. But hardly had he taken office before he suffered a heart attack in a New York hotel room. He was dead the next day.

That left Davis's interest in Panhandle, the controlling stock, temporarily without an owner. But soon there was an owner and the owner was not the Davis heirs. It was instead the United States Government, which seized the stock as collateral against an unpaid tax bill that Davis had accumulated. This seizure frightened Muller, for as soon as Davis had died Muller began hearing rumors that a major oil company had taken it into its head to get control of Panhandle. Muller knew that no major company would be even slightly interested in keeping Panhandle going. A big company would be interested in the proven reserves that Panhandle owned and nothing else. Panhandle would be taken over for its reserves, the reserves would be drained dry and everything else would be dropped. It would be no problem to absorb Panhandle. The big company would arrange a stock trade with the Panhandle owners, the Panhandle employees would be sent out to look for new jobs, and that would be that. To prevent all this an individual buyer was needed to take over Davis's stock. Somebody had to be found who would put money into Panhandle and thus save the situation.

Muller started looking. Davis was not buried before Muller was on the phone looking for a buyer. But buyers were hard to find. On the other hand it was easy to find a plenitude of reasons why Panhandle, which had never done much anyway, should be allowed to go under and be absorbed into the major oil firm.

Some days passed. Muller had no success in his search. He sat in his office all day long working the phones but no buyers appeared. Then one afternoon an aged man who rented space in Muller's office for $15 a month stuck his head into Muller's room. The man, a former vice-president of an important Manhattan bank, had some years earlier been taken in by a girl who with a band of friends had devised an effective con game based on the blackmail of older men who suddenly found themselves in very compromising circumstances with the girl just as the friends burst in threatening death and destruction. The then bank vice-president had proved to be a particularly fine subject for the girl's activities but the blackmail which followed had quite broken him and he had lost his position and had gone to selling annuity bonds out of the tiny room Muller rented him. Now he appeared, somewhat timorously, before his landlord. He announced that he was aware of Mr. Muller's problem and that he thought he might be of some aid. He knew someone, a European gentleman, who might be interested in such a matter. Or at least so the European gentleman had said. If Mr. Muller desired, he would send the European gentleman in to see him. Muller desired it very much. Later in the day the new prospect appeared, introducing himself as Oscar Gruss, a refugee just starting up in the New World, and requesting a look at the Panhandle financial statement. This was given him and he left, returning very shortly with the information that a friend of his was quite interested. The friend's name, he added, was Serge Rubinstein.

Muller had heard that name before. In fact, he had seen its owner several times in the Savoy Plaza Hotel, where Muller had at one time maintained a brokerage office. Although the office, like any office, was by way of being a public place, Muller had tried to keep most people out by hiring a cold-eyed former country club steward who, dressed in a blue uniform, stood by the door and was very slow about opening it to anyone who was not immediately recognized. The idea was that while several big customers were welcomed with open arms, no welcome at all was accorded to other men who might sit down next to the giants and try to find out their tradings for the day, thus hoping to pick up a good thing. Although it was surely not the chilly atmosphere that kept him out—more than that would have been needed—Rubinstein had never come into the office. It was rather that he had numerous accounts elsewhere. But Muller had seen him in the course of his comings and goings to the office. And he had heard a lot of stories about him.

"Rubinstein?" he said to Gruss. "That's your friend? That Russian boy with all those big blondes? And with all that stuff about Chosen? I don't want any part of that boy."

Gruss left. Soon after Rubinstein himself called. Muller refused to see him. But when Rubinstein called again a day later, Muller changed his mind. He had met with no luck at all in his quest for a Panhandle buyer and he figured nothing could be lost by seeing this prospect. He went to Rubinstein's office determined to keep his eyes open. And the first thing he thus saw was Ann Smith, Rubinstein's secretary. She made a very good impression upon Muller, who thought her an attractive and cultured girl. Possession of such an upper-drawer secretary scored a point for Rubinstein in Muller's mind.

He was shown into Rubinstein's office, where a conference was just breaking up. Rubinstein was just about to sign a contract made on behalf of one of his companies. The men representing the other contracting concern were standing by him, and with them was one of those men, very familiar to the Wall Street scene, who live off what are called "finder's fees" and whose days are spent poring over business reports for information which might enable the bringing together of two parties who, coming to an agreement, will give a small percentage of the money involved to the person who performed the introductions. As he bent over to sign the contract, Rubinstein looked up at the finder. "Now are we quite sure about your money?" he asked.

"Yeah, we're taking care of that," said one of the men representing the other concern. But Rubinstein ignored him and continued to address the finder. "If you're not satisfied in any way," he said, "I'll deduct the amount of your fee from their check and make out an individual check for you." The finder assured him it was not necessary and Rubinstein went ahead and signed. The matter was thus wound up and the men were shown out of the office leaving Rubinstein and Muller alone and the latter even more impressed with the former. He had seen too many cases where a finder brought together two parties who got along well and started wining and dining each other and playing golf and who in the end decided they would doubtless have found each other in any case and that therefore there was no real reason to waste money by giving it to the chap who claimed to have introduced them.

The two men sat down to talk about Panhandle. Muller at that time had talked up the subject to a score of men, but not one had reacted the way Rubinstein did. He immediately grasped what could be done to make Panhandle hum and he was filled with ideas about increasing the company's business. Unlike the others, he did not talk about how much could be lost, but about how much could be made. "I'll buy the shares," he said, an hour after Muller came into his office. "I'll take the presidency too, the way Davis did," he added. But Muller told him that would be impossible because of his questionable reputation on the Street. "You buy 300,000 of the 900,000 shares and you can have three directors," Muller said. "But no presidency." "All right, all right," Rubinstein said. His claim to the shares was made known to the government but the government ruled the shares would be sold at public auction. When Muller called Rubinstein with that news Rubinstein said it didn't matter, he'd handle the government and get the shares good and cheap. "I'll get things fixed up," he said, and left for Washington. Shortly after the shares were put up for auction in Texas. The highest bid, it was announced, was entered by the Midway Victory Oil Company, which was owned by the Victory Oil Company, which was owned by Norfolk International Company S.A., which was owned by Norfolk Equities, which was owned by British American Equities, which was owned by the Chosen Corporation—which despite all the litigation entered into by the British shareholders, was for all purposes owned by Serge Rubinstein. At the same time Midway Victory took 50,000 shares off the hands of a Panhandle officer. The average price paid for the shares sold by the government and the officer was $1.25.

It was July 1942. Rubinstein did not actually own the shares auctioned off to Midway Victory by the government, title not yet having been transferred, but at his direction a meeting of the Panhandle Board of Directors was convened in the Savoy Plaza Hotel. On that day, July 18, three directors offered their resignations, which were accepted. Then two Rubinstein associates, both well-connected American businessmen, were nominated and elected as directors. The man who had replaced the dead Davis as president, Henry Wilson, then took occasion to opine that an acquaintance of his, Serge Rubinstein, would also be a good director. Solemnly the name was entered in nomination. A vote was held and then a call was placed to the hotel's restaurant, where Rubinstein was having a bite. He was told that he was now a director. He came upstairs and told the board that great things were in store for Panhandle and that to aid in bringing them about he, Rubinstein, would recommend the hiring of a vastly talented oil production engineer. It was agreed that a good man should be hired to supervise things.

That was Saturday. On Monday, July 20, 1942, another Savoy Plaza meeting was held at which another old director resigned to be replaced by another Rubinstein man. The day after that a meeting was held not at the Savoy Plaza but at 63 Wall Street, in Rubinstein's office. There one more old director resigned, to be replaced by Gordon Foster. The Chairman of the Board also resigned, to be replaced by Rubinstein, who was unanimously elected to the post. As his first official act as Chairman of the Board, Rubinstein brought up the question of the oil production engineer of whom he had earlier spoken. He asked the Board to hire the man as assistant to the president and assistant general manager. It was done. Konrad Sztykgold thus became a Panhandle employee. Rubinstein then suggested that an executive committee should be formed and that it should consist of himself, the president of the company, Henry Wilson, and two of the new directors, with Sztykgold attached in an advisory capacity. It was done. Next, he introduced Hugh Duffy, a longtime employee of his and an officer of many of his corporations, and suggested Duffy's election as assistant secretary and assistant treasurer. Duffy was elected. Without owning a share of Panhandle's stock, the title still not having been transferred, Rubinstein now controlled five of nine directors, three out of four members of the executive committee, was Chairman of the Board, and had two close associates in strategic positions.

This was not exactly the way Muller had wanted things to happen, but he was afraid to make a fight of it—the publicity would hurt Panhandle. Anyway, at least Rubinstein wasn't president of the company—Henry Wilson was. But Wilson was becoming increasingly friendly with the new power in Panhandle. Rubinstein had arranged for him to receive a salary of $18,000 a year and also offered him a percentage of profits from some oil properties in the State of Washington —which were totally without value, although Wilson did not know that.

Wilson did not stay president long. Five months after Rubinstein's entrance onto the Panhandle scene, Wilson resigned. His successor was Rubinstein. Wilson also sold all his stock in the company. The buyer was Rubinstein.

Rubinstein now completely controlled Panhandle. At the time he went into the company an accountant of his, looking over the Panhandle statement and papers, offered his opinion that there was nothing, but nothing, to the company and that Rubinstein was certain to take a financial beating. Rubinstein laughed at that and said the accountant could find significance in the name of the corporation he had picked to buy Panhandle, Midway Victory. He was midway in his life, Rubinstein said, and this was going to be a great victory. (The name had nothing to do, of course, with the great Pacific battle which was to be fought in the future.) Now that he had Panhandle, Rubinstein was alive with plans for it. Panhandle was going to dominate the American oil industry. Panhandle was going to own a private fleet of tankers. Panhandle was going to expand into Europe and South America. Panhandle was going to do a lot of things, wait and see. But as things stood, Panhandle was limited in just what it could do by a charter which dictated that all the company's activities were to be connected with the oil business. That was a stumbling block to Rubinstein. The oil business had its possibilities, to be sure, but Rubinstein wanted more leeway, more activity, more kinds of things floating through his fingers, new deals and new angles. His operation with Chosen had been successful because he was able to move funds around from one corporation to another and from the corporations into new ventures, weaving and shifting and finding outside interests all the time. He wanted it to be that way with Panhandle also but here was the charter calling for involvement in the oil business and the oil business only. The charter would have to be changed. He caused a special stockholders meeting to be called and on October 8, 1943, by overwhelming vote, it was decided that "the officers and directors on behalf of the company be authorized to invest, own, hold and trade in stocks, bonds or other securities of other corporations whether or not engaged in the same business of the company." This move alarmed some of the people in the company who thought that like the shoemaker Panhandle should stick to its last but Rubinstein blew them aside, saying he was going to build an empire with Panhandle. Most of the stockholders, all but a very, very few, listened and were satisfied. Their new president and Chairman of the Board had a demonstrated ability to make money and if he did that for Panhandle it would mean the stock would go up. And whatever makes a stock go up is good.

Now he was free and Panhandle was his and all around him was the atmosphere which he loved and in which he throve. All day long he was on the telephone talking with finders and the people they found and all day long they were trooping to his office and to his home. Laurette did not see him half so much as she had during their courting period but often, all decked out in the finery he selected, she was called upon to go with him to this night club or that in company with the people with whom he hoped to do business. Ever since he had known her, he had been saying it was a shame Laurette wasn't a blonde—he always wanted them blonde—and now to please him she slowly started getting blonde. Each day she went to a beauty shop and there they lightened her hair so gradually and gently that even her sister Betty did not notice the change until one day when she looked at Laurette she saw her hair was practically the color of platinum. "My God, you're blonde!" Betty cried. Serge was with them and Betty's reaction delighted him. "It looks wonderful, doesn't it?" he kept saying. He himself attempted to improve his appearance with a series of nose-bobbing operations. No matter what a surgeon accomplished, however, Rubinstein was not satisfied. The end result was that his nose came to look like that of a veteran prize fighter—which lent credence to his tales of how he had been a star boxer at Cambridge.

Panhandle was thriving, due largely to the considerable oil wizardry of Konrad Sztykgold and the financial genius of Serge Rubinstein. Sztykgold spent almost all of his time in Wichita Falls, of which rather surprisingly he became fond, and in the oil fields. Often he went against the advice of the professional petroleum engineers to bring in new wells, being remarkable in his ability to scent the presence of oil. There is a saying in the oil business that you can have the best geologists and the best equipment but you have oil when you find it. Sztykgold could find it. "Frederick the Great was asked by Voltaire what the qualifications were that he sought in his generals," Sztykgold said, "and Frederick replied, 'I want my generals to be lucky.' That is the oil business. You must be lucky in many respects and unless you are, you must not go into that business." Frederick the Great and Voltaire. The idea pleased both Rubinstein and Sztykgold. Having luck and finding oil, that was Sztykgold's job under the hot Southwestern sun and in Wichita Falls. Rubinstein's job was different. It was to co-ordinate. His role in oil drilling was not to step up on the derrick floor, grab a wrench and tighten the fittings, although on the two or three times in his life he went to Wichita Falls he dressed up in elaborate boots and riding pants and went to stand by some equipment so that a camera could be snapped to show the heavy face looking solemn but resourceful as its owner pondered whether to drill for black gold or to give the word that would dismantle all. Actually he did not want to deal with underground lakes or pores of sandstone or shale although he began to study the oil business and soon amassed a great library on it and very considerable practical working knowledge. His job was to work with the finances and at that he was a wizard. He could read a report in an instant and decide what to do. All oil drilling is concerned with accumulated reserves which can be brought in when an old well dies. Wise direction wants to find and keep reserves in the ground to offset depletion, and at this Rubinstein was very good. Panhandle was never in a vulnerable position but always had money to look around and scout and explore. Sztykgold was sent all over the country, to Louisiana, Florida, Washington State, seeking new fields. In New York Rubinstein kept in his mind and had available at an instant's notice all the different ramifications of various oil rulings. He became an expert on laws affecting oil and in one moment could put his finger on the applicable point in any issue. He was also active in setting up new businesses connected with oil. Panhandle Steel Products manufactured oil-field equipment; Panhandle Drilling Company was available to drill wells for other oil firms.

Oil; yes that was very good. Rockefeller started with oil. But the other things, the other deals allowable once the Panhandle charter was changed . . . All the people and propositions pouring into his life . . . Panhandle bought into an aircraft corporation. Muller objected, saying he was afraid of getting the company into something they didn't know anything about. Rubinstein silenced him. "Don't you have confidence in the future of the air industry?" . . . A man brought him the opportunity to buy the controlling stock interest in a life insurance company . . . Panhandle bought 800 shares of Certainteed Products Corporation and the right to buy 6000 more in case, as was discussed, the two outfits should decide to exchange preferred stock issues . . . Panhandle Trading Company was formed to enter the import and export business . . . Purchase of the controlling stock interest in the Flushing National Bank of New York was contemplated and a percentage of the bank's stock was bought.

Deals, deals. There were people buzzing around him all the time. Each night he and Laurette went out and always at the night clubs they went to, a telephone was placed on the table so that he could get the calls of the men bringing him new things, big things, pieces of the empire he was making . . . The wax business . . . more oil wells . . . The Miller Marine Decking Company, brought to his attention by Gerhard Dahl from the BMT deal . . . Eight thousand shares of Buffalo, Niagara and Eastern Power Company . . . Half an interest in Monterrey Minerals S.A. . . . Talks about the purchase of the Ohio-Mex Company for $270,000 . . . some new oil fields for himself . . . a tract of land in Westchester

County gone into together with Sztykgold. . . . He was on the phone early in the morning no matter what time he went to bed. He might be up until four A.M. at a night club feverishly dancing with Laurette or with whatever was handy but still at nine he was at the office yelling to the girls to get him Wichita Falls or California or Boston on the phone. With Hugh Duffy devoting all his time to Panhandle, a new man in the office was needed, and so the job was given to Teddy Schulz. Schulz got a very nominal salary something like $100 a week, but he was grateful and loyal and happy in his work except for the times when he heard it said that Rubinstein had remarked that "Teddy was the highest in the class when we were in school but now look at him and look at me!"

Deals kept coming to him and he to them. . . . There was an attempt to borrow $2,500,000 from the Prudential Insurance Company and Massachusetts Mutual Life Insurance Company which failed because the two insurance companies wanted restrictions put on the use of the funds. He wasn't going to stand for that—no one tells me what to do with money. And no matter, anyway. The Republic National Bank of Dallas came through with $1,500,000 and no strings attached . . . The Fidel Association of New York, an investment trust, was bought by Panhandle for $146,000. Purchased, Fidel was made to buy a quantity of the stock of Warren Brothers Company, an old road-building outfit certain bonds of which had already brought Rubinstein personally a good profit. The bonds had been issued years earlier by an ousted government of Cuba and had been defaulted upon by a succeeding Cuban regime. They were considered worthless or almost worthless when Rubinstein had his Cuban company, Norfolk International, buy them from Warren Brothers. Shortly after, the American government entered into an agreement whereby certain loans would be made to Cuba contingent upon Cuba's redemption of certain bond issues among which were included the ones Rubinstein had just picked up for a song from Warren Brothers. How did Rubinstein know the Cubans were going to redeem the bonds? Who knows? Call it luck, instinct. Or perhaps one of the senators or congressmen hanging around him had something to do with it. In any event, it was a situation very similar to that of the BMT deal and besides making money for Rubinstein it also made him something of a power in Warren Brothers. Now with Panhandle's purchase through Fidel Association of 25,000 Warren Brothers shares and with Midway Victory also plunging in for 31,000 shares, Rubinstein controlled more than 30 per cent of Warren Brothers stock. He became a director and at once began talking of how he would take over the firm. Herr Professor remonstrated with him about that, pointing out that, there was a lot of unpleasant gossip around Washington concerning his fortuitous purchase of the old bonds, and that perhaps it would be best to keep a little quiet about Warren Brothers and not go out of his way to draw attention to the deal. Rubinstein did not agree. "Who shall have the power to stop me when I want to do something?" Who indeed?

Then came Stewart, the biggest deal. James Stewart and Company was a one-hundred-year-old construction firm with a tremendously distinguished record. To its credit was the construction of the Château Frontenac Hotel in Quebec, Madison Square Garden, the Idaho and Utah State Capitol Buildings, the University of Maryland, New York City's West Side Highway, the Grand Central Palace Building, and the United States Court House for the Southern District of New York. Stewart in 1944 was owned by two groups of stockholders. One group, consisting of the heirs to certain members of the original Stewart family, held 49.5 per cent of the stock. The other group consisted of the Stewart officers, who held 50.5 per cent of the stock and hence, acting in a body, were the controlling shareholders. Among these officers was the president of the company, Harry D. Watts. Watts was a good friend of Hamilton Pell, a New York socialite of most eminent background who came from an old and distinguished New York City and Long Island family. He had the reputation in Wall Street of being a professional board member who was selected for his score of positions of that type by virtue of the value of his fine background. He moved in an atmosphere of upper level business dealings and polite society and was well known. Well connected both in business and social life, he did a great deal of moving around, going to parties, meeting people. In the course of so doing he met, as did many another distinguished gentleman, the enthusiastic party-giver Serge Rubinstein. They became friends or, more accurately, Rubinstein cultivated Pell. When Rubinstein moved into Panhandle, he asked Pell to be a director. Pell accepted.

Pell was a member of numerous exclusive clubs, including the St. Nicholas Club of New York, of which he was president for many years, the Seminole Club of Palm Beach, Connecticut's Wee Bairn Golf Club, and a couple of yacht clubs. He was a golfer, of course. And one day as he went around the course of a Long Island club, he happened upon his friend Harry D. Watts, the president of Stewart. More business is done on golf greens than in board rooms and so it was not strange that Watts took occasion to remark that for the right price and the right buyer he and the other controlling stockholders of Stewart would be willing to sell the company. Was that really so, Pell asked. Well, He brought the news to Rubinstein and Rubinstein was delighted. "We'll have Warren Brothers and make it the biggest horizontal builder in the world, building roads everywhere, and we'll have Stewart and make it the biggest vertical builder," he cried. He was aflame to get into Stewart. Negotiations were opened at once, with Rubinstein dropping everything to take care of Panhandle's interests in the matter personally while he confidently told Watts that it was only a matter of time until Panhandle owned Warren Brothers outright and didn't Mr. Watts think the idea of combining Warren Brothers and Stewart was an exciting conception?

Actually Warren Brothers was presenting a problem. The management, initially happy to have Rubinstein interested in the company, soon began to hear frightening stories. Rubinstein was going around saying that the Warren Brothers people were old duffers way behind the times who didn't know how to run a company but that once he took over the firm and got rid of those useless hacks, you would really see Warren Brothers hum. After hearing these plans, the Warren Brothers people started fighting to keep control. Battle was joined when a director died. Rubinstein called for a stockholders' election to choose a replacement, but the Warren Brothers management, knowing Rubinstein could very well swing a stockholders' election, maintained that as the dead man's term still had two years to run, no vote could be held. They insisted they had the right to appoint a new man and went ahead with plans to do so. But it was not going to be so easy for them. Rubinstein had a restraining order served on the president of Warren Brothers. The order was not handed to the man at his Boston residence. It was dropped at the company's office in Delaware, where Warren Brothers was chartered. That office, in the tradition of Delaware-chartered firms, had nothing more of Warren Brothers in it than the name on the door. Perhaps after a few days some clerk retained by Warren Brothers and the fifty other firms with names on the door might get around to sending the restraining order up to Boston. But meanwhile Rubinstein had a little secret to spring on the Warren Brothers president. The naming of the new man was held off.

That was Warren Brothers. But things with Stewart went along quite smoothly. Working swiftly, Rubinstein conceived a plan for Stewart whereby the moment it was purchased it would go into the oil-drilling business as a sideline to its construction work. The expenditure of money for equipment would be immediately deductible for tax purposes and would thereby eliminate any Federal excess profit taxes that might be imposed on the construction firm for that year, 1944. The Stewart officers liked the sound of that. They were also pleased with the projected plan for the distribution of the $2,400,000 Panhandle was to pay for their company. The plan called for the officers, who it will be remembered held 50.5 per cent of the Stewart stock, to receive a flat $2,000,000. The heirs were supposed to be content with getting $400,000 for their 49.5 per cent. Everything went along very nicely until the heirs got word about what was planned. The heirs rushed to their lawyers, who immediately started suits to hold up the proposed sale.

The internal fight slowed things up, but it seemed clear that sooner or later the battle would be settled and the deal closed. So Panhandle started to look around for the money which would be needed for the purchase. The down payment was to be $700,000 and Panhandle did not have that sum readily available, so Rubinstein personally offered to buy 120,000 shares of Panhandle stock at $3.50 a share, thus providing the company with $420,000 which could be added to funds on hand to meet the down payment. But as issuing such stock could not be done without the approval of all the Panhandle stockholders, and as doing it might get the company into trouble with the Securities and Exchange Commission, it was decided to do the whole thing secretly and give Rubinstein not the stock, but an option to buy 120,000 shares at $3.50 a share regardless of what price it might stand at in the open market on the future date at which time he might choose to exercise his option.

The Stewart internal fight raged on. But Rubinstein worked full time on Stewart's affairs anyway. The year previous to Panhandle's entrance into the Stewart picture, the company had brought out a beautifully printed book which celebrated its one hundredth anniversary. The book showed pictures of all the important structures the company had built and was terribly impressive. Everywhere he went Rubinstein carried a copy with him to show anyone he met: Look, this is my new company. See these pictures? Did you ever hear of so many important buildings, all built by my company? Everyone did find the pictures impressive, including, Rubinstein let it be known, certain high officials of the Philippine Islands, then just liberated from the Japanese and in very bad shape following the destruction of the war. "I'm arranging a one-hundred-million-dollar deal to rebuild the Philippines," Rubinstein told people. "In fact, it may turn out to be a billion-dollar job. My new company, Stewart, will handle it. Our profit will be five per cent on the first one hundred million and three and a half per cent up to one billion. One of my other companies will float the bond issue the Philippines will need to finance the work. It's between eighty and ninety per cent certain that we'll get the job." At Panhandle board of directors meetings Rubinstein regularly reported that negotiations were speedily going forth and that as soon as Stewart was safely in the Panhandle fold final arrangements with the Philippine government would be concluded. The eighty to ninety per cent figure sometimes even reached the ninety-nine and nine-tenths per cent mark. "President Osmeña is an old friend of mine," Rubinstein would add. And there were all sorts of other things in the works for Stewart. Stewart was going to build an underwater tunnel in Rio de Janeiro. Stewart had big things cooking in Europe—in addition to rebuilding the Philippines the company was in a good position to take part in the postwar construction that would be needed on the Continent. The company was also going to build a giant housing project on the land Rubinstein and Sztykgold owned in Westchester County. God only knows where Stewart would end up. It was going to be the General Motors of building.

When he wasn't talking about Stewart's great future, he was busy outlining Panhandle's new oil operations. Panhandle, he let it be known, was working to get some oil concessions in Bolivia that were beyond measurement. The fields Panhandle would get would produce more oil than the rest of South America put together. There were just a few details to be ironed out and Panhandle would start its operations in these fabulous fields. There were just a few things to be taken care of.

In Stewart there were similarly a few things to be taken care of, but finally everything fell into place. The two groups of stockholders settled their differences and came to an agreement about how the Panhandle money should be distributed. They accepted a check for the down payment and the contract was signed, with the final closing taking place in very early 1946. Stewart became a part of the Panhandle empire. Immediately, Rubinstein moved in a new board of directors. He himself became a director, of course, and so did Sztykgold, Pell, Foster, and Duffy. Stewart was Rubinstein's, bag and baggage—Stewart the steppingstone to his greater future, Stewart the rock upon which he would build Tomorrow.

There is a question as to what Rubinstein actually knew and did not know about this wonderful James Stewart and Company. Many people in Wall Street later said he knew what the story was all the time and was happy about it because it gave him a chance to exploit the situation and turn it into a swindle. Give a crook a deal and right away he's looking for the dirty way to handle it. A crook's not happy with an honest deal. He doesn't know what to do with it. But there were other people, including those closest to the situation, who never thought Rubinstein actually realized in January 1946, when Panhandle took over Stewart, what the situation was.

And what was it?

It was that Stewart was on the verge of bankruptcy. Stewart was caught in a bind that was going to wreck the company. Stewart was a shell. The outside of the shell looked good but there was less than nothing inside. And things were getting worse with every day that passed.

What had happened to Stewart of the wonderful name and reputation was that in early 1945, months before Watts met Pell on the golf course, the company had submitted a bid for the construction of a naval hospital. At that time, early '45, the United States Navy was preparing plans to mount a mammoth invasion of Japan. The invasion was expected to cost hundreds of thousands of casualties and the Navy wanted to build a chain of hospitals to care for its wounded. One of the hospitals was to be in Houston, Texas, and this was the hospital for which Stewart had entered a bid. Unfortunately for Stewart, the bid was a successful one and the Navy awarded the contract to the company.

Stewart's fee for building the hospital buildings and their auxiliaries was to be more than seven million dollars, to be exact $7,355,890, but not a penny more. It was to be what is called a fixed-fee or lump-sum job as opposed to a cost-plus job. The latter kind of job would have called for the government to pay each and every bill for materials and labor, with the builder getting an agreed-upon percentage, usually five per cent, for his profit. Such a cost-plus job involves no gambling. No matter what happens during the work, regardless of what expensive troubles arise, the builder gets his percentage. If the job winds up costing X-hundred thousand dollars above what was expected, it need not worry the builder—the government will pay all the bills anyway. But a fixed-fee or lump-sum job, which is what Stewart had, is on the other hand very much of a gamble. If the job can be done cheaply, the builder stands to make a nice profit. If Stewart were able to build the hospital at a cost to itself of, say, $5,000,000, its profits would have been $2,355,890. But—and it is an immense but—if the job ended up costing a fortune over the agreed-upon $7,355,890, Stewart was going to have to pay that fortune all by itself.

Attached to the contract was a proviso. It called for a penalty to be paid by Stewart if the job were not finished within a stipulated period. The penalty was $1400 for every day past December 26, 1945, that the job remained unfinished, and $3400 per day for every day past January 9, 1946. That was the deal. Stewart signed contracts with the Chief of the Navy Department's Bureau of Yards and Docks and went to work. It was spring of 1945—April.

In August the atomic bombs were dropped on Japan and the war was over. With peace came the end of government controls on wages and materials. Prices soared. In addition a wave of postwar strikes began. Stewart was trapped with its fixed fee even though prices on everything were rising every day and work was being held up by the strikers. It was a desperate situation, a nightmare. By the end of August the Stewart accountants were figuring the company would lose $300,000 on the job even if somehow it was finished on time. By the end of September they upped the figure to $500,000. By December they were expecting a loss of $835,000 even if, as was impossible, the work was done on time and the penalties for lateness did not come into effect.

Under these circumstances, with this awful contract hanging over their heads, and with an almost inestimable loss facing them, the officers of Stewart came to a conclusion: It would be a very good idea to sell the company while there was still something left to sell. So thinking, president Watts went golfing one day and ran into his friend Hamilton Pell. And Pell went to Rubinstein. And Panhandle bought Stewart and with it Stewart's ghastly hospital project. By the time Panhandle took over, the estimated losses had reached more than $1,000,000 and the promised completion date was past.

Did Rubinstein know all this when he bought Stewart? Some Wall Streeters say he knew all along about the hospital disaster and welcomed it as a vehicle by which he could swindle other people and have a good laugh at their expense. Give a crook a deal . . . Others said all his hopes to become an empire builder were tied in with Stewart and that it came as an awful shock to him to find out the company was in such terrible shape. We will never know exactly what his thinking was. But we know his immediate reaction: Get the hell out of Panhandle before it was dragged under by Stewart. And get out with a bundle of money.

Now, Rubinstein had always been adroit at converting someone else's thrust at him into his own strong point. When Teddy Schulz's wife would call the office at eight in the evening to demand to know why Teddy wasn't home —dinner was getting cold—Rubinstein would say it wasn't his fault; he wasn't keeping Teddy and anyway Mrs. Schulz should have made it her business to tell Teddy to be home at a reasonable hour. Things would end up so that it was all the fault of Teddy and his wife that the dinner was cold—Rubinstein had nothing to do with it and was completely innocent. Sinned against, in fact.

So when Panhandle found itself with the ruinous Stewart deal—which eventually resulted in losses of $1,350,000 even though the government did not penalize the company for its lateness—Rubinstein converted it into an asset which would make him millions of dollars.

It will be remembered that his original purchase of some 200,000 shares of Panhandle stock, 150,000 from the government's auction of Davis's holdings and 50,000 from a Panhandle officer, had been effected at an average of $1.25 a share. Since those original purchases, Rubinstein had picked up an additional 100,000 shares, some of which were ostensibly sold by Panhandle to Konrad Sztykgold but which were immediately and secretly transferred to Midway Victory. The rest had been bought up by various Rubinstein corporations and by Laurette and Stella. His total holdings at the time of the Stewart purchase, not counting the option on 120,000 shares which he had gotten for advancing Panhandle the money for the down payment, amounted to just under 300,000 shares bought at an average of $2.00 a share for a total investment of $600,000.

He decided to sell. But at his own price, which was going to be a good deal more than $2.00 a share. Panhandle's stock was going to have to rise. He would make it rise.

Was he lying about all the great things he said were going to happen? Well, what is lying? Rubinstein always talked a lot about his doings and none of his conversation was intended to make him look small. He would meet a girl at one of his parties, step to one side with her, and invite her to dinner. She would accept—Laurette or no Laurette. (He was not, after all, the only married man in New York stepping out on his wife.) They would dine. Then in most cases they would go to a hotel. The next day he would be telling his people all about her and inevitably saying that she had been a virgin. "She couldn't resist me," he would say, flexing his arms. "It must be my physique." It seemed to the listeners a little strange that every girl Serge ever slept with had been a virgin before she met him, but they never said anything. That was Serge. Always with the big stories. It was the same thing with the Bolivian oil concessions that were going to produce more oil than all the rest of South America combined. And it was the same with the Philippines project. Hamilton Pell always used to nod along; yes, Serge, yes, Serge, sure we will, but actually (he later said) he was thinking to himself that it was all dreams, not to be taken seriously. For one thing, a special act of the Bolivian Parliament would have been needed for Panhandle to go to work in that country and in any event the cost of piping the oil over the Andes would have been tremendous. Yes, Serge, yes, Serge. In the Philippines the government of President Sergio Osmeña had fallen and the purely explorative talks that had begun were cut off by the new regime but Rubinstein was still talking about $1,000,000,000 projects. No one close to Rubinstein ever considered these projects really based in solid fact— "Crazy!" Sztykgold frequently said—but not everyone in the world was close to Rubinstein. Everyone in the world describes a lot of people and only a few of those people are members of the United States stock-buying public. But they are the key to what happened.

For even before Stewart was formally acquired by Panhandle, Panhandle's stock started rising on the New York Stock Exchange. Stewart was a great company, wasn't it? And Panhandle was enlarging, rising, going ahead, wasn't it? The stock kept rising and its progress was not slowed when Rubinstein let it be known that Stewart was in such great shape that it was very likely going to soon pay a $200,000 dividend to its new owner, Panhandle. The story was reported in the New York newspapers and by the financial services, and the stock kept rising. Soon other stories were printed, all originating in the office of the Panhandle president, Mr. Rubinstein. Stewart, said the stories, was getting, absolutely, without fail, a $15,000,000 construction job from the Ford Motor Company. It was all arranged. It would bring a five per cent fee—$750,000. Only a few details remained to be worked out. And Stewart also had worked out a contract with the Borden Company. The fee would be at least $150,000. At least. Stewart had built in New York City the West Side Highway, the United States Court House, Madison Square Garden! Look at this book with these beautiful pictures! My company!

The stock kept going up. Not a word of the murderous naval hospital story leaked out—but then, who likes to talk about his failures? And as the word spread that PanPR on the Big Board was a real jumper, a high jumper, there was more news from the office of the Panhandle president. This was oil news and added to the flow of talk on the Street which grew in intensity as the new information giving optimistic forecasts of oil production got more and more optimistic. This information was that besides the acquisition of Stewart and the other companies which, incorporated into the Panhandle picture gave a broader base to the structure of the outfit, Panhandle was now finding huge new reserves on protected holdings near the drillings of major companies. The stock kept moving.

It was not necessary for Rubinstein personally to run around the Stock Exchange Luncheon Club announcing that his company was going up. Legmen could be used for that. They were members of brokerage firms, customers' men dropping the word into conversation with their clients. That was how it worked. One man tells another.

Then Lester Miller entered his life. Did any general of Frederick the Great ever have such luck as that which brought Lester Miller to Serge Rubinstein? Probably not. It was a dream situation, coming at the perfect time. It was beautiful, too lovely. It was like the movies. Serge Rubinstein is sitting in his office thinking yes, yes, I've got to raise this Panhandle stock so I can sell out before all the bad news about Stewart gets around town. The telephone rings. Cultured Ann Smith puts through the call. Hello? Hello, this is Lester Miller. And who is Lester Miller? He is an economist and manager of the Investment Department of Laird & Company, members of the New York Stock Exchange. He is a man of the widest experience with a fine reputation and a large following among investors seeking good information about stocks. And why is he calling? Because he has heard all about Panhandle and noted its recent rise and wants to look into the situation because he is interested in low-priced issues with possible capital appreciation that he can recommend to the people he represents. What does he want? He wants to come see Rubinstein and talk over the Panhandle situation so that he can learn the facts about the stock. Like the movies.

Rubinstein asked Miller to drop in any time at all. Miller went to 63 Wall Street and repeated to Rubinstein that he sought information to help him form an opinion and that, frankly speaking, he was acquainted with Rubinstein's reputation for not being completely honest but that he was going to keep an open mind on that matter. Rubinstein understood Mr. Miller's feeling completely, completely, and had in fact foreseen it and to allay any doubts Mr. Miller might have, Rubinstein was now going to present him with a fourteen-page typewritten autobiography which would explain the entire story of his life, which was an open book in any case. The autobiography, written in the third person, told the story of the son of the eminent and distinguished Russian financier Dimitri Rubinstein and described the education of that son and his rise in Europe and America. With it went a memorandum headed "The Panhandle Group" which detailed the holdings of PanPR. Another memorandum was headed "Persecutions to which Serge Rubinstein has been Subject in the United States" and devoted itself to telling how Mr. Rubinstein had been vilified and slandered. The men were together for two hours and when Miller left he was inclined to think, as he said later, that the rumors and stories about Rubinstein were merely products of "jealous and small minds."

After this chat, Miller dropped in at Bishop's Service to look through the Rubinstein file there. The reports he found worried him a bit and he went from there to the New York Public Library on Fifth Avenue to read old newspaper stories about Rubinstein. But weighing everything he had heard from other people and from Rubinstein himself, and taking into consideration the written material he had perused, he decided in his own mind that perhaps Rubinstein was a misunderstood and persecuted fellow after all. He so reported to his immediate superior at Laird & Company, Benjamin McAlpin, a partner in the firm. He added in a note to McAlpin that he was inclined to favor a recommendation for Panhandle. A week later he again met with Rubinstein. Rubinstein this time had ready for Miller an extensive description of the vast oil reserves that Panhandle owned, reserves which alone, ignoring all Panhandle's other assets, were equivalent to seven or eight dollars a share for this stock which at the moment was selling for only five dollars a share. He also presented Miller with a copy of the famous Stewart book, which Miller bore back to Laird & Company and placed on a table in the customers' room for any visitors to read. But Miller was still a bit wary of the Rubinstein reputation. It was a hard thing to get away from. So he told its owner that he wanted to make it very, very clear that his, Miller's, reputation was by contrast a very good one and that he could not take the chance of lending himself to any kind of an operation that was not 100 per cent ethical and honest. Rubinstein said he understood and that he appreciated Mr. Miller's saying so. But, he pointed out, if he had ever done anything of a dishonest nature, anything at all, it was a certainty that he would have been prosecuted for it since his various enemies, particularly his late brother André, had frequently denounced him to several different government agencies. Even the FBI had investigated him at André's urging but he was yet, as Mr. Miller could see, free and under no indictment. If he had ever done anything wrong, didn't Mr. Miller think the FBI would have found out and done something about it? Miller had to agree there was something to that, and passed over the subject to ask if he could not meet with some of the management people at Panhandle. Rubinstein was happy Mr. Miller had asked that and was very anxious for him to meet the production boss, Mr. Konrad Sztykgold, who was currently in Texas but would soon be in New York at which time a get-together could be arranged.

In the following weeks the two met again several times and Miller told Rubinstein he had more or less made up his mind that the outlook for Panhandle was extremely interesting from a speculative point of view. By that time Miller was conversant with the entire range of Panhandle's affairs— save for the Stewart hospital situation of which no mention at all had been made. Instead Rubinstein contented himself with telling of his plans for the construction company, adding that he thought Fidel Association, Panhandle's investment trust, could finance several Stewart projects at an additional profit to the parent company. Miller now was convinced that the people looking to him for advice had been well served by his efforts. He had looked into the company and its president and he was ready to make a recommendation to his followers.

On August 7, 1945, Laird & Company issued a bulletin, prepared by Miller, which told about Panhandle. Eight paragraphs described, besides the flourishing oil drilling, all the outside interests of the company. Panhandle possessed, the bulletin said, "promising potentialities." Laird & Company liked the stock as an interesting speculation.

That same day Laird & Company customers started buying Panhandle, which was then selling at from 6⅛ to 6½. At the same time Miller prepared a memorandum for his superior in the firm, McAlpin. His report pointed out that Panhandle's acquisition of Stewart was going to be a very good thing, that it was likely Stewart would be able to average at least $50,000,000 worth of contracts each year for the next four years at a profit per year of about $2,500,000. The report also said that the other Panhandle companies were expected to continue doing well. There was no mention in the report of the murderous naval hospital job. Meanwhile, Laird & Company customers were buying the stock left and right, accounting for 35 per cent of the total volume of Panhandle purchases during August. The stock kept climbing, hitting 8¾ by late September. Even Miller himself plunged a bit, buying nearly 1000 shares. Miller also talked up the stock at meetings and luncheons of the New York Society of Security Analysts, a group of several hundred brokerage firm analysts and statisticians whose business it is to keep in touch with the market for the benefit of investors who depend upon their advice. The Society members, each with a following of investors anxious to know his views, have immense influence in the Street. They can generate tremendous buying power.

134

Miller talked with many of them at the Society's get-togethers. They listened to Miller and pushed Panhandle. The stock was traded more and more actively and it always went in one direction—up. This trend was not halted when in the fall of 1945 Panhandle announced the purchase of a wonderful new oil field in Throckmorton County, Texas. Publicity releases about the new field flooded into the offices of the financial editors of the New York newspapers, and were duly given space in print. On October 8 the New York *World-Telegram* said that Throckmorton was believed to be a major oil development that made the Panhandle officials feel justified in predicting big results. On the same day the New York *Sun* reported that Panhandle had brought in seven large wells in a row on its Throckmorton field. The day after that *The Wall Street Journal* also mentioned the seven-in-a-row wells. "It's pretty safe to figure Throckmorton'll return 15,000,000 barrels," Rubinstein told people—quoting a figure somewhat above the one given him by a geologist and oil engineer who had studied the field and reported that it would, at most, bring in a million barrels.

Panhandle kept going. By October 9 the stock went above 10 for the first time in its history, closing at 10⅜—five times the $2.00 per share Rubinstein had paid for his 300,000 shares. Since August, Panhandle had gone from 6⅛ to the new record high, a rise of 70 per cent in nine weeks. But its greatest jump was still ahead. For a friend and former classmate of Miller's at New York University, William F. Edwards, had become interested in the stock after hearing about it from his old school friend and was recommending it to his own customers with enthusiasm. Edwards was an important personage in the Street, a partner and research man in the investment counseling firm of Naess & Cummings, an organization offering advice to customers representing a buying power of between $75,000,000 and $100,000,000. Edwards believed that when the war ended the construction industry was going to boom, and when he heard from his friend Miller about Panhandle's link to Stewart, he asked Miller to effect an introduction to the head of Panhandle. It was done and Edwards emerged from the meeting thinking, as Miller had thought, that perhaps Rubinstein had been unjustly described in the past. After all, Edwards reasoned, if a fine upstanding company like Stewart is in with the man, he really can't be too bad. In addition, there was always Panhandle's 15,000,000 barrels of Throckmorton oil, plus all of Panhandle's other companies. The meeting took place in mid-October and, as usual, Rubinstein talked at length about the Bolivian oil concessions and the rebuilding of the Philippines. Only one doubt remained in Edwards' mind:

135

Was it possible that Rubinstein was thinking of selling out in this rising market? He asked Rubinstein that, saying that it was of the utmost importance that he know if that were Rubinstein's intention. For, he said, if he recommended the stock he had to be absolutely sure that there was no chance that Rubinstein, the man at the helm, would decide to pull out. Rubinstein assured him there was no chance of that happening. He was going to stay with Panhandle and its great oil fields and its fabulous Stewart forever. Edwards took his leave and said to his friend Miller that, well, perhaps the man is maligned. Ten days later Edwards wrote a memorandum for his firm saying Panhandle was a good buy and that although Rubinstein's reputation was not good it was nevertheless likely that his talents were largely responsible for Panhandle's good position. He also pointed out that he had obtained Rubinstein's word that he had no intention of selling his Panhandle holdings, and that he had definitely gotten the impression that Rubinstein wanted to become an important man and had chosen Panhandle as the company around which he was going to build up his position in America.

On the basis of Edwards' report, Naess & Cummings joined Laird & Company in recommending Panhandle to its clients. The clients started to buy.

At the same time Rubinstein began to sell.

The Securities and Exchange Commission was set up after the stock market crash of 1929 to curb stock irregularities, which until then had not been irregularities, but rather regular practices similar to those still seen in Europe. One out of a welter of highballing moves and shady dealings that the SEC wanted to stop was the undercover selling of a company's stock by officers of the company. The SEC feeling was that the investing public has a right to know if people close to a company are selling its stock—in other words it is not right for a stockholder to be without the knowledge that the insiders of a company are deserting the ship to which he is still clinging in the hopeful thought that it will sail on smoothly. To make sure that the holder would have this knowledge, a law was passed saying that it would be unlawful for an issuer of a stock to sell his shares without registering the fact with the SEC. The law also stated that when a controlling shareholder decides to sell the news must be registered. This regulation was one of two problems that stood in Serge Rubinstein's way when he decided to unload his Panhandle holdings before the news of Stewart's awful position became widely enough known to drive the price of Panhandle right through the Stock Exchange floor. His other problem was how to unload his tremendous holdings without himself driving down the market by the weight of his sales.

He solved the first problem with the aid of attorney Daniel Katz of Barron, Rice & Rockmore, his tenant at Nineteen East and frequent associate in many of his companies. What did Danny think, he wanted to know. If Midway Victory sold the stock would it be necessary to tell the SEC that he, Rubinstein, president of Panhandle, was unloading? Danny considered the question and finally announced that the answer was no. Rubinstein could go ahead and start unloading.

That took care of that. A day after telling Edwards he would never sell his stock, Rubinstein began selling through Benjamin Hill & Company. But in unloading some 37,000 shares, Benjamin Hill & Company drove the Panhandle price down 1½ points, thus quickly spotlighting Rubinstein's second problem, which was how to unload without slaughtering the market.

With his great holdings in Panhandle, a loss of 1½ points represented a decrease in the value of those holdings to the tune of more than $300,000. Rubinstein was furious. They had sold only 37,000 shares and already the market was down 1½! The way things were going they'd drive the price down to zero! He cut off his dealings with the firm. Someone with a subtler touch was needed.

So he sought out Frank Bliss. Bliss was a little old man, white-haired, very slim and short and neat, always smiling and courteous, who was called "The Silver Fox of Wall Street." He was by way of being a kind of legend in the Street by 1945. He had spent his entire life in Wall Street and in his time had handled the biggest deals of its history. He had bought and sold more stock than any floor trader in history, and was the smoothest trader there ever was. He would stroll about the floor of the market and perhaps run his right hand through his hair. Across the room, separated from Bliss by perhaps hundreds of men, a secret confederate would catch the gesture and know that meant sell 50,000. Half an hour later Bliss would blow his nose. A second agent would run to buy 50,000. Always smiling and making very quiet little jokes, Bliss was the most carefully watched man on the floor. But only he himself knew just what he was doing. The confederates, who might be hired just for the one transaction, never knew their fellow agents. They would catch their own secret sign—the finger scratching the chin; the hand placed on the hip—and would go to execute the Silver Fox's order. Who they were selling for they never knew. All that was locked up in Bliss's mind, behind the smiling face and under the smooth white hair.

Bliss had met Rubinstein a few years earlier when a friend

of his had found himself "short" in gold on the London exchange. Bliss had heard Rubinstein had means of arranging gold deals in London through his Chosen connections, and went to see him. The project had never been consummated, but the two men retained a nodding acquaintance. Now in his need Rubinstein went to Bliss. Could he quietly unload a substantial number of Panhandle shares? Without slaughtering the market? And quickly, before the news about Stewart got out and drove the price into the ground? Yes—Bliss could. He marshaled a corps of agents, instructed them in just what gestures meant what, and went out onto the floor of the exchange. The sell order was given by Rubinstein on October 18, a Thursday. Bliss spent Friday looking over the situation. That same day, Friday, Rubinstein had a meeting with both Edwards and Miller and repeated to them once again that he would not sell out Panhandle.

On Saturday morning—the market was open on Saturday at that time—Bliss went to work. In the nine remaining business days of October he unloaded 80,000 shares at an average price of about $10 a share. And he did not disturb the market a bit. In fact, Panhandle even went up. Naturally he did not tell anyone whom he was selling for. It was his little secret and Rubinstein's. Meanwhile Panhandle continued to be talked up all over the Street. By this time the Philippine reconstruction deal was being spoken of as hard fact, and it was said it would bring Stewart a profit of $36,000,000, which alone meant the equivalent of $37 a share for each share of Panhandle stock.

Eventually, however, word that the Rubinstein corporations were selling reached the ears of Lester Miller. He was horrified. He roared into Rubinstein's office demanding to know why in hell he had sworn, sworn many times, that he would not sell out his Panhandle holdings. How, Miller demanded, could Rubinstein possibly explain these sales? Well, explained Rubinstein, he had just needed some money. He had finally arrived at a settlement of his Chosen troubles—Mr. Miller remembered that, didn't he?—and he was paying off the suit by giving the Britishers $900,000 and that was why he had sold a part of his stock. In addition, the lawyers who had handled the claim for the British shareholders were threatening to sue him for their fees, which they estimated at $400,-000, and to counter their claims it was necessary for Rubinstein to deposit $300,000 in cash in a bank as a guarantee he would pay if he lost the suit. (Actually this was not quite true. The very day he told Miller the story, Midway Victory's board of directors voted to allow Rubinstein to deposit securities, not cash, in the bank. As a result not a bit of cash had been deposited.) And that was why he was selling. He hoped Mr. Miller would understand.

Miller did understand—more or less. But he wanted to be sure that now that the Chosen question was settled there would be no more sales. He wanted a letter from Rubinstein saying so over his signature. Would Rubinstein send him such a letter? Surely. A letter was written and sent to Miller. But it was not exactly what Miller wanted. It simply said the stock had been sold, 80,000 shares. It did not promise anything about what was going to happen in the future.

Edwards was not at all satisfied when he heard the explanation from his friend Miller. He constantly tried to get Rubinstein on the telephone but the reaction to his calls at 63 Wall Street, once so warm, was now very chilly. Mr. Rubinstein never seemed to be in the office when Edwards called. Finally he got Rubinstein and was told the same story Miller had heard. With it came the promise that no, there would be no more sales. Edwards accepted that with reservations. But meanwhile all he and Miller had done continued to bear fruit. Panhandle kept climbing, hitting 11⅜. Rubinstein, through Bliss, kept selling, disposing of another 28,000 shares. When Miller and Edwards found out, they gave up on Rubinstein. Miller shouted at him over the telephone that he had done just exactly the kind of thing that had given him such a bad reputation on the Street and that now Rubinstein was in his eyes a person for whom he could never have any feeling or faith. Rubinstein replied to this by offering Miller a job as his personal economic adviser—"I'll pay you $15,000 a year." The investment counselor hung up in a rage.

So much for Miller and Edwards. "You can't trust a skunk even if he changes his spots," Edwards told Miller, somewhat jumbling his animals but making his point anyway. But neither Miller nor Edwards could now precipitately halt the purchase of Panhandle by investors who had gotten the word that the stock couldn't miss—and who never dreamed they were probably buying directly from the president of the company. The stock moving, hitting 13⅝ by the end of December. (Rubinstein's sales in that month accounted for just under 50 per cent of the total sales of Panhandle on the exchange.) Frank Bliss was doing a superlative job: he was unloading left and right and the stock not only wasn't being hurt but was actually climbing. Sixty thousand shares were sold in December but Rubinstein still dropped a line every now and then to Miller and Edwards to say he really wasn't going to sell any more. The two stock experts were reduced to gibbering at each other and, when they could get through to him, which was not often, at Rubinstein. The essence of

139

their message to him upon the occasion of such chats was that this was no way to do business.

Newspaper articles continued to appear, each telling of sparkling new developments for Panhandle. Standard & Poor's financial publication, *The Outlook*, appeared with an article saying that for the first time in history Panhandle was paying out an extra dividend and that future prospects looked excellent. The article was written by Standard & Poor's oil analyst, Burton St. John, after an interview with Rubinstein. Panhandle went to 12⅝. Rubinstein kept selling.

In January of 1946 Rubinstein accounted for almost one-third of all the Panhandle sales on the exchange. The stock reached 14¼. By the end of that month he had sold 246,-000 shares and had only 50,000 left. He held onto that amount for a while and then went back to selling. By April it was ended and he was finished with his work as head of Panhandle. But not quite. He appeared for the last time at a Panhandle board meeting, announced he had divested himself of his interests in the company and resigned his positions. He also tendered a $12,000 bill for various expenses he had met with in his work but had forgotten up until that minute.

On April 23, his resignation became effective. On that day there also went out to the stockholders the company's annual report for the year ending December 31, 1945. In it, for the first time publicly, the truth about Stewart was told.

The effect of this revelation can be imagined. The news meant the stock was going straight down. Pity the poor devil who bought at 14! But Panhandle was still good for something in the life of Serge Rubinstein—the opportunity it offered him to sell short. Selling short is to make an arrangement to sell today for today's price, but to make delivery of what you have sold not today but next week or next month. If you sell today for 14 for delivery next month, and if next month you can pick up the shares for 7, you have made seven points profit. What you hope and pray for is that the stock drops. Knowing that the Stewart revelation would drive Panhandle down, and also make the public take a new, skeptical, second look at all those claims about Bolivian oil concessions and Throckmorton reserves, Rubinstein proceeded to sell Panhandle short. In preparation for this, he had asked "Judge" or "Pop" Miller, his old English friend, to come over and act as his agent, or nominee, in the matter. He also hoped to have Madame Rubinstein play the same role for him, and gave her $100,000 to deposit in an office of Merrill Lynch, Pierce, Fenner & Beane. But the firm soon found out who she was and who her son was, and declined the account, returning the $100,000 three days after they received it. Judge Miller was, however, not so well known in

America, and no one realized he was selling short with Rubinstein's money and for Rubinstein's profit. So the English gentleman dutifully sold Panhandle short—very profitably, as it turned out—as the stock dropped and dropped, taking with it the hopes of anyone who bought it to know in the sweetness of happy day dreams of progress in the Philippines, Bolivia, and Throckmorton field. Inevitably, as it had to, Panhandle went to the dogs. Six months after Rubinstein left, the stock hit 5.

He was in Panhandle Producing and Refining for four years and invested $600,000. He made $3,500,000.

Chapter Twelve

The Draft

On Sunday, December 7, 1941, Mr. and Mrs. Serge Rubinstein and Mrs. Rubinstein's twin sister Betty went for a ride on Long Island to look at a house the Rubinsteins had rented for the following summer. The plan was that they should eat en route, and the sisters were talking about what restaurant to go to when suddenly Rubinstein cried out that they should be quiet. It was, from him, not too unusual a request, for often he demanded absolute silence from the people around him in order that he might think. Quite regularly he would order that there be no talking in the car while he worked out details in his mind about impending deals, and upon such occasions all with him would have to sit without talking until they were told that it was now all right for them to continue. Sometimes the chauffeur would be commanded to stop the car so that its owner could get out and stalk down the roadside deep in thought and planning what wonders the others could not know. The car would follow him slowly and at a distance, the other travelers whiling away their time as best they could until he signaled that he had mentally arranged things to his satisfaction and the trip could be continued.

But this time he demanded silence for another reason. He had caught the words of an announcer interrupting a program of music coming from the car radio. He ordered the chauffeur to turn up the radio and as the man did so the announcer repeated the bulletin. It was, of course, the news of Pearl Harbor.

When he had digested the information, Rubinstein told the chauffeur to turn the car around and go back to town. As one who—but naturally—expected to be observed by everyone everywhere he went, he told his wife and her sister that they would not eat out in a restaurant this day "It wouldn't look right." So they drove back to New York where Rubinstein sat down and like the youths lining up before enlistment offices, volunteered to come to the aid of the newly embattled United States. He did not address himself, however, to recruiting sergeants and petty officers, but to the Commander in Chief, Franklin D. Roosevelt. I OFFER MY SERVICES IN THIS GREAT EMERGENCY, he wired his some-time White House host. MY EXPERIENCE AND KNOWLEDGE IN RECENT EUROPEAN AND ESPECIALLY JAPANESE MATTERS MAY BE OF VALUE AT THIS TIME AND I AM MOST EAGER TO DO EVERYTHING I CAN TO BE OF SERVICE TO THE UNITED STATES. A while later Presidential Assistant Wayne Coy acknowledged the wire, and Rubinstein took the answer and pinned it to a copy of his own telegram, carrying the two papers with him everywhere and often showing them as evidence of his desire to do his bit. But nothing more was ever heard from the White House about the offer. When he showed the telegrams Rubinstein remarked— it almost became his trademark—that "I gave the Japanese their own Pearl Harbor in 1938 when I got a million dollars worth of yen out of Japan and pulled the rug out from under their currency." Sometimes it was a "Pearl Harbor in advance" and sometimes a "Pearl Harbor in reverse." Konrad Sztykgold's part in the operation was not mentioned.

Meanwhile, there was the war. He had prior to December 7 engaged the Champagne Room of El Morocco for a New Year's Eve party, but he canceled the arrangements because of the war—again, it wouldn't look right. El Morocco did not see it that way and Rubinstein was thenceforth ever barred from the premises. But being restricted from El Morocco was not a really important matter. He had other things to think about. After the White House kept its silence about his telegram, he tried to get a job in the War Production Board, the Board of Economic Warfare, in the office of the Alien Property Custodian and eventually in the Office of Strategic Services. An appointment was made for him to meet former Governor William H. Vanderbilt of Rhode Island, who was serving in the OSS with the rank of Navy Commander and recruiting potential espionage experts in the New York area. The appointment, which was arranged by Herr Professor, was for four o'clock one day in the Oak Room of the Hotel Plaza. Vanderbilt was on time; Herr Professor was on time. But 4:15 came and went and Rubinstein did not appear. Finally he strolled in. Herr Professor leaped up and went to him, saying, "But Serge, why are you late? This is an important man with little time." "Why shouldn't I be late?" Rubinstein returned. "He wants something from me; I don't want anything from him." He sat down with Commander Vanderbilt. "I gave the Japanese their Pearl Harbor years ago," he said. "I destroyed their currency with one fell swoop." The tone of the conversation did not appeal to Vanderbilt and after a while he excused himself and left. Rubinstein never heard from the OSS ever again. And with that he lost interest in the war. He had wired the President, applied to this board and that board, been interviewed by the Commander—enough! Besides, by then he was just getting into Panhandle—his entrance into the oil company via the purchase of William Rhodes Davis's stock took place in July 1942—and he had other things on his mind. Rubinstein then was thirty-three and eligible for the draft but it did not seem likely he would be pressed into service. Before the outbreak of the war, in June 1941, he had appeared before his local draft board to say he was the sole support of his wife, his wife's mother and two sisters, his own mother, his Aunt Genia, and George Shiskin, the old man from St. Petersburg who received a regular monthly stipend. Itemizing all these people one by one, he added that his income for the preceding fiscal year amounted to some $12,000 and that while he was worth in the neighborhood of $300,000, he had debts amounting to three-quarters of a million dollars. The board gave him a dependency deferment and that seemed to settle the matter. Now and again he reappeared to inform the board that he was still in no position to provide for his dependents were he to be drafted, and the board accepted what he said. So putting the whole matter of possible service out of his mind, he went to work on the Panhandle situation.

And when he was not working, he was playing. "I work hard and I play hard," he said. Laurette in those 'ays was stunningly beautiful—Teddy Schulz thought her perhaps the most beautiful girl he had ever seen—and Rubinstein loved to show her off although he became enraged if another man looked at her. Winter weekends the couple, often accompanied by sister Betty, went to Lake Placid where the two girls sat sipping hot chocolate and waiting for the loudspeaker to boom out that Mr. Rubinstein was now coming down the special bobsled course over which not everyone could ride but only those who had a permit gained by possession of superior bobsled skills. Then, always shooting down the very center of the run, which is the most dangerous and gallant way to go, his sled would hurtle into view while the girls clutched each other; it was so reckless and dangerous and proved, they said, that he had more courage than sense. On the ski slopes he would be a noisy but rather sloppy skier, hiring instructors to follow him about and yelling his head off at them, reminding one man who saw him of the fashion in which a kid with a new bike wants to show off before everyone on

143

the block. Or he would hire a horse and hanging on the long reins, ski behind it as it cantered over the ice. Now and again he would fall and be dragged for hundreds of feet as he tried to halt the animal, and then the girls would tell him he was crazy to risk life and limb that way. But he would laugh at that, saying that he didn't want to grow old anyway; he'd rather die. He often said that—I want to die young—but he often said also that he was afraid of that death. And when upon rare occasions he became ill it was as if the end of the world had arrived, with doctors and nurses scurrying about trying to calm down the impatient occupant of the sickroom.

Summers he rented homes within striking distance of New York. One summer he decided to take a mansion in Oyster Bay, but found that there were problems involved in such an undertaking. The owner was no more likely to make welcome Rubinstein than were the owners of certain hotels in Lake Placid, so the Archduke Franz Josef was sent to rent the house. (Gordon Foster had been used to make Lake Placid reservations.) But when Rubinstein moved in and gave a party or two the neighbors telephoned the absent owner to announce who the tenant actually was. That brought the man flying back to say that renting to the Archduke was one thing, but renting to Serge Rubinstein was something else. No matter; he took another home along the Nave in Red Bank, New Jersey, and bought a sailboat to go with it. Laurette and Betty looking wonderful in shorts and pullovers, they sailed up and down the Jersey waters and even found a place which served Russian-type food. Often he had guests down and when he telephoned in advance the restaurant would set apart half the place for him and his party and make a great to-do when he appeared spouting Russian and talking about how, ah, this was like the good old days in the old country. One day a haphazardly invited guest brought down to the house as part of a cosmopolitan group transported in half a dozen rented Cadillacs found himself in a room containing electrical equipment and radios and remembering the recurring rumors that Gordon Foster was actually in the employment of the British Secret Service spread the story that Rubinstein must be a foreign agent of some sort. The story gained currency and Rubinstein never bothered to deny it or the somewhat parallel story that he had masterminded a world-wide scheme to unload Czarist art treasures on behalf of the Soviet government. Both tales went to embellish his reputation of mystery man and internationally important operative in many fields.

He was, of course, not faithful to Laurette for very long past their wedding date. (The image of Serge Rubinstein faithful to one woman is a picture difficult to conjure up.) But he always dictated just what his wife was to wear and how she was to do it. Under his tutelage she affected great splashy hats sitting atop her upswept blonde hair and elegant low-cut dresses adorning her tall body. She went in for a great many doodads such as dangling earrings and very fancy shoes with enormous spike heels, and was practically a caricature of what a New York night-blooming glamour girl should look like. He wanted her to look like the plaything of some very big man or, more kindly put, like the mistress of some European grandee, and in fact she did. At home he hired and fired servants, decided what the meals were to be and with Gordon Foster's aid arranged the furnishings. Her role was to be that of the kept woman—a role she fulfilled. He was in the European manner always sending her little gifts: flowers, niceties, a ring. She in turn—it must be remembered she was nineteen when she married him—depended upon him for everything and her family along with her. She had nothing to defy him with, he was in charge, and she in those early days used to worry a great deal about him, thinking that when he flew the plane would crash and so forth. She was perfectly frantic—at first—when he left her alone to go somewhere on a deal and yet as time went on, always the cold and unapproachable one, she tended to stand up to him in an uncompromising way. "Let's drive down to the shore," he would say and she would say "No." Just No without alternatives. He would suggest something else and something else again and finally she would say Yes and it would be Yes. But it took awhile before things came to that pass. Perhaps it was what Americans would call his cheating that made her take these attitudes. For him, of course, it was not cheating. Where was the European man of means without a mistress here and a girl friend there? Who criticized the son of Queen Victoria when he went each week to Paris and one of several apartments where he could find relaxation? Had not Nicholas, as Czarevitch, kept a leading dancer with the full approval of all who mattered in Russia? Laurette did not know of these things but she knew full well of her husband's activities. "Serge thinks he's so smart," she said to Teddy Schulz, "but I know he's going out with So-and-so." She said it many times for there were many So-and-sos in his life and at every party before Laurette's eyes he was circulating around getting phone numbers which would be called in a day or so in order that an intimate little dinner for two might be arranged. But yet there was only one Laurette— there always was. Once at the Copa a luncheon was given for prominent models and Laurette, as a John Robert Powers alumna, was invited to attend. She went with her mother and caught the eye of a man who was to select the most outstanding model in attendance for presentation of a large bottle of rare perfume. The man walked to Laurette's table and put down the bottle and said, "This is the most beautiful woman in the room." Her husband could not tire of telling the story. He had a life-size full-length portrait of her painted and hung it in the living room so that he could draw attention to it and to its subject, who monosyllabically greeted the guests and impressed the Europeans as being immensely dull but just right for a financier and boulevardier. Actually Laurette did not enjoy being on display and alone, away from Serge and his crowd, she could unbend and talk with animation, mostly about art. She outfitted a studio for herself and spent most of her time there working on paintings, not portraits, which were not her forte, but still lifes and landscapes, and on her sculpture. Things passed her by and she was untouched: big deals, nobility kissing her hand, headwaiters bowing, houses in the country, her husband rising Chairman of the Board—she did not care. He dressed her up and treated her like one of his many blondes, she was his doll, and it did not seem that even that mattered to her very much after a time. He treated her in his *savoir faire* style as a big beautiful blond dumbbell; it did not matter. Nothing of his empire building penetrated and if she sat silent during his interminable discussions of how he was going to build Stewart and Warren Brothers and conquer the world it did not mean she was really listening. She did not care to be the *grande dame* of his salon, introducing all kinds of people to one another, all in different walks of life and each coming to the fascinating meeting place of the great Wall Street operator and his brilliant and beautiful wife. So by default that became more Stella's job, while Laurette retired to her art work and, in time, to her children.

Meanwhile the war went on around them. It was a period of general austerity but at the same time the New York night spots were blasting out of their walls to the tune of the spending of many dollars earned in booming wartime. Rubinstein had been at it for many years, but his interest in partying never slackened and he played best to a large audience. It was possible to say, "Serge, I'd like to pay my share," but he would never hear of it; it was absolutely out of the question, you were his guest, it was his pleasure —please, no more discussion. Laurette was by his side, the focal point of many eyes, and Gordon Foster was there seeing himself as something like a Grand Duke's agent to Teddy Schulz's office boy or accountant or person in trade, something like that, and Hamilton Pell was present as esteemed fellow businessman engaged in great works.

The early war years went on and back in England the Chosen matter was finally dragging itself to a close. The British government was dollar short and, anxious to have the thing wound up, was putting pressure on everyone concerned to have done. The British shareholders themselves were weary with it all and fearful that if they didn't get their money pretty soon, or at least a share of it, Rubinstein would end up not giving them a penny. A big drive was undertaken to get the shareholders to vote for an official receiver to take over Chosen. But when in 1943 the vote was tallied in London it was found that 300,000 proxies voting "nay" had been flown in from Rubinstein in the United States via an American Air Force bomber. The proxies were all carried in a diplomatic pouch and this coupled with the use of precious bomber space for such a purpose raised a tremendous hubbub. A question was raised in the House of Commons and Foreign Secretary Anthony Eden endeavored to explain as spokesman for the government. His speech was a masterpiece of double talk and no one exactly understood what he was saying, but it was nosed about among the members that certain people in Washington would prefer that the matter be not too noisomely pursued. That did not prevent one or two British papers from saying the whole business was more than a little strange, as was the fact that Rubinstein in America got information faster than the shareholders living in Britain. It also did not prevent Mr. Justice Bennet of the High Court of Justice, Chancery Division, from ordering that the matter be compulsorily wound up whether or not "this highly unscrupulous and clever tactician, this unscrupulous gentleman Mr. Rubinstein" liked it or not. So at last an arrangement was made whereby Rubinstein would pay some $800,000 to the British shareholders in full settlement of their claims. On April 30, 1943, he went to the office of Percival F. Brundage of Price Waterhouse & Company, accountants for the British shareholders. It was late in the afternoon when he marched into Brundage's office. He bore in his hand a large black satchel. In it was $195,000 —in cash—which he was offering as the first payment on his settlement. He insisted on counting the money in front of Brundage, an operation which consumed considerable time and which rather set Brundage back on his heels, he in common with most people never having seen $195,000 in cash spread across his desk. After the counting was finished, the men had a minor disagreement about whether to deposit it or not and Rubinstein scooped up all the many rolls of bills, put them back into his satchel and departed holding his burden (perhaps not unexpectedly) rather firmly in his hand. Chosen's settlement was not yet to be.

Two months before this drama, Rubinstein had been called to his draft board for re-examination as to his dependency deferment. He again repeated his insistence that he had no assets with which to provide for those dependent upon him. The draft board accepted the statement at the time, but after he talked up the business of spreading the money all over Brundage's desk, word reached the board that perhaps their man was not as impoverished as he claimed. Perhaps not unnaturally the board began to suspect that anyone who walked around with $195,000 in cash was not a pauper. The board called him down once more and there began a new series of affidavits and examinations. But their tone was somewhat changed, with Rubinstein now pointing out that Panhandle produced more than one per cent of all the aviation gas used by the Army Air Force and that, as President and Chairman of the Board, he certainly deserved a deferment in order to further the company's business. There were several orders for induction and several more postponements. In the midst of this the immigration people arrested him and held him for a day on the charge that he had entered the country with a fraudulent Portuguese passport and was therefore illegally in the United States and liable to deportation. But the immigration case collapsed, or appeared to collapse, when certain Portuguese authorities came to Rubinstein's aid by averring his passport was completely on the up-and-up. (Not long afterward, a young lady who became the best friend of Konrad Sztykgold's daughter but who was then living in Portugal heard from her Lisbon hatmaker a description of how the living standards of a certain Portuguese official involved in the passport validation had suddenly risen. The hatmaker was, of course, happy at the precipitate change in the spending of the official, for his wife had become the shop's best customer, spending more money on her hats than she had formerly spent on her entire wardrobe. Nosing about, the young lady in question heard it quite openly said that this Mr. Rubinstein, our fellow citizen, had said to certain officials of the Portuguese government, they being either based upon or passing through Washington, that a sum of $250,000 existed for the validation of his citizenship in the honored homeland, Portugal.) The brief arrest, however, offered Rubinstein a chance to point out to one and all that although he had been completely willing to serve the United States, he must be excused now from feeling anxious to enter the Army of a country that was working hard to get rid of him and would doubtless take advantage of any military absence of his to complete its plans.

But regardless of the immigration situation, the Selective Service people were not through with him. They were on the spot for two reasons, the first being the idealistic one that in a democratic country it is important to preserve the citizenry's faith that the drafting of men is done in a completely fair way; the second one being that increasingly the New York headquarters of the draft system was receiving regular mail, signed and unsigned, asking why in hell this Serge Rubinstein was on the loose night-clubbing when millions of other men were in uniform. Eventually all the letters and the Rubinstein file landed for review on the desk of Colonel David Brady, a New York lawyer in civilian life but a draft official during the war. Brady had hardly begun to look into the matter when he received a phone call from Senator Brien McMahon asking him to lunch. The two men had known each other before the war and talked about old times over their cocktails. Then the senator asked Brady if he knew about this Serge Rubinstein draft question. Brady said yes, he was looking into it just at that time. "Listen, Brien," he added, "stay away from it." McMahon said certainly, of course, but he had represented Rubinstein in various matters and was just interested in what his client's draft status was. Brady said that whatever it was, the Selective Service System would deal with it fairly. "Well," said McMahon, "I just wanted to know because I heard someone mention your name and say you were out to get him, out to knife him." They finished their lunch and parted. A few days later a lawyer—now a federal judge—who lived near Brady and who was a former Rubinstein attorney, called and asked if he might stop over for a moment. It was quite late at night but Brady told the other man to come on down and have a drink. "Can I talk to you about Serge Rubinstein?" the lawyer asked. "Anyone can talk to me," Brady said.

"Well," said the lawyer, "I understand Rubinstein is saying you personally are being unfair to him in trying to have the whole business re-examined and reconsidered." Brady told him that wasn't so. A great many other people called him in the following days, but the colonel continued his inquiry. Then a higher-up in the Selective Service System called Brady in and suggested that with the things the way they were it might be best if Brady disqualified himself from having anything to do with the case.

Meanwhile other wheels kept turning. Colonel Arthur J. McDermott, New York Director of the Selective Service System, was called down to Washington at the instigation of Representative Andrew J. May of the House Military Affairs Committee and there, as he later said, "grilled" on the subject of Rubinstein by H. Ralph Burton, the Military Affairs Committee Counsel. "Burton went into every conceivable phase of the situation," Colonel McDermott said, "and was highly argumentative and critical in his manner of talking . . . It was an extraordinary and very unpleasant procedure. To the best of my knowledge it has never happened in any other case in the millions and millions in the six and one half years of Selective Service."

But the case was still under consideration; the board was still discussing a reclassification. Finally they decided to put Rubinstein into 1-A. He immediately made an appeal to have the 1-A classification changed back to either a dependency or an essential industries deferment, but the board voted unanimously to keep him in 1-A. Rubinstein then reached the ear of Major General Lewis B. Hershey, national head of Selective Service, and Hershey asked the Presidential Board of Appeals to take up the case. This group, set up to act as President Roosevelt's adviser in draft matters, at once began to look into the Rubinstein matter. (Theoretically, the board members worked directly under Roosevelt but it is not likely he personally dealt with every file the board looked at.)

Meanwhile, money was flowing out to prevent a draft call. It was the commonest thing for the members of the Rubinstein entourage to remark to one another that Serge had just taken care of this congressman for twenty-five thousand dollars, that one for twenty. Rubinstein himself talked with complete freedom on that subject—with enjoyment and braggadocio, even . . . One day there was a somber ceremony at the Panhandle office in which a medal was presented to a company official, Thomas Eakins, on behalf of his son killed in action overseas. An Army officer and an aide came to the office with the medal on a pillow and there presented it to the stricken father. Together with other Panhandle people, Rubinstein and Romeo Muller witnessed the brief ceremony. Half an hour later they went down together for lunch. They walked into the elevator car which was filled with people heading for the street, most of them silent, as people are in elevators. Muller's thoughts were still on the bereaved father and the dead son when Rubinstein began to speak in a loud voice, as he always did. "I got another of those damned 1-A notifications today," he said. It was impossible for anyone in the quiet car not to hear every word. "I wouldn't mind," he went on, "but I just paid Senator"—he named the man—"another $50,000 to keep me out of the Army." The car arrived at the ground floor. The two men walked out. "For God's sake, Serge!" Muller exploded. His anger surprised Serge. A little later a Rubinstein lawyer went to another senator with twenty-five one-thousand-dollar bills and quite openly talked about it, saying to many people that really it was just throwing money down the drain for not one good reason in the world but that Serge wanted it that way so there you are.

The whole business of Rubinstein's involvement with the draft could not but hurt Panhandle and that worried Muller. He suggested to Rubinstein that the two of them journey to Washington together and there confer with a lawyer who was friendly with Muller (and with certain people in the government) and might be able to offer a little aid in presenting to the certain people the viewpoint that Rubinstein was, after all, very important to Panhandle and thus to Panhandle's considerable contribution to the war effort. Rubinstein was pleased with the idea and the two men went to the lawyer who listened and said it appeared to him that Rubinstein had a legitimate position and that as a favor to Muller he would try to bring the matter up with the right people. The talk ended and the two visitors stood to go. But Rubinstein had one more thing to say. "I'd like you to be the Washington attorney for Panhandle," he said to the lawyer.

"Very fine," answered the man.

"Suppose I give you a retainer," Rubinstein went on, reaching for a checkbook. But the lawyer stopped him, asking just what the duties of the Washington attorney for Panhandle would be. Rubinstein was already bending over the check with a pen, and simply said there would be no duties—but in case something came up, the lawyer would be on hand.

"No duties?" asked the lawyer. He did not seem to understand.

"No," said Rubinstein. "How about $10,000 for the retainer?"

Finally the lawyer understood. "Mr. Rubinstein," he said, "I never accept a fee I do not earn. We are wasting each other's time. I said I would try to help you and I meant it and there was no need for you to try to make me more willing to do so by giving me money. Good day."

Outside, Rubinstein said to Muller that the man would be of no use at all, a man like that couldn't do anything for anybody. A man either had something to offer that was for sale or he was nothing. This man was nothing.

But Muller was still worried about what all this would mean to Panhandle. After leaving the lawyer's office he made his way, alone this time, to a friend in the government with whom he had often played cards socially and asked the man just what was behind all this fuss about Rubinstein's draft status. The man told Muller that it was just that the fellow attracted so much attention, that was it. Did he continually have to give parties for three hundred people? Did he have to go to a night club every evening? Did he have to hang around Washington bragging all over the Willard and the

Mayflower about how many senators he'd taken care of? The thing for him to do, the man said, was calm down, keep quiet, not draw so much attention to himself, just do his job for Panhandle. Then it was more than likely the government would lay off. That Rubinstein was widely known as a Russian might redound to his service, the man added. The government was anxious to be on good terms with every Russian, any Russian at all, even those who had fled the Soviet government.

Muller went back to the Mayflower, where he and Rubinstein were staying, filled with the importance of making it clear to Rubinstein just what the unofficial government attitude was. He went into the hotel expecting to find Rubinstein upstairs in their suite, but as he passed the cocktail lounge he heard a familiar voice and saw a familiar sight. It was his Russian surrounded by a dozen people, talking at the top of his lungs and running his hand over a tall girl. Muller stepped in and asked Rubinstein to come with him a moment. Rubinstein did so and Muller repeated all his government friend had said. Ah, said Rubinstein. Then it was all clear. He went back into the cocktail lounge, paid the bill and went upstairs with Muller. That night they took the train back to New York.

Two weeks later Muller was in Washington and dropped in to see his government friend. "I told Rubinstein all you said," Muller announced. "I guess he's out of your hair now."

"That right?" asked the official. He sent his secretary for a report on the subject of their conversation. Then sitting back at his desk he read it to Muller. The report was dated the previous day and detailed how upon that day Rubinstein arrived in Washington and again checked in at the Mayflower, taking a large and high-priced suite. After changing his clothes, the report continued, Rubinstein went downstairs, made a phone call, and then went to stand by himself in the lobby. He wore a double-breasted blue suit and had his hands jammed in his pockets as he rocked to and fro on his heels. He was smiling to himself. Five minutes after Rubinstein made his call, the hotel desk received an outside call asking that Sir Serge Rubinstein be paged and asked to come to the phone. Sir Serge, the caller said, would be found in the lobby. A bellboy was sent off on the errand and paraded into the lobby calling out "Sir Serge Rubinstein! Telephone call for Sir Serge Rubinstein!" Rubinstein heard the bellboy's call but did not go to the youth and identify himself. Instead he stepped in front of him, some three or four feet forward, and as the boy continued his chant—"Paging Sir Serge Rubinstein"—Rubinstein walked in front of him until the two of them, two marchers, the one smiling left and right, the other calling out loudly, had circled the entire Mayflower lobby. Then Rubinstein gave the boy a coin. "Thanks. I'll take that call."

Muller gave up. And Rubinstein went on as he had before. When people said to him, "But Serge, the government . . ." he would throw up his hands: "Ah, so, the hell with the government!" He was dismissive of all that foolishness, government, gas coupons, little stamps for rationed meat and butter—nonsense, stupidity. In the night clubs there were steaks whenever you wanted them, meatless Tuesday or no meatless Tuesday, there was plenty of everything. But he watched his eating nevertheless, knowing his tendency to balloon up. He was forever weighing himself and asking people if they thought he was getting fat or if they hadn't noticed that he'd dropped three pounds—he really looked slim now, didn't he? Yet in his face there was beneath the great charming smile—or at least there was in the eyes of some of those who saw him—something of the demimonde, the *untervelt,* something that said that its owner could walk over bodies. Such as saw that, or said they saw it, found that for all the opulence of the shirt that was a little too stiff and the cologne that was a bit too strong there was something lacking that might be called inner refinement; that there was something there which you could find in the pugilist or truck driver who might have, with certain differences, owned that face. Women meeting him for the first time often tended to be a little repelled, or rather a little set back on their heels. He was so clean and gleaming, so perfectly well groomed, his hair so smoothly combed and his nails so well manicured that there was something, something . . . decadent? Too cunning and designing? But then he kissed their hands and after doing that did not relinquish his grip on their fingers while his other hand reached up toward their elbows. One young blonde meeting him thought to herself that he was like a snake, a great smooth snake with a brilliant smile. She mused to herself that it would be interesting to count a snake's vertebrae, find out how they intersected. He in turn spoke of her smile—was she in movies? She was so pretty! No? What a pity! Ah, but she was an actress? Yes, he'd known it. Yes, there was something about her that would look just right, just perfect on a stage.

. . . But she never really did find out just how the vertebrae intersected.

The government moved toward a final classification. He had had a total of twelve changes in his draft status but by middle 1943 it began to look as if there would be no more. Everyone around him told him to have done and go into the Army and get it over with. All logic demanded it: he was in his mid-thirties and hardly prime combat material; he would gain a commission and end up with a desk in Washington and a chance to gain respectability once and for all with the immigration people. Did he think they would be able to deport ex-Major Rubinstein once the war was over? Or maybe even ex-Lieutenant Colonel? Stella was after him to go in because she was afraid there would be terrible trouble if he did not, but he told her that once he was in the Army Konrad would take over all of his business interests and leave him high and dry. To Konrad he said that he would go in save for his fear that the British with their long memories would contrive with the Americans to have him, without a moment's training, sent to a combat zone so that he could be conveniently killed off and removed from the Chosen situation. To Herr Professor he said *Ach,* the Army, that was *zuchthaus, zuchthaus,* the German word referring to the kind of degrading prison service done by serious offenders. His mother-in-law, Mrs. Kilborn, told him he would be made an example of once the war was over, the way they did with a similarly rich man in the First World War. Gordon Foster told him to go in for Christ's sake, the war would be over soon anyway and even before it was he'd end up owning half the U. S. Army and make contacts worth millions. But Rubinstein answered both of them by saying he couldn't possibly go—how could he look after his interests once he was in uniform?—and Foster at least concluded it was that money, that money, all that money pouring in like rain. Teddy Schulz went off into the Army and when he came home on leave he dropped up to the office to say hello to everyone and have a chat with his ex-schoolmate and ex-employer who said they wanted him to go too but that he could not; he had too many responsibilities. (Teddy decided that maybe Serge was afraid he'd lose Laurette once he was away from her. Teddy had always been impressed with Laurette.) To anyone who questioned his attitude Rubinstein explained that they were after him because he was in finance, "which is reserved for older people and people who are longer established in this country." Or he said it was that he was being "persecuted for my assets—I'm being bombed and strafed by my business enemies; I'm being blackmailed."

He discussed the subject endlessly but he changed his grounds with every sentence and there was nothing in his talk of the clear thinking and piecing together of one thought and another that characterized his approach to other problems. Some of those who heard him put it down to his ignorance of the U. S. Army that was so different from the East European forces of which he had heard much during his youthful St. Petersburg days of the First World War. But others said it could not have been simple lack of knowledge and that he surely must . realize that the lot of an American conscript of modern times in no wise resembled that of a member of the peasant hordes of 1914–18. "Serge," one woman said to him, "you've never seen anything of American middle-class life, which is what the Army would be like. By the standards of any kind of Russian or Polish or Imperial Army you live like a king."

"I know, I know," he said.

"Well, if you know," she said, "then go on in." But he was hardly listening and was off again about how the British would do him in or Konrad would steal all his companies away. "That's ridiculous!" said the woman. "Well, I feel that way!" he blazed back.

Finally the Chosen business was about to be concluded; there would be a settlement and it would be over at last. He did not exactly consider the payment of $800,000 in several installments a defeat—after all he had had the use of Chosen's money for years and had used it to begin his career in America— but still it could not be deemed a victory that he had to give more than three-quarters of a million dollars to the British shareholders. Lounging around the courtroom during one final hearing, he nosed it around that a part of his trouble with Chosen derived from the fact that financial writer Burton Crane of the New York Times had been out for his hide. Crane, Rubinstein said to several people sitting around him, had come to him asking for $5000, threatening that if the money were not forthcoming the Times would run a series titled "The Life of Serge Rubinstein" and that in content it would be something other than complimentary. One of those who heard the story from Rubinstein's lips told it to Crane when the newspaperman arrived to cover the hearing and Crane immediately asked if the man would sign an affidavit telling what he had heard. The man said he would. Crane then rounded up half a dozen other people who had heard Rubinstein telling the story and got them to promise to sign affidavits. That done, Crane rushed back to the Times office and one of its lawyers. The lawyer said it was an open-and-shut case and that the Times legal department would sue on Crane's behalf for $500,000 for defamation of character. But shortly after, Rubinstein got a very eminent lawyer to charge around to the Times and all but get down on his knees to explain that Serge was just being playful. To Crane's anger, the paper decided to forget the whole thing.

But in the background to the final negotiations for an end to the Chosen matter there lingered always the spectacle of the Army swooping down to claim what it said was its due. On Columbus Day, 1943, Rubinstein tried to bribe the chief clerk of his local draft board at 155 E. 88th Street in order that the man might give him a little help here and there. The offer was rejected but Rubinstein continued on and tried to give the man a little advice about how to beat the market. This was also rejected. Rubinstein then appeared before the board to say he was now associated with an airplane manufacturing company doing most essential work and that his continuing value to the company lay not only in his financial involvement but also in his vast experience in things aeronautical which he had gained in France before the war. The company, he explained, Taylorcraft Corporation of Ohio, had a man in Chile who had invented a new kind of wing which made landing speeds of only fifteen or twenty miles an hour quite feasible but it had been "going on the rocks" until he, Rubinstein, got into it. The board listened, but noted that he had never before in any of his numerous affidavits referred to Taylorcraft, and told him to get ready to be a soldier. (Meanwhile in Ohio, negotiations were going on to have an Ohio board declare him essential.) A week or so after this last appearance, the board made its final, irrevocable, decision. Rubinstein was told to report for induction on Wednesday, November 17, 1943, at 6:15 in the morning at the Grand Central Palace—which Stewart had built.

On that day, November 17, Colonel Brady remarked to an associate that it was a toss-up whether Rubinstein would be rejected as a mental case or whether he would end up owning whatever Army post he went to. As it turned out, Brady was wrong on both counts. For Rubinstein did not show up at the appointed place. The previous evening he had gone to the board to request a copy of Federal Form 301, the application by a neutral alien for relief from military service, submission of which would automatically assure his non-entrance into the Army but which would also mean he was forever barred from citizenship in the United States. When he arrived at the board, in company with lawyer Danny Katz, the office had just closed for the day, but he pounded on the door until someone came to see what was going on. He asked for a Form 301 and while a search was made to find one he departed the premises, leaving Danny to pick up the paper and bear it to his client after remarking to the draft board people that Mr. Rubinstein did seem a bit nervous today.

So that was that. He had a perfect right to file Form 301 and had always had that right. Now he was free of the worry about the Army and free also to devote himself to Panhandle and to his personal affairs. The apartment at 1016

Fifth Avenue was confining and he had the desire to own a town house, so he began to look around for a suitable one, shortly finding one just a little south on Fifth Avenue, at 814, which was between 62nd and 63rd Streets, than which there is no better in New York City or, for that matter, in the entire world. The house, a six-story limestone affair, was the former home of the late financier Jules S. Bache, and along with many pieces of Bache's world-famous art collection had been left to the Metropolitan Museum of Art. It was more than a town house; it was close to being a palace, having twenty-eight rooms, ten fireplaces, accommodations for a dozen servants, eight master bedrooms, ten bathrooms, two elevators and quantities of immense closets. During Bache's lifetime the building was used not only as a residence but also, upon certain days of the week, as a private museum for the Bache art collection, with visitors being admitted by special pass. In 1945, however, the Metropolitan had little use for the building and was not asking too great a sum for it. Rubinstein got it for a $25,000 down payment, with $75,000 to be paid in several installments. Once purchased, the house was given over to Gordon Foster's decorating talents and Foster worked on it for six months, buying everything only at wholesale prices to comply with Rubinstein's order that the bills be not too excessive. Spencer Samuels, whose family owned the renowned art firm of French and Company, and who was a frequent guest of Rubinstein's, was asked to submit to the new owner some *objets d'art*. Samuels went to work with the happy idea in mind that the Wall Street millionaire head of Panhandle Producing and Refining Company was going to emulate the showplace collection of Bache, but within a very short time found that this was not to be the case at all. Everything he offered Rubinstein was deemed too expensive by far, and finally Samuels was reduced to showing works of art that had been, in the art phrase, attributed to various masters. One such work was a massive study, "The Notary," which one expert had in the long ago attributed to Rembrandt. As dozens of other experts over the years had decided that it was in fact not the production of the master but only of a talented student, the work could be gotten for the rather modest price of $2000. At the top of one flight of stairs Bache had had an important (and indisputably genuine) Rembrandt, and with the idea of replacing the other painting with "The Notary," Rubinstein bought it and had it hoisted to the same spot where the other painting had been. Immediately it was put in place Rubinstein began saying that guests must come and see his wonderful new painting, it was attributed to Rembrandt, and soon all who came to the house automatically described the painting as Serge's Rembrandt, which was worth God knows how much. Eventually the price universally quoted somehow settled at $75,000. Rubinstein never corrected the off-center impression and in time the possession of such a valuable work—Did you see Serge's Rembrandt; he paid $75,000 for it?—cast an aura over the entire house. "Ah, Mr. Samuels, it's beautiful," the art dealer heard on all sides, to which he reluctantly had to reply that it certainly was an interesting work, wasn't it? In a Vienna museum there existed a genuine, validated, Rembrandt called "The Notary," but happily Vienna was a long distance from 814 Fifth Avenue.

Rubinstein did have one very fine painting, this being Romney's "Sir William Lemon, Bart.", a life-size portrait of an English nobleman standing resplendently in blue cutaway coat, knee breeches, white stock, and powdered wig. With the painting came a long recitation of who owned it and what experts had validated it, but to it Rubinstein added a collection of attributed-to-Romneys which rode along on the blue cutaway coattails of Sir William Lemon, Bart., and came to be known as Serge's great Romney collection. In the interests of artistic conscience Gordon Foster battled this conception, his weapons being repeated statements that for God's sake Romney-no-more-painted-this-junk-than-I-did. But no one listened to him as carefully as they did Rubinstein's remarks that yes, I rather like Romney's work. Eventually Foster gave it up as a bad job and managed to get it down when the guests raved over the Romney collection.

The finest adornments of the house were two gigantic Brussels tapestries, each 11-feet-7 by 12-feet-8. One represented the Finding of Moses, complete with Pharaoh's daughter and five handmaidens, the whole surrounded by a rose crimson border. The other saw Joshua with helmet and sword and prancing charger scattering Amalek and his warriors. The same border surrounded the sight. The tapestries, which were of the seventeenth century, were from the castle of Viscount Halifax and had been installed by him at the British Foreign Office during his tenure as Foreign Minister. When their owner came to the United States as British Ambassador he brought them with him, but finding they were too large for the British Embassy he put them out for sale, consigning them to Frank Partridge, Inc., where Foster came upon them and brought news of their existence to Rubinstein. Rubinstein was enchanted and dashed off a letter to Lord Halifax telling his Lordship it would be a pleasure to purchase these beautiful items and that any price his Lordship suggested would be met, the entire transaction being regarded as a high honor. Even before the letter went out Rubinstein was envisioning a meeting with the British

158

diplomat which would be followed by complete entrée to him and (although he did not say so in as many words) all kinds of gracious assistance in the settling of the Chosen matter and the finding of new business opportunities in England and the Continent. But back came only a cold letter from a secretary saying the tapestries were in the hands of an agent, Partridge's, and that the agent would be the one with whom to discuss the question of a possible purchase. Rubinstein bought them anyway, paying $10,000 for the two. In time those who did not think that French and Company had furnished the house from its choicest collections (which it had not) came to believe that at least half of everything had come from private sales between Serge and his good friend Lord Halifax. Actually Rubinstein never said the dozens of paintings covering the walls—"Fox Hunting Scenes" by Jean Baptiste Lemoyne (attributed to), after "Self Portrait" by Marie Louise Elisabeth Vigee-Lebrun (the copy having been done by one E. H. Suplee), all the others—he did not say they were priceless masterpieces and it was not a question of saying they were and borrowing money off them, but everyone assumed they were terribly costly. With them went dozens of pieces of French furniture (slight imperfections), a statue of Europa seated on the back of a bull (minor repairs), Limoges painted enamel playettes of the Crucifixion, early sixteenth century (some restorations), fourteen spode Imari-pattern porcelain soup plates and eighteen dinner plates decorated in royal blue, iron red and gold with a wide median band of reserves of formalized floral arrangements (minor chips), acajou and blue silk moiré side chairs mounted in bronze doré (covering stained), Khorassan carpets, 19-feet-4 by 16-feet-10 (some wear) and multitudes of Russian ikons—Virgin and Child, Christ and the Archangels, Virgin of Kazan and Hierarchy of Saints complete with God the Father, angels and saints, castles, haloes, and a demon and skeleton mounted on an animal grotesque.

The house was opened with a great party in mid-1945. Laurette sulked all through the festivities, perhaps because she had been against buying so large and grand a place and had had nothing to say about its furnishings. Gordon Foster came across her sitting in her dressing room, which he had furnished in Directoire style; she was in the dressing-room chair, a revolving affair covered with damask bought (wholesale) for $38 a square yard and she had dripped grease from a sandwich on it. Foster fled the room, thinking to himself that, well, what could you expect from such a couple—here he, Foster, had furnished the whole place and bought all the antiques and bric-a-brac where a gentleman would have

159

done it all himself and in addition not have been married to someone who dripped grease on damask.

Downstairs Emil Coleman's orchestra was playing and there were floral displays everywhere, and great high plants. A fine group of waiters bringing their own faultless silverware served from a buffet and there must have been seven hundred persons in the house. Herr Professor came across the host standing off by himself, alone for just a moment, and said to him, "Ah, Serge, now you must be happy; you have this mansion, all of this."

But Rubinstein waved his hands depreciatingly and said, "Yes, but on the other hand the right thing for me is the hall of a big hotel: Lots of people saying hello, hello, hello; at every moment the hall will be filled, every moment there will be footmen and elevator boys there and you give them a dollar, a dollar, a dollar—all of them at my disposition, everyone there; that would be better."

The year was hardly out when the government had an indictment dated January 30, 1946, charging the unlawful "making and being party to the making of false statements as to the non-liability of a registrant under the Selective Training and Service Act of 1940 and conspiracy to do so, against the peace of the United States and their dignity, and contrary to the form of the Statutes of the United States in such case made and provided." In plainer words, draft-dodging.

Chapter Thirteen

Trial

Named with him in the indictment were James C. Hart of Taylorcraft Corporation, the Ohio airplane manufacturers, and Gordon Foster in his capacity of Panhandle officer. But that the three of them were indicted did not mean that the trial was just around the corner. The basic questions a jury would have to answer were firstly did he misrepresent his financial status in asking for a dependency deferment and secondly was he essential to the war effort and deserving of an essential job deferment by virtue of his associations with Panhandle and Taylorcraft. These were complicated questions. To help answer them Rubinstein had it put to the office of the United States Attorney for the Southern District of New York that as many of his operations had a foreign base and as witnesses from those countries could not be forced to come to the United States, he would be willing to pay the expenses of government lawyers going abroad to question such witnesses. The United States Attorney, thinking it possible that a prosecution might be aborted by a higher ruling that the trips should have been allowed, consented to the plan and dispatched Irving H. Saypol, the Chief Assistant U. S. Attorney who would try the case, on a long series of trips outlined by Rubinstein. Saypol went to England to take depositions on the Chosen business and was trapped there for a month and a half when all the air and ship lines went on strike. Then he went to France to check into Rubinstein's claim of aircraft knowledge gained in that country. Then he trudged off to Brazil and Chile to look into Taylorcraft's man who had supposedly invented the wing that allowed planes to practically come to a halt in the air before landing. After that there were Bolivian oil deals to look into. Most of the witnesses did not have much to say that was material. One, in fact, a man who was supposed to discuss Rubinstein's air knowledge, turned against him when he learned his bribe, which had been agreed upon as $2500 in French francs, was going to be calculated at the low official rate instead of the high black market one. The man did not hold Saypol responsible for this breach of responsibility on Rubinstein's part, but he did protest vigorously to the government lawyer. Saypol consoled the man and went off on the next leg of his Odyssey.

Meanwhile, back in America, Rubinstein was out of Panhandle, which was glad to see him go. The draft-dodging indictment had cast a cloud over the company and the drop in the value of its stock when the revelations about Stewart and the oil hopes came out did not help endear the ex-president, controlling stockholder, and Chairman of the Board to those who had to clean up after him. Rubinstein maintained that a part of his reason for resigning from Panhandle was that he did not wish the company to be embarrassed because of the indictment, but that did not stop Panhandle from instituting suit against him, charging that he had caused the company to go into businesses only profitable to Serge Rubinstein and made it assume the burden of $300,000 worth of rent, office and salary expenses he should have personally met. The suit also charged that he forced the company to rent oil leases from him personally to the tune of almost $100,000, the leases legitimately being worth about one-twentieth of that amount. Named in the suit were six Rubinstein corporations into which Panhandle money had been transferred, they being mere "instrumental ties" for the "carrying out of wrongful acts." Panhandle also protested that Rubinstein had the company pay "extraordinarily large unearned fees, commissions, bonuses and gifts" to people associated with him, including Stella and Laurette. Romeo Muller, disenchanted, led the fight to press the suit.

Finally the case was settled out of court for $203,000.

With Saypol ranging all over the world (and feeling a bit foolish about it) and with Panhandle now a thing of the past, Rubinstein concentrated on the new house and the finding of new business opportunities. In the house the fourth floor was turned into a nursery for a baby daughter, Diana, who a year and a half later was joined by a second girl, Alexandra. As far as business opportunities went, nothing very exciting turned up and so the family, including Stella, went that summer, the summer of 1946, to Hollywood where Serge rented a large house in Beverly Hills hard by the residences of Mickey Cohen and Buggsy Siegel. In New York a Negro handyman, James Morse, lived in the house alone, taking good care of it and rarely going out except to perform various chores for other members of the Rubinstein crowd—Sztykgold's daughter, Mrs. Kilborn, Gordon Foster, the girl friend of a Rubinstein lawyer. The Hollywood people took up Rubinstein as a kind of smoother Cohen or Siegel, whispering to one another that he sinks ships, dispatches munitions, makes millions, dodges the draft and is therefore a most exciting character and a much desired guest. Each day he played tennis on his private court, displaying good form and a tremendous will to win, but very little speed in getting around. He had immense lasting power and energy and never wanted to quit, but kept on calling for one more set. He did not flagrantly pull illegal stunts on the court but if the ball hit just this side of the baseline he'd be pretty sure to call it out. But if he played for money it was never for very much—perhaps $50 a match at the top—so no one minded too much. Almost every day he had one of several famous professionals in to give him a lesson. As a swimmer he was very strong and spent a couple of hours every day in his own pool or in the pool of the Beverly Hills Hotel. At night, of course, he was at the Hollywood clubs, best table, front. But such play could not completely occupy all his time and so he looked into the movie business and found that for the investment of a little money he could become a producer in fact if not in name. There was a European friend of his in Hollywood, Seymour Nebenzal, and he agreed to back Nebenzal in the making of a picture or two. Outfitted with Rubinstein's money Nebenzal made a deal to shoot on the lots of a major company with the release of any films being handled by the company. The actual cash outlay by Rubinstein was not considerable, being in the neighborhood of $300,000 which was obtained from banks anyway, but he had the last word on everything about the project even so. He proved to be brilliant in his casting and his ideas. It was quite amazing to those who watched him; he never had an office and operated out of Nebenzal's place or in the Hollywood tradition out of his swimming pool, but he was the guiding force of the movie that emerged, which was called *Whistle Stop* and starred George Raft and the young Ava Gardner, who was personally picked for the lead by Rubinstein. Later he and Nebenzal collaborated in the same fashion on *Summer Storm*, starring Linda Darnell who, as had been Miss Gardner, was personally selected by Rubinstein. After that an immensely prominent part of his chatter with sweet young things was to the effect that he'd made Ava a star—I had her in my picture—and that the same was true of Linda also; she became a star because of my other picture. Nebenzal never got mentioned in such talks, but there was enough truth in what Rubinstein was saying to make it a rare, rare starlet who didn't want to meet and get acquainted with the man who'd made two big stars just as a kind of part-time activity. Both pictures paid off in more conventional ways also, each proving to be a money-maker.

Back home his lawyers fought off attempt after attempt to bring the case to trial—"a series of moves calculated with but one object, delay," Saypol said—and it began to be said it would never get before a jury. But it was also said that the government was in too deep and that for it to back off would raise many questions very difficult to answer. The sparring went on. Originally Rubinstein had been allowed to go free in $20,000 bail after an arraignment that the presiding judge said was the longest he ever sat at, but when one day Rubinstein went out of the court's area, to Washington, without asking permission, Saypol moved to increase the bail. He pointed out that Rubinstein owned a four-engine Army surplus C-54 he had picked up when still head of Panhandle as the first of a projected fleet of planes to do air cargo work, and that as the plane was capable of flying the indicted man out of the country, a very high bail should be imposed upon him. Saypol had in mind the figure of one million dollars but the judge he applied to, James P. Leamy, thought that was too high and settled for a bail of $500,000 —the highest amount ever required of a defendant in a New York court. The Rubinstein lawyers fought the gigantic figure, pointing out that their client was a man of property with a home and large stock market investments which would tend to keep him in the country, an argument which prompted Saypol to remark that it was then strange, wasn't it, that only a couple of years earlier he had been too poor to go into the Army. The bail was reduced, however, by suggestion of the Circuit Court of Appeals, to $50,000.

Fifteen months passed, fifteen months of the indictment hanging over his head and Saypol scurrying here and there, fifteen months of estimating who might compose the jury, their business, religious and patriotic orientation, fifteen months of figuring just who might be the lawyers to successfully conduct the defense. At the end of that time, all time ran out, all appeals, all stays, all bids from congressmen and senators for just a little more money. Rubinstein appeared in court. It was March 4, 1947, a day upon which President Harry S. Truman asked Congress to end the life of the draft. "Oyez, oyez," cried the clerk of the court. He was on trial.

Before the trial began, the lawyers Rubinstein retained to defend him spent months preparing their case. These men were of a different breed from the regular Rubinstein attorneys, whose participation in the trial was limited to acting as intermediaries in discussions with the trial lawyers, who all found it pretty impossible to communicate with their client and were happy to have a little help from fellow barristers more practiced in that difficult art. The lawyers appearing in court were called in simply for a one-shot, emergency performance. They were courtroom practitioners, showmen of a sort, generous in their gestures, filled with presence and the ability to talk. There were in all eight or nine men sitting at the counsel table, of whom the most important ones and the attorneys of record were Leo C. Fennelly, Francis W. H. Adams, George Wolf, and Harold H. Corbin. Adams, later Police Commissioner of New York City, was there to handle the case of Hart, the Taylorcraft man. Wolf, forever identified with Frank Costello, whose affairs he handled for many years, was Foster's lawyer. Fennelly and Corbin were present on Rubinstein's behalf, and it was Corbin who with Saypol for the opposition dominated the trial. None of the lawyers found Rubinstein very palatable; they early learned he would order them around in conferences, advise them continually during the pre-trial hearings (leaping out of his chair to whisper loudly to first one and then another), barge past their receptionists into their offices where he would all but put his feet up on their desks, and call them at all hours of the day or night. Just before the trial began the whole crew of them met for a final discussion, adjourning at lunchtime to go downstairs to a nearby restaurant. The place was filled, but Rubinstein pushed by a line of waiting people, as was his habit, and ignoring the angry murmurs grabbed the first table that became free, ordering his group to sit down in chairs he directed for them. Luncheon was eaten and at the end Rubinstein stood up, walked to the food counter and after rummaging around among the desserts, finally grabbed a piece of cake which he unconcernedly bore back to the table. Back at the office, one of the lawyers asked to speak to the client alone. "Mr. Rubinstein," he said in his slow rolling court-room-lawyer's way, "what I am about to say is an important feature of the preparation of this case and has to do with the conduct and behavior of a defendant during a trial, in-cluding his getting to the courthouse and leaving it. It is far better if he arrives unostentatiously—not from a town limousine from which, stepping out in state, he is liable to be seen by prospective jurors or jurors. He should dress modestly, with not too many changes in clothes. In fact, it is best for a defendant *never* to wear a different suit to court.

"Now, his behavior in the elevator—taking into account he might meet there a number of jurors—he should not push forward to be the first one out. Also, he should not hang out in the corridors; jurors going to the juryroom and passing by might see him or hear his loud voice. He should instead go directly to and sit quietly in the courtroom. During the recess he should take a walk, go to the lavatory, take a smoke, and then come back and sit quietly. He should, in short, suffer a little bit. It is very important that he sit quietly during the court sessions and not take part in the trial, giving advice and orders to his lawyers. The jurors will resent this, thinking the defendant is just too damned smart. Jurors, you see, particularly in the cases of colorful defendants, have their attention greatly drawn to the de-fendant's appearance and demeanor.

"Now, Mr. Rubinstein, these are generalities. But with you, Mr. Rubinstein, if you won't resent my saying it in your own interest, you must exercise a great deal of control. For you are a boor. You are boorish. But we must try not to let the jurors know that."

As the lawyer talked, Rubinstein turned white. At the end there was a short silence and the lawyer said that was all for today, and now as it was late, he would be getitng on home. Rubinstein nodded and then looking up said, "Let me drive you." "It's not necessary," the lawyer said, "but if it's no trouble . . ." Together, in silence, they went out to where the Lincoln stood at the curb with the waiting chauffeur. They got into the back seat and the lawyer leaned back and closed his eyes. It had been a long day. As they headed up-town the lawyer dozed off, but came awake to the sound of very loud whistling. Rubinstein was whistling an air from Mozart. It went on, very loudly, and the lawyer knew it was for his benefit. "I see you like good music," he said. "Oh yes," Rubinstein answered, "Mozart, Beethoven, Bach . . ." They arrived at 814 Fifth and Rubinstein asked, "Could you do me a favor?" "Surely," the lawyer said.

"Come in," Rubinstein said. "I want to introduce you to my wife." They went in and Laurette was there and Rubinstein said, "Laurette, what do you think? He said I was a boor. He said things that would shock you." But Laurette laughed. "Serge," she said, "maybe it'll do you a lot of good." It did not, of course.

The chief defense counsel, Corbin, also found his client very hard to take. Corbin had a distinguished reputation and an impressive courtroom manner. He had been involved in litigation work, civil and criminal, for many years, but Rubinstein paid him no respect at all, interrupting him as they talked, telling him how the case should be handled. Corbin and his assistant, Edmund Bennet, found him the most difficult client they had ever seen; he always had his own ideas and it was a case of his wanting to do what he wanted to, and wanting to do it all the time. Corbin and Bennet wore dark suits with light stripes and vests; their office had paintings on the dark walls with the names of the artist below along with the date of birth and death and the initials which stand for Royal Academy of Art. Corbin smoked cigars and sat in his office behind a heavy desk adorned with a barometer indicating the temperature and the pressure, and when in court spoke in a rumbling voice even as Bennet, thin and small, made notes. Both of them took note of the clothing tastes of their client. They themselves reserved a Homburg for evening wear.

Their fee was substantial, approaching $100,000. The arrangement they made was for Rubinstein to pay half when they undertook to handle the case and the other half when they went to trial. (Trial lawyers, being usually transitory in the lives of their clients, must use a little caution to make sure they get paid.) Rubinstein paid the first half of the fee promptly, but when it came time to pay the second part, he suggested that instead of cash the lawyers take the balance in an interest in an oil well. If it came in, he pointed out, you had an oil well. If not, you had a good tax deduction. Corbin and Bennet said no. A couple of weeks later, Bennet checked out the proposed well. It was a dry hole. They laughed together about that; a dry chuckle from Bennet, a throaty rumble from Corbin. Neither of the two men were optimistic about the fate of this most difficult of clients but they went to work searching for witnesses and points of view that could help their case. They found only one man who would go all the way for them, and that was Konrad Sztykgold. That there was no plenitude of good witnesses did not bother their client—that Muller would hurt him and cultured Ann Smith also did not seem to affect him. Nor did the question of what his lawyers thought of him have any

166

particular importance in his mind. There arose a situation where everyone was called by his first name but there was never any discussion of children or hobbies or wives or anything like that. Neither Corbin nor Bennet ever asked him why he didn't want to go into the Army; they dealt with facts, not whys. They felt no shame at defending him, no emotion at all. When a man is indicted, trial counsel is no different from a doctor; you may not believe in the man but you see he gets all the protection the law of the land affords. When they dealt with him they called a spade a spade, trying to point out that this factor or that, in the way it appeared, might appear to an outsider to look like larceny. But that this was so did not bother their client; the important thing was that he was clever in manipulating things and that it had been a good job he did. He was offended, in fact, when they grasped what he had done in various dealings; he seemed displeased, they thought, that it was possible for anyone to fathom his methods.

So they went to trial—a trial which would have never been had he simply filed Form 301 in the first place. The courtroom was filled with what are called benchwarmers and churchmice, and the atmosphere was horrible. There had been just too much publicity about big deals and night clubs, too many articles about millions made and spent while other men went to war. A great percentage of the men in the courtroom wore discharge buttons in their lapels and a great number of the prospective jurors were if not openly hostile then not safely neutral enough so that the defense could pick them. Corbin thought the feeling against Rubinstein hung over the trial like a fog; used to courtrooms as he was he felt from the start that the general trend was unfavorable and he saw in the faces of the prospective jurors and heard in the reactions of the benchwarmers that which although difficult to define made him each day less optimistic than he had been before. For the government, Saypol was quick, active, driving. He appeared terribly anxious for a conviction.

During the first days as the jurors were being selected Madame Rubinstein was in the courtroom, but then Corbin and Bennet noticed that she fidgeted as she sat dressed in what they thought was a loud fashion and they decided that she was liable to make a poor impression on those who must decide her son's fate. There was something about her that was contrary to what you would expect of a mother; ordinarily a mother is an appealing person to a jury but for Stella there would be no sympathetic reaction in Rubinstein's favor. One day at recess in Longchamps they put it to her that it would be best if she stayed away. As for

Laurette, they had the impression that she resented being in the same restaurant with Rubinstein, let alone in the court-room. They thought her very pretty—a little flashy, perhaps.

Before long the first group of talesmen was exhausted and a new group was impaneled. Then as the selection was coming to an end, one juror already chosen raised his hand and asked to be excused, saying that he was now not so sure he could be unprejudiced. He added that although he was in his early forties he had tried to enlist in the Marines when the war broke out. (It was all done quietly but surely it did not help the defense.) At length the jury was chosen and the government presented its case. Saypol began by going to the heart of the first issue at question: Did the chief defendant have no assets which could have provided for his dependents had he gone into the Army? Rubinstein had said in an affidavit to his draft board that he had not and that if he were inducted his wife would have to live solely on the $50 a month she would get from the government, his mother on $15, his aunt on $5 and his other dependents on nothing. Saypol developed the idea that in fact Rubinstein owned stock in companies owning other companies owning great resources and that in fiscal 1940 his tax returns showed earnings of $337,000, mostly made in the BMT transaction. (He had told the draft board his earnings for the period were $12,000. The rent on his apartment exceeded that figure.) The defense countered by saying that he spent more than he earned in making friends who could lead him to new business ventures, but to everyone in the court it was obvious that the jurors found it hard to quite stomach the idea that a man pleading poverty had made more than one-third of a million dollars in one year. His walking into the office of the Chosen accountant to offer $195,000 in cash as the first payment of a settlement was brought up and painstakingly examined. Brundage, the accountant, testified that after he and Rubinstein argued about a point of the payment he had said to Rubinstein that he would keep and deposit the money anyway, but that Rubinstein, grabbing at the money, had said "No you don't; that's mine." That is mine? One hundred ninety-five thousand dollars in *cash*? A man pleading poverty to his draft board? The jury seemed set back on its heels.

Then came the most crushing moment of the trial, the calling of the draft board clerk Rubinstein had tried to bribe. The man, Charles Hanel, was about Rubinstein's age but the contrast between them was shattering. For while Rubinstein was sleek and powerful looking, Hanel suffered from a physical disability which gave him a pronounced limp. As he made his way up to the witness stand, a silence fell upon the courtroom. The limp is not in the record, but at that moment

Corbin's hopes reached low tide. They never rose again. Hanel spoke:

". . . he then told me that he realized he had been quite a pest and that I had been quite courteous to him and he wanted to show his appreciation for the courtesies I extended. He told me that he had contemplated bringing me two hundred shares of Taylorcraft aviation stock to show his appreciation. I told him I did not like that manner of talking. I merely did my job; I treated him in the same manner as I did any registrant. He then told me the stock was very low and would go higher. He said it could be bought over the counter in Maryland. He advised me to buy some, saying I could make a few dollars. I told him that it did not interest me . . ."

. . . . The jury had just filed out at the end of the day when from the courtroom audience a man came running toward where Rubinstein sat with his lawyers. "Yellow slacker!" shouted the man. There was a discharge button in his lapel. "You and your millions and your lawyers who defend you! You'll walk out of here free!" he reached Rubinstein just as the bailiffs closed in. "I'll kill you myself!" he screamed. They hustled him out. The jury had not seen, and as all juries are, this one had been told not to read newspaper accounts of its trial, but perhaps there were jurymen who did read nevertheless. Corbin was afraid of that, and Wolf also, afraid the man's shouts would have put into words what surely must have gone through the minds of many people, including jurors considering the case of a millionaire on trial on such a charge. They wanted to poll the jury and see if any of the members had read of the incident, but Saypol opposed that and Judge J. F. T. O'Connor ruled in his favor. There were other things the jury might have heard or read, one of them being the fact that it was openly said that Washington was very anxious for a conviction for political and idealistic reasons, the political one being that almost all of Rubinstein's contacts had been with members of the Democratic party and that the Democratic administration wanted to show they were as worthy as the Republicans any day when it came to prosecuting sin; the idealistic one being that it would do the country good to see that a rich man could go to jail for draft-dodging. (Governments everywhere are never happy with the perennial claim that it's a rich man's war but a poor man's fight.) Did the jury read of the incident of the shouting veteran? Did they wonder the next day why there were four extra guards? No one ever knew. It was fully reported, that was certain. Rubinstein had spent a lifetime wanting to be read about, talked about, photographed, and he had done well in this aim. He was a celebrity; the trial got full coverage from the New York newspapers and the national wire services.

The government's case went on: Stella was getting money all the time from Sweden because of her late husband's interest in a Swedish insurance company and therefore she would not have been left penniless had her son gone into service. Rubinstein had large resources, owned companies, had money—how could you justify his plea of poverty? Saypol then turned to the question of the chief defendant's essentiality to the war effort. His participation in Panhandle, the government contended, was simply that of a financier, and if every man with a financial interest in a war industry deserved to be exempted from the draft, then anyone with money could easily arrange to stay out of service. And how essential was Panhandle anyway? The Panhandle steel-making subsidiary made, among other things, bobby pins. Were the bobby pins essential because doubtless a number of them found their way into the hairdos of the WACS and WAVES? As for Taylorcraft, the government contended, the situation there was that on October 4, 1943, two days after being told he was absolutely going to be drafted, Rubinstein asked the Executive Committee of Panhandle to invest money in Taylorcraft, which was in the business of making small planes for the U. S. Army. The Panhandle Executive Committee had reservations, but Rubinstein had promised he would personally make up any losses incurred in an investment in Taylorcraft. Then he had flown to Alliance, Ohio, to meet with two directors of the company, including defendant James C. Hart. Taylorcraft at that time was being financially backed by a man who had announced his intention of merging the company with another firm—which would have meant the end of Hart's $18,000-a-year job. Hart, not a rich man, was anxious to hang on to his Taylorcraft job. Rubinstein, arriving in Alliance on October 10, a Sunday, offered to invest in the company and keep it going. Hart then telephoned the company's personnel director with instructions that the man come to the plant as soon as he got back from church. When the personnel director came out to the plant, Hart introduced Rubinstein and said this was Taylorcraft's new executive assistant in charge of finances. On October 11, a list of Taylorcraft's essential employees was flown to the headquarters of the Ohio Selective Service System. Rubinstein's name was on that list. The next day Rubinstein appeared before his New York board with a letter from Hart telling of Rubinstein's involvement with Taylorcraft. The letter said the involvement had begun many months earlier. The letter, Saypol pointed out, had been dated August 2 and had been dictated by Hart to Mrs. Hart—her initials were on it.

But, Saypol brought out, Mrs. Hart on August 2 was just about to enter a hospital to give birth to a baby. Would she have been typing letters in the office at such a time? And the wording of the letter was interesting—it used the word "whilst." Was "whilst" a part of Jim Hart's normal vocabulary? Or was the letter dictated by Rubinstein and typed in October with an August date? And that was why Hart was a defendant in the court. Foster was there because he had signed a statement giving as a Panhandle officer his opinion that Rubinstein was essential to the company. That was the government's case. One, Rubinstein had plenty of money and no need for a dependency deferment; two, he was not essential to either Panhandle or Taylorcraft and Hart and Foster had lied along with him when they said he was.

Corbin rose to the defense. All through the trial he and the other lawyers had opposed putting Rubinstein on the stand. Ten minutes of his loud voice, one reiteration of "I gave the Japanese their Pearl Harbor in advance," three or four remarks about how he was smarter than anyone else in the Street, half a dozen snappy answers to Saypol—and the case could be closed right there because there would be no point in going on. He could get right off the stand and head for the nearest Federal penitentiary. Rubinstein, as expected, opposed this idea. It was his conviction he could absolutely stampede the jury in his favor and make a fool out of Saypol while he was about it. But the lawyers prevailed. They would not put him on that stand.

It was the only time they managed to overrule him. They begged him to sit still in the court, but he would not. He constantly was jumping up to give instructions and Saypol came to know that whenever a particularly damaging government point was in the offing, Rubinstein would be the first person in the court to spot it. You could tell because at once one hand would begin stroking his nose and the other would scratch his hip. In between these gyrations he would be quickly and feverishly whispering to his attorneys who vainly pleaded with him to save it all up and give it to Sonny Wolchok during the recess so that Sonny could give it to them in a quieter way. But with all this, Corbin had to conduct the defense. His best witness was Konrad Sztykgold, who said that Rubinstein always wanted Panhandle to be in defense work, that Rubinstein himself had been very active in finding new oil sites which Panhandle drilled to feed the engines of America's war planes, that upon occasion Rubinstein, saying, "It's my hunch" ordered drilling to go ahead on wells everyone else thought were useless but which turned out to bring in a lot of oil, that Rubinstein worked Saturdays for Panhandle which in fact was "chaotic and sleepy" before Rubinstein, a "lucky genius," came into it. An oil field roustabout was produced to say he had seen Rubinstein, "dressed up just like the roughnecks" and personally working on oil wells, "all over the derrick, up around the machinery, up where they are drilling and looking over cores and in fact taking quite an active interest, yes sir." (Saypol blew holes in this by proving Rubinstein had been in Wichita Falls, the Panhandle headquarters, twice in his life.)

Then it was finished. It had taken thirty-six days and 1,000,000 words of testimony were heard and 5000 pages of record had been transcribed. The three defendants stood up in the courtroom of the United States Court House which like the Grand Central Palace induction center to which he had never gone was built by James Stewart and Company, that firm which had been meant in his life to be the rock upon which he would build glory, empire, future.

Guilty, of course.

Chapter Fourteen

Lewisburg

At the moment the Bronx bank employee who was the jury foreman pronounced the verdict, Rubinstein shrank back, very pale. It was ten minutes past ten at night, April 22, 1947. The jury had been out just short of seven hours; now dismissed, its members filed into Foley Square and on home. Inside, back in the brightly lighted courtoom, there were questions called out for the prisoners to respond to—their pedigrees. Your age? *Thirty-nine*. Do you smoke? *A little*. Do you drink alcoholic beverages? *A little*. Are you a user of narcotics? *No*. Mother's name, father's name, place of birth? *Estelle, Dimitri, Russia*. To the reporters in the courtroom it seemed as if he was in a daze. Dimitri, Russia . . . Grand Dukes Boris and André coming into Dimitri's house . . . "I am your God and your Czar" . . . Then Dimitri went to prison . . . But Stella visited Rasputin and soon Dimitri was out . . . Vienna was so beautiful. Villa Chaire . . . The future belongs to a dictator elite . . . The little chorus girls . . . Valuta, valuta . . . Cambridge, Paris; the parties of the Marquise . . . Japan; the chess games deliberately lost to the Prince. Bribery is the best investment . . . America; do you know what this White House is? I can go in and out of there whenever I like . . . The parties, the gifts, the handouts . . . All the deals. A letter to Konrad Sztykgold, introduced in testimony: "Purchase of this insurance company would eventually make our group one of the largest financial

172

groups in the United States." Another: "I believe this vehicle in our hands would enable us to play a predominant part in world affairs after the war." . . . Who shall have the power to stop me when I want to do something?

They handcuffed him to Gordon Foster and took him downstairs. A police van was there to take him to the West Street Federal House of Detention for the night. (In the morning the judge would impose sentence. His maximum term could be twenty-five years in prison.) "I'm not going to ride in that," he said. "Get me a taxi." They pushed him up into the van. He was clumsy with one hand linked to that of Foster; his Homburg was askew. Tears were running down Jim Hart's face.

What had he done wrong? Once with a grand gesture he had said to Herr Professor: "What do you believe I earn?" Herr Professor said he did not know. Rubinstein wrote a sum on a piece of paper and said, "For myself I keep 20 per cent; the rest I give away" . . . Miss Smith, make out a check for $150 for this gentleman; he knew my father in St. Petersburg . . . Two hundred . . . Three hundred . . . Konrad Sztykgold's daughter came soliciting for a children's school in Switzerland. She hoped for—what? Fifty dollars? He sat at his desk and wrote a check. Five thousand. I can break mountains.

All around him the Americans were tossing down their bourbon and waters, saying son-of-a-bitch draft-dodger for Christ's sake . . . The Americans. They can't drink . . . They don't understand things . . . The girls, even. They don't have the passion of our European girls; they think ah, I'm going to be something, all this money, give me something. The Americans. Who was it years ago saying Serge, you're going to have trouble with the Americans? Oh yes, it was the widow of the Englishman who had been so terribly rich with a summer place in the South of France and a Rolls-Royce with footman and chauffeur. But she ended up with very little living in a tiny apartment on the East Side and coming to dinner saying I can tell you you're going to have trouble with the Americans, the Americans like new people, but they get everything they want from them and forget them and get new new people . . . Could she have been right; was that why they were this way, so against a man simply because he was a foreigner and a Jew and a man of brains? But what was there to understand? Should there be any code, approach, philosophy other than the one saying the world should be ruled by brains, by those who sway people and get results accomplished?

At the Federal House of Detention they climbed down and went into a large cell block with a lot of people already in it:

173

Chinese awaiting deportation, pimps on the way back to Europe. They sat together on a bench, Hart crying, Foster saying what the hell—screw them. "Gordon," Rubinstein said thickly, "how did I get you into this? But never mind, everything will be all right, you'll see." He subsided. They sat side by side. "Gordon," he said, "what have I done?" It was very late, three or four in the morning. "Gordon, I wish I were dead. I want to die." Oh, Serge, Gordon said. Oh, what the hell. "But why are they against me . . . ?" In Panhandle's field labored hundreds of roughnecks deferred from the draft because they were bringing oil up out of the ground. Was the company president and Chairman of the Board to go play soldier boy? The Army . . . Sergeants saying do this, do that. To be a soldier is weakness, helplessness. You do what others tell you. You sleep on a cot like all the others; you eat just exactly what they give you. You go where they say when they say it. You do what they tell you. You are a number. A soldier is ordered what to do and he does it. But I can break mountains.

In the morning the New York *Times* had an unkind lead paragraph for one of the stories on its front page: "Serge Rubinstein, a man accustomed to having his own way and to overcoming problems beyond the imaginative scope of the average person, came foursquare yesterday against an obstacle with which, temporarily at least, he was unable to cope."

The van took them to court for the sentencing. He was unshaven and when he came in the reporters noticed the eagerness with which he had followed the developments of the trial was gone. He looked done in. His face was sallow. He slumped in his seat. The judge was nine minutes late in getting to court; the three prisoners sat with guards by them. The judge arrived, apologized.

"Mr. Rubinstein, will you stand up? . . . It is the judgment of this court that you shall be sentenced for a period of two and a half years in an institution to be selected by the Attorney General of the United States." Two and a half years and a $50,000 fine. For Foster and Hart, $10,000 fines but no jail. "The defendant will be committed." At that moment his sister-in-law Valerie came into the courtroom. A reporter asked her what she thought of the sentence and she said that the judge hadn't given him enough, it should have been a longer jail term.

The lawyers asked that he be allowed to go free on bail while the case went up on appeal; it was denied. So he was going to prison. That night Herr Professor said to a friend that Rubinstein lived at the wrong point in history; that he should have existed in medieval times when a great feudal

174

lord could do as he liked, have no moral responsibilities, be above law but balance it out by giving gifts of his own choosing at his own time. It was, Herr Professor said, the tragedy of the man's life that he had been born just in time to see the closest modern approximation of that period: the life and ways of the court and nobility of Czarist Russia. "The answer to this impossible man," Herr Professor said, "is that the ideas of the East have come to the West, which put aside those ideas five hundred years ago. Perhaps it was only possible in our time. Never before, surely, was there such a physical nearness of East and West."

"I don't think, you know, that Serge believes he ever did anything wrong," the other man remarked. "I think he lives well within his own code of ethics."

"Ah," said Herr Professor. "You don't understand. You are too American. Even to say he 'lives well within his own code of ethics' betrays the evidence of Western thinking. The phrase is misapplied. The way he was educated, what he saw, made things like a code of ethics not binding. It is the same as a Buddhist monk brought to a Catholic church. The monk believes in no God but still you would not call him a Godless fellow. Rubinstein may look like a Westerner and he is a master of Western techniques, but he has only learned the techniques and not the game. A boxer may win every match by hitting below the belt; he has mastered boxing but the rules mean nothing to him."

"But how," asked the friend, "can you talk so much about the East and Russia in relation to him? Must I remind you Serge is a Russian Jew and not a Grand Duke?"

"Yes," said Herr Professor, "but look at the surroundings he grew up in. Only a part of his thinking was connected with the Jews. Much of it was that he did not depend on and was independent of the Jews. He grew up admiring the behavior and the way of thinking of the high Russian overlords and he ended up by trying to emulate it. He continued his father's way in the United States—and would you call his father a typical Russian Jew with his palace and important friends? And what was his father's way? It was that you need not have scruples and that in a jam, money or something else would get you out—the way Stella got him out of jail by seeing Rasputin. Moral foundations did not exist. In the circles in which his father moved, who believed in anything?

"But I will tell you something. You cannot in the last give a draft-dodger a good press but something which makes him palatable is his own viewpoint. The West held him guilty when he first came here and took advantage the way he did. The West could not understand how this disgusting little Russian Jew had the effrontery to bribe and connive as he did. It was an impertinence, unallowable. That was the view of the West when it held him guilty. And yet, to him, what he did was logical; it was the only way to be. He came here, after all, with the idea of having money, of being a modern Grand Duke. And he did help people when he wanted to, we must say so, and that was a part of it too, that was Grand Dukedness. Do you think he thought he would be convicted? Not for a moment! In his own eyes he had done nothing wrong and besides, Grand Dukes aren't convicted of things!"

Weeping, Stella called the editor of the New York Russian language paper, *Novoye Russkoye Slovo*. "This is a second Dreyfus case," she cried. "The Americans are doing the same things, but no one touches them. They are hounding Serge because he is an immigrant."

The editor, M. Weinbaum, said: "I am sorry to disappoint you, but I completely disagree."

Stella hung up.

Laurette came to see him in the House of Detention, driving down in the Lincoln with her mother. Mrs. Kilborn waited in the car as Laurette went up and came back weeping and quite wordless. Sister Betty went to visit Laurette later that day, thinking to herself that it was all because his holdings were a one-man operation and that he thought the world was sitting here waiting for someone to do things to it —he couldn't say, as with a plate or saucer, here, hold it while I'm gone. At the same time Stella went to see her son and he gave her the keys to his safe deposit vault and told her to take whatever she needed. A week passed. They took him to a train and to the Lewisburg Federal Penitentiary in Pennsylvania. "I guess they'll make Saypol a judge now," he said to the man taking him down. (But he somewhat anticipated; Saypol first became United States Attorney for the Southern District of New York before taking the bench as a New York State Supreme Court Justice.)

. . . . Lewisburg. In court during the trial he had followed every word of testimony and when the proceedings of a session seemed favorable to his cause he had the next day not changed his tie—"I can win with this tie." And when he lost a garter in court he searched everywhere for it—it would be a bad omen if he could not find it. He had spent more than a million dollars on the trial, what with Saypol's travels and all the lawyers. But in the end it was Lewisburg, an easy prison of the Federal system reserved for conmen or tax evaders or offenders with no records of violence, but a prison nevertheless—clanging doors, regulated exercise pe-

176

riod in the yard, line up for meals, slop buckets in the cells filled with disinfectant. (Its rating of "easy" stemmed from the fact that there were considerable recreational activities and the guards didn't massacre the men the way they do in hard prisons.) He arrived on May 5, 1947. They put him in a two-man cell and there he found little gifts left for him by convicts: cigarettes, shaving cream, toothpaste, things the government did not immediately make available to new inmates. They were there not only because he was rated a big shot with connections but also because of the feeling which is never lacking in prison that people have to be taken care of.

In the next days Lewisburg tried to get friendly with him. For some reason the men addressed him as if his name were Sergei instead of Serge and everywhere he went men said hello, Sergay, how you doing? In the prison yard he was invited to join in the daily handball games and he was very good at that; the sport was after all somewhat akin to tennis. The games were played for stamps, the currency of the prison, and he rarely lost. But within a short time he was having trouble with his cell-mate, a former restaurant official who had come to the attention of tax agents who noted him night after night losing great sums at the Miami gambling tables and, checking, found the money with which he played was not declared income but simply cash receipts casually removed from the register. The trouble was over who would clean the cell. Prison regulations called for cell-mates to rotate the duty, but what did Serge Rubinstein know about mopping or sweeping? Soon word spread in Lewisburg that the man thought he was too damned good to clean the cell. In the yard during recreation periods he was at first the center of attention with men asking hey, Sergay, how about teaching us to swindle people and he answering that he never swindled anybody; you bums are crazy. He used the word bum too often and one day a man resented it. Rubinstein used the word again and added the man was descended from filth while he himself was the son of multi-millionaires. He pointed out that his mother lived on Central Park South and inquired just where the other man's mother lived. "Do you think I even want to talk to you?" he asked. "Do you think I'd talk to you on the outside?"

But most of the time he tended to talk in monosyllables, answering questions with a sullen Yes or No. When he did upon occasion open up the convicts found he talked about only one thing: Serge Rubinstein. I could escape in a minute; the Russian government would take care of me. My arm hurts. I wish I were home. He never asked about another man's plans (or fantasies) or arm or longing for home. People still went out of their way to know him, he being wealthy and all, but he never wanted to know anybody. If you asked him how he was feeling he would answer rotten, but there was never a follow-up question about how you were feeling; he never asked about another convict. There were just short of 2000 convicts in Lewisburg, and the gossip about the new man spread quickly: he was nasty, not nice. Convicts have an instinct for good defined as a quality of generosity, but Lewisburg found no good in Rubinstein. None of the men got to know him, but they knew, or said that they knew, that he was all bad. There was no generosity in him.

He was put to work in the library and to teaching in the prison school where his subjects were mathematics and economics. He was tremendously good at it but that did not gain him the affection of Lewisburg—a man who even attends prison classes, let alone teaches them, is practically by definition a no-good to his fellow inmates. Outside, the appeal from the jury's verdict was turned down, but word spread that Rubinstein was living like a prince in prison, with women being vanned in for his amusement. A New York columnist even reported seeing him on Broadway. It was a delicate situation for anyone in Washington who had known him before, and a delicate situation for the Federal penitentiary system. Perhaps there was a fear that if this noted prisoner kept an easy job as teacher there would be those who would say that he had it because certain officials had been at pains to arrange it. So he was taken out of the prison school and put to work at a harder task in order that the gentlemen in Washington could not have it said of them that they were allowing a draft-dodger to have it easy in prison. Representative Francis Walter of Pennsylvania came to the prison one day and emerged reporting with satisfaction that no special privileges were being given Rubinstein; that he was, in fact, the "gentleman who cleans out the gentlemen's room." It was so; that was his job. To those who had known him before, and to those who would know him afterward, the picture always seemed incredible, impossible to imagine— Serge cleaning *toilets?* But beyond the harsh duty he was not doing well in prison. He was not rolling with the punch. The man who does do well figures what the hell, I wear a drab suit and it's a lousy way to live but there're angles here and there and I'll try to get along with it. Rubinstein did not adapt and arrive at that approach. He never saw himself as a convict with, for the time being, a convict's goals. For years he had lived in a special way in a grandiose manner and with an elaborate structure of himself caught in his own mind. Now in prison the picture stayed, held intact by the vision of what would come in the glorious future even though today all the toys were taken away: No great deals

178

in the making, no big men to see, no companies, no webs of front men, no gratification and no replenishment. Later, soon, ah, he would show them all. Wait and see. Tomorrow.

There was one other thing missing: women. But that this was so did not mean there need be no sex for him. All prisons operate with a deep cushion of homosexuality underlying the lives of the inmates. The opportunty is always there and a lot of men, a great percentage, make use of that opportunity. There were no women with emotional needs to recognize, but there were men to conquer. He became what Lewisburg called a working homo; this guy today, that guy tomorrow. He was never the Chicken, who plays the woman's role, but always the Shark. Some time after the visit of Representative Walter he was transferred to duty in the prison laundry, and it was there that he did the greatest part of his Sharking. In Lewisburg, as in all prisons, men live by doing favors for others, and those who worked in the laundry were in a position to give out extra shirts—a man was allowed only two a week—extra towels, socks. Behind the big automatic machines completing the washing cycles, Shark and Chicken could be alone, with the latter paying off the former for clean clothes. Also there were the postage stamps. But primarily there were promises, the allusions to what could be done once we get out. Rubinstein was widely talked about in Lewisburg and the estimates of his wealth were gigantic. How many men with untold millions come the way of the ordinary convict? His attitude was that he was surrounded by the absolute scum of the earth but that maybe on the outside, what the devil, he'd slip a grand here, a grand there to those he'd known back in Lewisburg. There was enough possibility that he would do so to keep men circulating around him in a strange parody of the parties at 814 Fifth. Some of the men were Chickens. Others were harsh shakedown artists with friends on the outside. The year after he went in, two rough-looking types accosted Stella in the lobby of the Hotel Navarro and told her that her son would be in real trouble down in Lewisburg unless she was nice to them and nice right away. Stella was terrified, but went to a bank and withdrew a few hundred dollars which she gave to the two. They left but said they would be back by and by. A few months later they were. She gave them more money, never knowing who they were or who their friends were, but thinking it was the only thing to do. In the prison meanwhile Rubinstein was getting progressively more unpopular. ("Most hated man in Lewisburg," said the warden.) A rumor spread among the convicts that he had betrayed an escape plot by going to the principal keeper and announcing the plotters hoped to escape via the subterranean passageways which were the weak link of Lewisburg. It was to be a tunnel effort through the passages under the hospital, the story went, and Rubinstein had queered it by telling the PK while asking that the PK contact the Federal Commissioner of Prisons with an aim of getting Rubinstein's time shortened. That placed him permanently as a 4-F along with the stool pigeons you couldn't trust. In the laundry his behavior seemed to one fellow-prisoner to be that of the typical Mafia criminal without the violence. He always wanted to be in on things, was always afraid of being left out of a deal where someone was getting away with something. He had to be in on everything; when he'd see a man getting extra towels for someone he would raise his voice to shout hey, what are you doing with those towels? The hack on duty could not help but hear and would come and that would be the end of the extra towels. Usually a squealer is looking for something, but Rubinstein did it for no reason at all. It was resented, of course; bitterly so. One day there was a showdown of sorts. He came into the laundry with a big bundle of dirty clothes and threw it messily on the floor, taking out some postage stamps and indicating he was tired today and who wanted to do his work for him? A convict up for mail robbery in the State of Washington took exception. "Who're you, you big-shot son-of-a-bitch?" he demanded, and kicked the bundle out into the hall. The two men closed together and exchanged a few blows before the hack broke it up. Thereafter the mail robber cursed Rubinstein all day long but was totally ignored. The men seeing it did not like it that Rubinstein showed so clearly his feeling that a mail robber's four-letter words and snarls were similar in value to the barking of a dog, and that this valuation could also be placed upon anything that might be said or done by any other of the useless swine in this damned place. Shortly after, a friend of the mail robber who suffered from a heart condition was late getting to supper after a hospital appointment and therefore missed falling into line at his usual place. (In Lewisburg as at most prisons the men line up in the same order and sit in the same seats at every meal.) The guard told the heart patient to fall in any place and the man stepped into the mass of dark uniforms without looking to see who his dinner partners would be. After he had gotten his tray filled and was seated, he saw he had stepped in front of Rubinstein and was therefore seated next to him. The man started to ride Rubinstein, calling him a queer and a 4-F and a woman in man's clothing. As he had the heart patient's friend, Rubinstein ignored this new enemy. The other eight men at the table mutely looked on. The heart patient's diatribe grew wilder and wilder. Rubinstein ate in

180

silence and when he raised his eyes he looked straight ahead. Finally the man, almost in a frenzy, plunged his hand into his mouth and yanked out his false teeth. Then he dropped them into Rubinstein's cup of coffee.

A few days later at lunch Rubinstein raised his hand as a signal indicating he wanted more stew brought to his place by the prisoners serving seconds out of big pots they wheeled around the mess hall. The server came up and doled out the stew into his tray. Then bending over so that no guard could see, the man spat down into the food he had just ladled out. Rubinstein looked into space. But shortly all such demonstrations ceased. Every prison has a prisoner called The King who bosses things, and The King of Lewisburg in those years, on the outside a conman, approached Rubinstein. "You like to do your time in an ordinary way, a nice way?" he asked. "There's a guy on the outside, get some money to him. See your lawyer pays something every month." One of the Rubinstein lawyers took on the assignment and two giant prisoners became Rubinstein's bodyguards, going about with him whenever it was possible and letting it be known they would deal with anyone who bothered their charge. But no bodyguards could make him popular (although it is possible The King arranged for the harassment before making his bid to Rubinstein) and in the yard's handball games he always had to play with new men; the old ones would walk off the court when he appeared. In his cell he regularly did calisthenics and as he was very clean and never needed a shave and lost a lot of weight, he looked quite well. In the laundry he began to talk a lot about women and all the good times he'd had with them, but the convicts had the uneasy thought that he was doing it in a strange attempt to get them excited so that they would play Chicken to his Shark. It was not a pretty thought. Many of the men cursed him and purposefully bumped into him, but with the two bodyguards hovering about, nothing could be too overtly done. Still it was obvious what the feeling about him was and he went to a prison official and asked to be transferred to the tier where the misfits were kept, they being mostly aggressive homosexuals. The misfits lived in single cells and were not mixed so freely with the rest of the prison population and he wanted that, to be away from the other men. He was transferred to the misfits' tier and remained there for the rest of his time.

Outside, the government was moving to get an order which would deport him when his term ended, his conviction being pointed to as an indication of moral turpitude. The same month he went to jail his lawyers had appeared in court to ask that he be held definitely not deportable, but the request was turned down. The authority appealed to, Judge John C.

181

Knox, studied the FBI report on him and said it showed not "a creditable thing he has done." How, asked Judge Knox, could he "subject the American people to the machinations of this man for the next thirty or forty years?" The government lawyer arguing the question, harking back to the original matter of Rubinstein's Portuguese citizenship, said that "any man who would go to court and say he is the bastard son of his own mother has sunk to such a depth that he deserves no consideration." The Rubinstein lawyers continued to fight the government's averred hope to deport their client; pressing his claims were Lemuel B. Schofield, former head of the country's immigration and naturalization agency and Edward Ennis, its former general counsel.

At home Laurette was suffering badly from the publicity that attended her husband. Sister Betty had married the son of a Rubinstein business acquaintance and gone to live on Long Island, at Locust Valley, where she and her husband belonged to a country club on the Sound. Often Laurette went there with them and eventually she decided to bring the sailboat up from Red Bank, New Jersey, to dock it at the club pier. She went down to Red Bank with a friend, a doctor, intending to return with the boat. But when she was gone a trustee of the club called in Betty's husband and said to him that it was an impossible situation that the wife of Serge Rubinstein should be seen on the club property. Betty was distraught and couldn't think of what to do. A day later the sailboat came up the Sound and under power made for the club pier. Laurette was standing up with the boat's line in her hand when Betty's husband came up to the ninth hole of the club's golf course and saw her. The boat was just about to touch the pier when he came running off the golf course waving his fists and shouting, "Get out of here! Get out!" The experience broke Betty; things thereafter were never the same with her husband and soon they parted. As for Laurette, it was a crucifying experience. She began to drink and to brood. From Lewisburg, Rubinstein wrote asking her to stand by him, saying in a curiously childish way everything would be all right if she did that. "But if you abandon me—if you don't write and say kind things, I'll hang myself in my cell. Then it will be on your conscience for the rest of your life."

Spring came, spring of 1949, and his parole, held up by a nervous government, came through. He had been away two years to hear each day the heavy doors slamming shut, to dress always in the same dull uniform and eat the same dull food, to be a number and never hear himself called mister and to have his face shoved into a toilet once by two unknown assailants who jumped on him from behind one day when the two bodyguards were not present. With the announcement that parole would be granted came another piece of news: Laurette was leaving him.

Laurette had had enough, enough of people saying that was the draft-dodger's wife over there, the blonde. The month that saw him come out of jail saw her go to Las Vegas with her brief asking a divorce. "Soon after our marriage," the brief read, her husband "told me I would have to recognize and tolerate his association with and being in the company of other females without criticism or objection." He had told her, she said, that she was "a dampening influence on him." He had also beaten and cursed her. In reply to the suit he said he could not have been more stunned "if the roof of the prison had fallen on me." Columnist Cholly Knickerbocker, who had so often criticized him, this time sympathized, saying even animals stick with their wounded own. But Laurette was gone. He had never loved any other girl as much as Laurette; he never would. When she had come down, as she did on occasion, to visit him in prison, bringing with her the older daughter, Diana, it had been for him the great moment of the month. For her it had been something else again. Although she never had before, she drank very heavily in those last days of 1948 and all through the early months of '49, and her family worried about her. But no one thought she would divorce him while he was helpless in prison. Her people were against even the idea; her mother told her she *must* wait until he got out, not hit him with this while he was behind bars like an animal. But Laurette said she wouldn't be able to face him down in person and so she was doing it now when he wasn't around. She went to Las Vegas with the two girls; the divorce was granted days before an escort of guards took him out of the gates of Lewisburg. He was wan, terribly thin compared to what he had been, almost emaciated, and in fact he was not free. Waiting for him was a United States marshal with an arrest warrant based on an indictment brought just as the statute of limitations ran out. It was for stock manipulation of Panhandle back in 1945–46. He was but a moment out of Lewisburg when the marshal joined their wrists together with handcuffs and took him aboard a train bound for New York and arraignment. On the train he ordered coffee but the marshal would not release his right hand and so he clumsily drank it with his left, hot liquid spilling down and hurting him and staining his suit. They went to court immediately and bail was set. The money was put up and so for the first time since the foreman of the draft-case jury said "guilty on all counts" he was his own man. He went to Stella's suite and into her room and into her arms. A little group of friends

183

and old business acquaintances waited with his mother to greet him and he went among them shaking hands and shakily saying he appreciated it so much that they were there. Then he sat down and burst into tears. The people drifted out of the room with their heads averted but they could not escape the sound of his sobbing—I can break mountains—or the memory of the tears running down his cheeks.

Chapter Fifteen

Freedom

He went to 814 Fifth, to home. Handyman James Morse waited for him in the lobby. "Hello, Mr. Rubinstein," the servant said; the master ducked his head and looked away—shyly, Morse thought. Laurette's absence then for the first time seemed real as he walked upstairs and through the empty rooms. Almost everything that had once been there had disappeared: all the furniture, all the paintings, everything was gone or in storage. Morse went and got the family dog, Mitzi, the only thing Laurette had left behind. Rubinstein fell on his knees to let the animal lick his face. It was, he said, the worst moment of his life—only a dog waited to greet him.

The next day a few people dropped by to see him. But not many. He seemed to them gentler and softer than he had been before. Thin, very pale, much quieter, he seemed more understanding, less flamboyant. There were those who thought that perhaps it was all for the best—he had been riding for a fall anyway. But after a few days the people who were willing to see him had come and gone in their small numbers. Where once there had been hundreds, now they came in handfuls. The others, or almost all the others, ignored him. There were no telephone calls or messages for ex-convict draft-dodger and indicted stock manipulator.

Then after three or four days a note was delivered. It was from a girl. She was the daughter of an eminent European and she had known Rubinstein before he went to prison. Her father had known his father in the long ago and so it was natural that when he came to America they should meet and that she should become a frequent guest at his parties. She was attractive but not flashily beautiful and she was different from most of the girls at the great Rubinstein parties of before he went away. She had not liked Laurette very much, thinking that the mistress of the house looked like the lovely little cold dolls you see in the hairdresser's window, but she felt something for Serge although she found it strange that he would try to date her up practically under his wife's nose. She thought him not good-looking but attractive as a man—so full of vitality, with such dash and eagerness. Yet as she was not anxious to be the lover of a man with whom she could one day be number one and the next day number ten, nothing happened between them although that it did not was very much against his wishes. He tried very hard to arrange something with her, and that led to a break between them. It occurred in the middle of the war, when she told him that her brother was slated for overseas shipment from his Army post and that she and her mother were certain he would be killed and never seen again. "I tell you what," Rubinstein said when he heard this news. "I know every general in Washington; come down there and I'll arrange things for your brother so that he can have a nice safe job." The offer seemed too tempting for the worried girl to ignore and so she promised to meet Rubinstein in Washington the following weekend in order that talks with high military officials could be begun. But as she was packing it occurred to her that perhaps Serge had been a little too anxious about it, too ready to reserve her a suite at the Mayflower. She asked her mother to go with her. They went down on the train and to the suite which they found filled with flowers and baskets of fruits—and also connected via an easily unlocked door with Rubinstein's own suite. They had barely arrived when through that door walked Serge. But when he saw the mother he at once dropped the matter of helping her brother, and did it in so obvious a way that the girl felt very cool toward him. There were no generals to be seen and the weekend was so wasted that she lost interest in Rubinstein. "That wasn't nice," she said, "to do that to a girl who was really desperate." Their relationship, such as it was, ended. (The brother went overseas as scheduled, was wounded, got a Purple Heart, came back.)

The memory of the incident stayed with her but she felt badly for him when he went to prison and when he came out she wrote saying he could come to her house at any time, that the door was open to him and he must drop in. He called her the moment he got the note and the next day went to see her. It seems to have been his first post-prison and post-marriage date. The girl was tense about the whole thing —not knowing any ex-convicts or their ways—but Rubinstein boasted about how interesting prison was and how much he learned there. "You are probably disappointed that I'm not acting like a beaten dog," he said, but she said that although he was much quieter than he had been he was not *that* different. His attitude seemed to be, or he tried to act

185

so, that prison was not really so difficult after all and quite an education, all things considered. When later on he talked once about how the French threw him out of their country she was struck by how similar was his talk about Lewisburg. Pierre Laval kicked me out but I showed him! They threw me in jail but I learned all sorts of things, you'd be surprised! It had not been a defeat, not at all, don't think it was.

That night they went to a little Viennese place for dinner and a day later she invited him to come for a homemade goulash with wine. He arrived carrying flowers and was exceedingly gracious and terribly appreciative. The girl had a set of new English china and told him she would christen it with the goulash; when she said that, that the china was new, he picked up a soup tureen and went into the kitchen and said, "In Russia this is for good luck," and smashed the tureen into the sink, breaking it into dozens of pieces. The girl and her mother would have been furious with anyone else in the world but from him somehow they did not resent such behavior. "So uninhibited!" said the mother. "Like a boy—so young!" She gave him a four-leaf clover she had found in the park. "I really love it," he said, "I really appreciate this." It seemed he really did, for he took it and saved it and often mentioned that the mother had given it to him. And after that the mother was often included in plans made with the daughter: a drive to Montauk Point where the couple could go riding while the mother sunned herself; a visit on Sunday to a Long Island pension run by a fallen Russian aristocrat.

Evenings in New York they went to small East Side places with a European flavor. There were no big night clubs or great splashy entrances. Konrad Sztykgold liked the girl and hoped she would marry Rubinstein; Konrad Sztykgold also thought Rubinstein was doing the right thing by keeping out of circulation and living quietly. Rubinstein seemed somewhat in agreement with the first of Sztykgold's thoughts, but did not agree with the older man's belief that keeping his light under a bushel was the answer to the problems of the most publicized draft-dodger of World War II. He was instead filled with plans to be implemented once he had gotten back into the swing of things, which would be right after that summer of 1949. Meanwhile he would just coast along, pick up a little weight, take it easy, and make ready to leap again into the financial world downtown.

That summer he and the girl went to the beach, went riding, went to the summer stock theaters on the Island. In town accompanied by Madame, Aunt Genia, and the girl's mother they went to dinner in the European places. Rubinstein spent money freely enough but did not fling it around; he seemed able to enjoy a quiet meal with his relatives and the girl and her mother. It seemed enough for him that he was free. The girl's birthday came and he went to her home with a dozen orchids, but as they sat together the doorbell rang and a Western Union boy arrived with twenty-four roses sent by an admirer who lived in South America. Rubinstein was furious to see the bouquet twice as large as his own, and grabbing the flowers rushed with them to the kitchen where he flung them into the garbage pail. As with the smashed soup tureen, the girl could not be angry with him; from Serge somehow you accepted it. (She retrieved the roses when he went home.) They continued to see a great deal of each other. She was not wealthy, although in the old country the family had been, but Rubinstein did not play on that although after a while he said to her that it was ridiculous for her to keep her job in a dress shop and should give it up—he would keep her and give her $50 a week spending money. She laughed the idea down. (Her mother said he was fresh to suggest such a thing.)

At 814 Fifth he began to work on the house to make it an office as well as a residence. He installed secretaries in upstairs rooms and gave Teddy Schulz a room and had a switchboard put in. The files which had been stored in the basement of 19 E. were brought to 814. Another change was also effected: Madame was brought to live with him. She was not anxious to leave the Navarro but he insisted, saying there were so many rooms in the Fifth Avenue house that it was foolish to pay rent for her to live elsewhere. She was given her own floor and there once a week she gave a little party for her Russian and European crowd, everybody eating sweets and sipping tea served by her maid brought from Europe, but nobody getting any liquor save for Madame's friend Robert Wyner, to whom a single cocktail was solemnly served by one of the house's two butlers. Madame had almost nothing to say about running the house; her son dictated what the meals were to be and also made it clear that at certain times Madame would eat upstairs and not disturb him in the main dining room. Any work done on house furnishings was completely under his control, and the purchasing of new pieces was done in the same way as before: of the period but not of first quality.

So the summer wore on and it seemed to those who knew them that he and the girl would marry. Such was the hope of those who were not of that great number of persons who fell away from him and who would say with totally straight faces that they had never been in his home or done business with him. But Madame was against the match. She had never cared for Laurette or for any other girl her son favored, and she was against this girl. When as a group Rubinstein and the girl and the relatives of both would go to stay the weekend in the Russian aristocrat's summer hotel, Madame made very certain that the girl would sleep in a different guest house than her son. And before long she produced her own candidate for son Serge's affections. This was Betty Reed.

Betty Reed was a blonde from Tennessee. She was very tall, several inches taller than Rubinstein, and very beautiful in a distant, cold way. She wore her hair up and long earrings dangled almost to her shoulders away from which plunged the low neckline of her gown. Everyone who saw her was impressed with the great beauty which was hers; sooner or later everyone used the words "statuesque" or "Junoesque" to describe her. She had come into Madame's life one day in the elevator of Madame's Hotel Navarro, a tall blonde girl wearing a demure dress with a high, high collar telling the older woman that she was a singer new to the city and terribly lonely. Madame said to her that she must come and have tea one day—they would talk about music. Betty came and the two became friends. It was in the tradition of old Europe that Madame should play protector to this young artiste seeking to establish herself in the world of song. It was also in the tradition of Madame's kind of motherhood that she should produce this beautiful creature to divert her son's mind from the other girl he seemed about to marry. Soon Betty Reed was a frequent visitor at 814 Fifth and soon she and Serge were going out a lot together. But Betty, so different from the other girl, was not made for the intimate little European places where the waiter and the violinist had accents and the patrons ordered in the language of the old country. Betty was instead of the night clubs and staying out late and drinking in the after-hours spots. She was not in fact as new to the city as she indicated—and not as young as she said she was—and within a short time Madame turned venomously against her. By then it was too late; Serge and Betty were going everywhere together and when one friend of Serge's, an older woman, admired Betty's skin, Betty was able to casually say it was that way because she never allowed it to come into contact with outdoor air, which was bad for it. "I don't go into the street," she explained to the other woman. "I sit in my apartment with my hair in curlers and cold cream on my face, waiting for Serge to call." The other woman was slightly taken aback but managed to say Betty's skin was the most beautiful she had ever seen on any woman and that she had also long admired Betty's ornate hairdo of which not one strand ever seemed to be out of place.

The romance with the other girl faded. They still saw each other and, noticing his home lacked an ice bucket, she gave him one. It touched him very deeply. She had done it first because she thought it was a necessary item in his house and second because she thought that if a person had been used a lot, the way she thought he had by the many people who had come to his house before prison only to drop away after, then it was only right that such a person should be given a gift even if it was only a little thing. But the romance was ending and although their friendship continued—he would come to the dress shop where she worked and take her out for lunch—they were no longer being seen together.

But his interest in Betty Reed grew and he envisioned her as a great singer and a star in Hollywood. Konrad Sztykgold had a brother who taught music and Rubinstein sent Betty to him for lessons and had her sing in his home to the accompaniment of a piano. "She has the greatest voice in the world," he told people. The lady friend of one of his lawyers, herself a veteran of many years in show business, took exception to that. "Betty has a lovely voice but she's a rank amateur," this woman told Rubinstein. "Some day, with work, study, experience, she'll develop—but right now let's be sensible. She is a good long way from stardom." Rubinstein was not even listening. "She'll knock everybody on their ear," he said. "She has the greatest voice in the world." The lawyer's friend lost her temper. "How can you tell me she's so great?" she demanded. "How dare you tell me what I know is not so?" "Well," he said, "I know and I can judge and she has a great, great talent." The lawyer's friend went off talking to herself. You couldn't tell that man anything, not a damned thing, she told the lawyer. Not long after Rubinstein and Betty went together to Hollywood and to the Beverly Wilshire Hotel—mail and telephone calls to Betty's New York place were routed to Rubinstein's secretary at 814 Fifth. They frolicked each day in the hotel swimming pool while he arranged for her to debut in a local night club. On the night she was to sing he made reservations for eighty people, among whom were numbered some of the top figures of the movie industry whose members, less conservative than the Wall Street men, still more or less made welcome the sub-rosa producer of *Whistle Stop* and *Summer Storm*. The lawyer's lady friend went out for the great moment and sat with Betty a few hours before, where she learned that the star-to-be had no jewels to wear. The lawyer's friend loaned her some to go with the sensational gown and then sat in the audience next to director William Wyler as Betty did her stint. The arrangements were that it was to be a guest appearance and that if she did well she would go on to greater and greater things in Hollywood. "If she doesn't make good . . ." Rubinstein said grimly to the lawyer's friend. "Well?" asked the woman, and Betty, hearing, broke into tears. When the performance began Betty proved to be good enough—not bad; adequate—but no better. Her natural voice was good and her looks magnificent, but she did not have the personality needed to effect a chemical reaction among the listeners; she came over as dull and unintelligent. The applause was mild and that was the end of the matter. Rubinstein and she hung around Hollywood for a while, but no offers were forthcoming. Rubinstein was with her a great deal but he was not to her as he had been to the other girl; he was stingy with money and she had to ask him for five dollars or ten dollars in front of other people. After a while they returned to New York and Betty went to live in an apartment on Central Park West from which she went, between dates with Rubinstein, to occasional voice lessons about which was based the fiction that she was still by way of being a voice student destined for greater things. Perhaps Betty herself knew otherwise, but Rubinstein often alluded to her great future. He would make it so.

Increasingly Betty strove to look like the vanished Laurette, wearing her hair just as Laurette had, and dressing as Laurette had. When Laurette's sister Betty came to call upon her former brother-in-law, the other Betty, Betty Reed, arched herself to say, "Everyone says I look just like your sister." Laurette's sister said, "Do they?" but thought to herself, You don't look like her at all. For all that she was the main woman in his life, Rubinstein was not faithful to Betty. Through her he met another singer, this one with a greater talent but with an equal need of aid, and he doled out support to the girl in a niggardly way: a lesson here, a train ticket to an out-of-town audition there. But for such gifts and the promise of more he wanted a return. The girl went to an older woman, a friend, and told her of the situation. "He keeps insisting on romance," the girl said. "I don't want any. What do you think I should do?" The woman thought it wasn't cricket at all for Rubinstein to try to go around Reed's back to Reed's friend and said so. "Tell him to put a ring around your finger if he wants anything," she said. A few days later Rubinstein went to the woman. "Why are you spoiling my romance?" he asked. He wore a big smile. "Why shouldn't I?" she demanded. "Well," he said, "it really doesn't matter. I had her last night. She was a virgin."

"You liar," said the woman. "Oh, you bastard."

"So what's so terrible?" he asked. He smiled in the most charming way.

"You filthy liar," she said. But it was all true. The girl

190

was nineteen, and from Rubinstein she went on to a notable career. Ever after he would say he had made her a star. Ever after the older woman looked at him with fascinated horror. "She doesn't like me," he would say in front of her, and his mother or aunt would say, "Now why should you say that? Of course she likes you." "No, I don't," the woman would say. "I think he is the world's greatest bastard." He would smile—charmingly. The woman had a son, an Army veteran who hated the sight of Rubinstein; on the few occasions they met the son turned his back on the ex-convict and draft-dodger when the latter tried to begin a conversation. But that the son did so did not irritate Rubinstein; he would laugh. The son's wife similarly found him unpalatable and treated him with the utmost contempt. Upon one occasion at a party given by her mother-in-law he put his arm around her and that threw her into a frenzy. "You slimy thing," she spat at him and her husband got a pin and jabbed it into the offending arm. But Rubinstein laughed and the young couple marveled to each other that here was a man you simply could not insult. Both of them hated to see him on companionable terms with someone near and dear to them, but the friend found it hard to break off the relationship. Rubinstein was anxious to have her as part of his circle. When she gave parties he would send Jimmy Morse and his butler, William Morter, to help out, and he would send with them a case of champagne. In time he drew her into a situation where she was close to his mother and aunt and it became impossible to break away. And though she hated many things about him she found also that when he wanted to he could be charming and thoughtful and even, in a way, sweet. They talked on the phone regularly and for all that she called him a swine and a bastard, she still found in herself a feeling for a person whom she thought could have been the greatest man in the world but threw it all away.

Time was passing; he began to talk about getting back into the forefront of the business community. With the desertion of the quiet European places and the entrances into the big night clubs there came a flood of adverse publicity—Draft-Dodger Who Wallowed in Luxury While Our Boys Overseas Suffered Now Back to Old Haunts—and that worried Konrad Sztykgold who saw that things could not be the same. He tried to dissuade Rubinstein from attempting a business comeback and making a big public display but Rubinstein would not hear of that. "I have to go out or people will say I'm washed up and I lost out," he said. "I'm a big man; I can't run away." "No, Serge!" Sztykgold would cry, and say again that he must keep out of the limelight and go into semiretirement. Rubinstein's temper would rise and he would shout that Sztykgold was old and crazy and didn't understand things. Teddy Howard, the press agent whom he met years before at the Long Island beach clubs and in Hollywood, also tried to talk to him. "You've got to change," Howard said. "Lie low. Be a little bit humble. Don't go making a big splash." But Rubinstein hardly listened and went on about how he was going to be bigger than ever and make a comeback and be a J. P. Morgan. "Why *should* I change?" he demanded. But if he could not change, the ways of the world in relation to him could most decidedly do so. The government was still trying to deport him and in Washington it was absolutely death itself to mention his name and slowly it became apparent that in this case Wall Street wasn't going to forgive or forget. Sztykgold tried to put him into various oil transactions, but when the opposite parties learned the principal in the deal was to be Serge Rubinstein, they backed away at once. Lawyer Edward Ennis, who worked on his immigration problems, tried to do other things for him but found it a difficult assignment. "Serge," he asked, "don't you realize that anyone can double cross you and you're helpless to do anything about it? They can go to court and accuse you of raping Cleopatra in the park last night and the jury will come in with a verdict of guilty. Can't you see that?" Rubinstein could not. Long before Cape Canaveral became world famous Rubinstein somehow learned a government operation was planned for the spot and that the land could be bought cheaply. He sent Ennis down to look into it and Ennis physically tramped all over the area but came back advising his client not to buy. "Serge," he said, "don't go into it. If you own it the government will go to a condemnation jury to establish the price you'll be paid and the word will be that this Goddamned draft-dodger is dickering around trying to screw the government and the jury will end up awarding you less than you paid in the first place." Someone else buying Cape Canaveral could have made a million dollars easily but for Rubinstein it was an impossible deal. The client sent the lawyer looking elsewhere for deals but everywhere he went Ennis found that the name Rubinstein scared away most people and that those it did not were all too anxious to do business with the aim in mind that any contract entered into could be safely broken at will. Wall Street was absolutely closed to him as an active principal. When he walked into the Stock Exchange Luncheon Club all in his wake could be seen men looking angrily after him saying, "That son-of-a-bitch." Romeo Muller, his old associate in Panhandle, heard a former president of the New York Stock Exchange say that most of what the Street felt was not contempt but envy, and perhaps it was so, but no reputable firm would take his business and few men would even be seen talking to him. The impending trial on the stock manipulating charge was put off but still it was in the forefront of Wall Street's eyes and he was prejudged as being even more guilty than he had been in the draft-dodging case.

In the wake of his prison term and the way America regarded him, ever more and more people fell away from him. Less and less they came to his home. Even Herr Professor preferred not to see him, not because what Rubinstein had done offended him as a patriot but because of the immense stupidity of his refusal to serve in the Army. Herr Professor was affected in his capacity of European intellectual; another former friend, a New York newspaperman, was offended in his capacity of old-line American socialite. He mused to himself that while Otto Kahn and the Rothschilds had been capable of penetrating the nuances of a society and doing the right thing—as a boy sitting in his family's box at the Metropolitan Opera House he had often seen Otto Kahn—Rubinstein had proved wanting. Rubinstein the ex-convict seemed to typify, the newspaperman decided, the unrest and boiling of a Europe that was not appealing. Perhaps the good Lord invented such as Serge to test the mettle of those on the Lord's side, he thought to himself, and forthwith banished Rubinstein from his list of friends. (Before, it had all been very different; before, the newspaperman and his wife were frequent visitors to the Manhattan town house and the New Jersey shore place. But that was before.)

But Rubinstein was still confident of eventual triumph. Ennis was too cautious. Sztykgold didn't understand. Herr Professor was old and foolish. The newspaperman was an ingrate. Laurette was a poor girl he had tried to make into a great lady and it had been too much for her to absorb. The government and the American people were not even worth discussing. He had been innocent of any wrongdoing, unjustly convicted, the victim of persecution and malicious envy. They were all wrong, everyone was wrong, and he would yet make his comeback and be bigger than ever, richer, grander. His doubt never seemed to waver yet those who knew him noticed disquieting things. He was starting to drink a little, something he had never done before. He drank Gibsons, one here and another there—nothing serious, but strange in the eyes of those who had known him when in the course of a five-hour party he would sip perhaps the equivalent of half a shot of liquor. And he took up smoking. Often he would ask for a cigarette, take the pack out of the hands of the giver, remove one cigarette and hand it back to the donor, and then pocket the remainder. A few hours later he would be asking for another cigarette.

The stock manipulation indictment hung over his head even as the deportation matter went on and on. The former charge could bring twenty years in prison. He shopped around for the right courtroom lawyer to handle it, or rather sent others shopping for him, but it was terribly difficult to find a man who would even consider the case. The top New York lawyers simply wanted no part of him. Every lawyer who handles defendants with notorious reputations learns to expect piles of condemning mail and the frowning disapproval of other clients, and when Rubinstein sought a lawyer for the stock matter he did so as a man with one of the worst reputations in America. Few lawyers would want the letters and frowns such a client would produce. He had been in the country just a little more than a decade but he was very well known and commonly described as a thief, a cheat, an ungrateful foreigner, a parasite, a braggart, a skirt-chaser, a cheap skate, a liar, a man who killed his brother and defamed his mother and, of course, as the pre-eminent draft-dodger of World War II. That he had gotten a two-and-a-half year term for this last, and had served less than that, seemed unfair to hundreds of thousands of veterans who had put in three or four or five years in the country's service. It was said of him that his sentence should have been at the very least the same amount of time that the longest-term draftee had served. It was pointed out, with bitterness, that boys aged eighteen who deserted under the stress of combat were given terms of fifteen or twenty years in prison, ten times the amount he had served for sitting around New York amassing money and living it up. As he got back to his old night-clubbing ways his name appeared more and more regularly in the papers, always mentioned with loathing. He was an open target but in a way his people found insane he seemed to gloat over the notoriety which made him better and better known. No newspaper story about him ever began without designating him as a draft-dodging ex-convict, and few failed to mention he was under indictment for stock rigging. Now and then he would fly into a rage at such stories and call Ennis with futile demands that suit be instituted for hundreds of thousands of dollars, but more regularly he would cut out and save the clipping. Once a newspaperman came to him saying that for $250 an upcoming story could be killed, but Rubinstein sent the man way, saying it was better to have your name in the paper than to be ignored. When the story came out he characteristically changed his mind and wanted Ennis to sue the paper. The lawyer told him to save his breath; it was hopeless. On the other hand Rubinstein himself was not immune from suit: only weeks after he got out of jail he was appearing before an Official Referee to contest yet once again the claims of his sister-in-law Valerie. David Brady was her choice for a lawyer for this final attempt to get what she said had been coming to her late husband André—the same David Brady who, as an Army colonel in Selective Service, had run afoul of Rubinstein the unwilling registrant. "This is only one more part of Mr. Brady's persecution of me," Rubinstein said, but he got a cabaña next to the one occupied by the lawyer and his family at a Long Island beach club and there tried to strike up a friendship. "I would like to shake your hand, Mr. Brady," he told the lawyer. "In other circumstances we might have gotten along very well together." "That is quite true, Mr. Rubinstein," Brady said, "if you and I had been two totally different people." He ignored the outstretched hand. Rubinstein laughed. In the hearings Brady openly called him a liar and a fraud but he ignored the accusations—they were beneath him, not worthy of notice. He came to be the same way with almost everyone else who slighted him: night-club owners barring him from their premises, unemployed domestics refusing to work for him, the man standing at the Stork Club bar saying if that dirty draft-dodger drinks here I won't (Rubinstein was asked to leave), the newspaper reporters nastily jabbing at him in court hearings, the American Legion saying it was a disgrace that New York's Armistice Day parade on Fifth Avenue should have to pass the house of the draft-dodger, the girls telling him they wouldn't be seen dead with him, the charity people sending back his contributions with the notations that his money was not acceptable, the underworld types sidling up to him to intimate he was one of their own, and, most hurtful of all, the businessmen saying they wouldn't even sit at the same table with him, let alone go into deals—deals that he knew might make him richer and bigger and prove that he was right when he said, as he said over and over again, that it was yet true that God had His arms around the Serge Rubinstein who was destined to rule the world.

But he could not always laugh. One night, very late, Jimmy Morse came in and found him wandering the first floor, with a bottle in his hand. "Mamma! Mamma!" he was screaming. "Maa-maa!" Morse stole silently away.

Chapter Sixteen

Not Guilty

His search for an attorney to defend him on the SEC charge continued, his people scurrying here and there to the great downtown law firms seeking a name lawyer willing to defend him in the same courthouse from which he had left for Lewisburg. Finally, after several pleading visits, Sonny Wolchok secured the services of the right man. He was the renowned Isidore Kresel, seventy-two years old, frail, thin, tiny, but one of the most brilliant of New York's lawyers. Kresel had prior experience with his new client. Once, years earlier, in a fit of rage, brother André had flung out at Serge that he would go to the famous Mr. Kresel and get him to press his claims. He would go the very next day, André cried. That afternoon Serge himself went to see Kresel. He explained that his insane brother was after him; would Mr. Kresel take the case? Kresel said he would and asked for a $2500 retainer fee. Serge wrote out a check. When the next day André appeared, Kresel had to tell him that he had been badly beaten to the punch. Crestfallen, André went away. A day later Serge called Kresel telling him to forget the whole thing. A second contact took place at the time the indictment for draft-dodging was handed down. Kresel was approached and considered taking the case but demurred upon the advice of his son-in-law, who was his partner, and who was just back from the Pacific war and not in the mood to see the office doing business with an alleged draft-dodger. But when the SEC indictment came in the son-in-law urged Kresel to undertake the defense, saying that Rubinstein was finding it impossible to get a lawyer of any standing and that although the fellow had been a bad boy once, it was not right that he thus be spanked twice for it. So the firm took the case. Rubinstein came down for a series of conferences and immediately took a dislike to the son-in-law because although the man was two years older than he was himself he looked younger. Rubinstein's cool behavior became an office joke, with secretaries and junior members telling the son-in-law that he should be ashamed of himself for daring to look younger than the new client and that he should apologize. The son-in-law admitted he was a rotter for looking younger than Rubinstein, but added that he found the fellow too sleek, oily, and unctuous by far and that therefore the two of them were square with each other.

It took months for the case to be prepared. Witnesses

were lined up in many states and in foreign countries, with Sonny Wolchok even sailing to Manila to consult with officials there about the Stewart scheme to rebuild the Philippines. (The Assistant United States Attorney assigned to the case took exception to the time Sonny was gone, saying that the journey must have been undertaken on a "slow boat to China," and that it was a "public scandal" that the case was taking so long to go to trial.) But eventually, on June 20, 1951, selection of a jury began before Judge Charles A. Deway. Several jurors had been picked when one talesman, a housewife, remarked on the stand that she already knew something about Rubinstein—"That's the draft-dodger." Kresel immediately moved for a mistrial but his plea was denied and the selection went on. Had bets been taken at that moment on the trial outcome, Rubinstein would have been odds-on to be convicted. That the Korean War was at its height was a factor of great importance; Rubinstein knew it and was inclined to favor behind-the-scenes negotiations which would allow him to plead guilty in return for a government promise that he would not have to go to jail but would simply be allowed to leave the country forever. Kresel opposed any such move, saying he had been engaged to defend Rubinstein, not plead him guilty. Kresel's attitude arose from his pride in himself as a lawyer and not from any affection felt for his client, whom he considered an intolerable person—loud, flashy, opinionated. Once the two, leaving Kresel's office, had trouble finding a taxi and the old man said that it was foolish to wait, and that they'd take the subway. They went down to the train together but once inside Rubinstein irritated Kresel, who did not feel himself above this means of transportation, by saying this was the first time in his life he'd ever been in the subway. "That's strange, isn't it, considering how much money I made in the BMT merger?" Rubinstein loftily said. Kresel grunted. In court he forbade his client to speak to him and sat as far from him at the counsel table as possible, placing himself at one end and Rubinstein at the other. Rubinstein turned sulky at that and sat in brooding silence.

The government lawyer, Eugene F. Roth, was a dapper man with good courtroom presence. It was said that as Saypol had graduated to U. S. Attorney on the basis of his draft case conviction of Rubinstein, so would Roth move up to the same post if he did the same to Rubinstein in this new matter. He was assisted in his presentation of the case by SEC personnel who had investigated Rubinstein's doings in Panhandle; they, like Roth, were confident of a conviction. Of all the men at the government table, the one who knew the defendant best was John W. Schwegler, the SEC man who

197

had conducted the original investigation of the Panhandle situation. He was a much-decorated veteran of the First World War and as such was not inclined to think much of Rubinstein. In addition, during the course of his investigation, Schwegler had been forced to jump through hoops by the man he was investigating. Rubinstein was convinced that Schwegler was planning secretly to record anything said between the two men at face-to-face conferences, and often irritated the SEC man by jingling coins in his hands as an attempt to render ineffective any recording devices that might be in use. Upon other occasions, again in an attempt to undo any buggings, Rubinstein refused to talk with Schwegler unless both had their heads out the window. This led to conversations carried out with both men leaning far out into space as they went over complicated financial transactions. Once, off the record (but not out the window), Schwegler asked Rubinstein why in hell he hadn't gone into the Army, and got in return the answer that the British had long memories and would have arranged to have had him sent to England where he could have been prosecuted on various criminal charges the wily Londoners would dream up. Schwegler did not buy the story, and decided in his own mind that it was simply Rubinstein's own typical way of looking at things that would make him take such an attitude; that with holdings of one hundred million he would still have been a devious soul reluctant to return a penny to the Chosen stockholders.

The government's requirement was basically to prove that Rubinstein spread rumors about Panhandle that were untrue. Kresel's defense was to try to show that the government allegations depended upon sinister interpretations and that if the jury convicted, it would have guessed Rubinstein into jail. Despite his age and unimpressive appearance, the lawyer's courtroom tactics were brilliant. The trend of the case was from the start in the defendant's favor, but Rubinstein nervously failed to see it. During one weekend recess he had a big blowup with his lawyer about the handling of a witness. "I want you to recall that man, and do the job right!" he shouted at Kresel, who icily dismissed his views and went home. The next day a note was delivered to the lawyer. It was from Rubinstein and, couched in the most high-handed terms, told Kresel that he, Rubinstein, demanded that the witness be recalled, that Kresel must do it, that Kresel had a responsibility to Rubinstein and ought to live up to it. The note was delivered to Kresel's home on Sunday afternoon as he sat with an assistant, Irving Weinberger, going over certain details of the case. Kresel was beside himself at such language from a client. (He had

198

been in practice for more than half a century, and did not feel much in need of a lecture about his responsibility to a client.) He shook with rage and was almost incoherent. As Weinberger tried to calm him down, the phone rang. It was Rubinstein, demanding to know that his written orders had been complied with. Kresel refused to speak to him but went back to work with Weinberger. A couple of hours later Rubinstein called again to apologize, but Kresel never forgave him.

The actual trial was dull for spectators looking for sensation, and soon the court was almost free of visitors. Laboriously Kresel was able to show that there was a logical explanation for every one of Rubinstein's moves that had sent Panhandle's stock skywards. He even managed to get dismissed a count of the indictment, which had been drawn up by the young Roy M. Cohn. Roth, on the other hand, made a bad tactical mistake by dragging in the question of Rubinstein's sworn allegation that he was his mother's bastard son. In the draft case the act had been material, but in this one it was not, and it seemed to observers that mentioning it made Rubinstein a more sympathetic character in the eyes of the jury. Stella, sitting in a purple dress and purple-trimmed straw hat, with Genia by her side, suddenly took on the appearance of a mother with a son in bad trouble; the jury looked at her with compassion and an SEC official looking on took out a pencil, wrote "Not guilty on all counts" and passed it to the investigator, Schwegler. Schwegler looked over and slowly nodded. Konrad Sztykgold made a particularly good witness for Rubinstein. He was in poor health and testified in disobedience of his doctor's orders, but he parried all of Roth's thrusts and spoke well in Rubinstein's defense.

Nineteen days after the trial began, Roth summed up by characterizing the defendant as "the architect and guiding genius behind a scheme to defraud investors." Rubinstein, he said, was "not primarily a businessman, not interested in the business of his companies. He was primarily interested in the manipulations shown in this case."

"Is this the kind of businessman," Roth asked, "we want representing our society, our way of life, when it is under attack? Rubinstein is not here because of his business reputation, his previous conviction. He is here because he did these things wrongfully, unlawfully, willfully."

Kresel vented some of his feelings about his client by telling the jury that Rubinstein was the "worst fool" he had ever met. He stressed the point that there was a reasonable, logical, legal explanation for everything Rubinstein had done. The jury retired to deliberate and one of the SEC officials remarked to Weinberger, Kresel's assistant, that if the government got Rubinstein sent away it would be only right that the New York Bar Association, so many of whose members Rubinstein had long supported, should be draped in black. Weinberger laughed and agreed. But it was not to be, for after two hours of deliberation the jury returned a verdict of not guilty on all counts. As soon as the foreman spoke, Rubinstein leaped out of his chair and ran around the counsel table to embrace the unwilling Kresel and cover him with kisses. Fuming and raging, the tiny Kresel tried to shake him off, but Rubinstein clutched him harder, only interrupting his kissing to cry out affectionate phrases. Finally Kresel broke loose, only to be overwhelmed by Stella, who came pounding up the aisle to repeat her son's performance. The judge was infuriated by all this, and pounding his gavel, shouted to attendants to clear the court. But first Rubinstein insisted on shaking hands with the jury. Every juror had to individually shake his hand, which Rubinstein presented to each in turn in a fashion reminding one man of the way a Prince might give a servant a gratuity: Thank you. Excellent. Very good.

The SEC people walked out of the courtroom, several with a feeling of pride that an American jury at the height of the Korean War would acquit the foremost draft-dodger of a greater war only six years past. It was a strange feeling, considering the positions of the men who felt it, but deeply realized. Kresel also went out, furiously wiping his face and the top of his head. But as he went down the stairs of the courthouse, a Rubinstein lawyer, one of the regulars, caught up with him. "Mr. Kresel," said the man, "Serge wants to invite the jurors to come up to his place for a little party."

"My God!" said Kresel. But he was very tired and finished with the case and en route for home and he had no heart left to joust with his client. "All right," he snapped, "but only for a few minutes." He also ordered Weinberger to go along and make sure the guests left in a hurry. Weinberger and the regular lawyer and Rubinstein went up in a cab together, Rubinstein jubilantly talking of how he was now vindicated. He also handed Weinberger a little advice on how to beat the market: buy on the decline but never buy unless the total net worth of a company divided by the number of shares outstanding does not indicate that the shares are worth more than the prevailing price. They arrived at 814 Fifth and Rubinstein tipped the cab driver five dollars. "That's the biggest tip he ever gave, and he'll never give another like it," the regular lawyer whispered to Weinberger. They went inside and soon afterward the ex-jurors started drifting in one at a time. To the women of the group Rubinstein was particularly gallant and charming. For the men he had fine brandy and champagne. Soon music was coming out of a phonograph and Rubinstein was dancing about with first one and then another of the ladies who had so recently sat in judgment on him. The jury verdict had come in at five in the afternoon; the party began about six-thirty. At seven-thirty Weinberger was called to the telephone. Kresel was on the other end, talking in measured, controlled terms although over the phone Weinberger could almost hear him grinding his teeth. "Are those women still up there?" Kresel asked. Weinberger had to admit they were. He did not see fit to add that at the moment two of them were Lindying with Kresel's recent client. "Listen," rasped Kresel, "you tell Rubinstein to get those women out of there!" Weinberger said that yes, sir, he would. He hung up and made his way to Madame, who sat contentedly watching the festivities. "Mrs. Rubinstein," said Weinberger, "Serge has been through a grueling experience. Don't you think that perhaps the celebration ought to be curtailed now?" Madame said maybe that would be best, and called to Serge, who came dancing over with an ex-juror in his arms to say that he wouldn't think of cutting the party short, wouldn't think of it. Why, it was just starting to get going! Weinberger fled. The party went on and on.

The jury verdict was brought in on a Friday. On Monday in an article in the New York *Times* it was disclosed that a massive drive to deport Rubinstein was being mounted by the government—the Immigration and Naturalization Reviewing Board was going over his immense folder bit by bit and point by point. At the same time government income tax experts began to re-examine his statements yet again although this had been done before with no criminal irregularities having been found. Most of his money by then was in investments of various kinds which were held in the names of various dummies, so actually Rubinstein did not have too much to fear from the investigations. Previous government tax moves had begun with the imposing of an order tying up his money so he could not flee the country with it or shift it to different accounts, so he had converted his holdings into voting trusts in which the dummies who ostensibly owned the stocks vested all control and voting rights in Rubinstein. But that this was so necessarily curtailed his use of his funds. He could not move with the speed he had shown in the past.

And there was something else that was holding him back. It was what he had become, what he was. He had changed. It had not happened that one day he was a man who was the next day gone, but after Lewisburg and after the SEC trial, after all the newspaper articles and calculated snubs, after all of that, he changed. He worked terribly long hours and talked endlessly about making his comeback, and enlarged his collection of Napoleon statues and busts, and still spoke about himself in conjunction with J. P. Morgan, but in fact he was afraid to take chances and the great judgment of the time to pounce was not there. He had been slow in losing what he had been and to many people it seemed as if it was still in him, but it was not. Teddy Schulz saw that this was so but could not really believe it for a very long time, until slowly Teddy came to admit to himself that Serge just was not Serge any more. . . . A Greek shipping man came to 814 Fifth with a deal involving the purchase of a steamer held in the name of a Panamanian company and flying the flag of that country. Ship, papers, flag rights were all for sale for a little more than one million dollars, which was a bargain in the shipping market of that time. There had been a time when Rubinstein would have leaped at such a proposition, immediately envisaging himself as a new Onassis. But now he hesitated. Lay out a million dollars? He went with the man to a Greek festival in Manhattan which was held in a modest dance hall, and there, sitting by the Greek consul, he flew into a rage about the arrangements: the unpainted walls, the cheap glasses in which the drinks were served, the non-affluent Greek-Americans who made up most of the crowd. "This is disgusting," he shouted. "It's impossible to stay here!" He stamped out and that was the end of the Panamanian ship deal. The Greek was enraged at this insult but he had mistaken the reason for Rubinstein's disinclination to deal with him. Rubinstein had done business in worse surroundings than the dance hall—in the laundry room at Lewisburg, for one place. It was not the dance hall, it was himself. He was afraid to take a position, afraid to risk money, afraid to come out of a self-built shell the walls of which were very quickly hardening. Not long after an obvious swindler, a man with conniver written all over him, came to Rubinstein with a deal involving the financing of a so-called new electrical invention. The deal was ridiculous; it stank. "Now he is really crazy, your friend," Sztykgold cried to Schulz, rushing out of Rubinstein's office after an hour-long session of screamed Russian curses and pleas. But to the new Rubinstein there was one thing about the deal that was appealing and brought him out of his shell: it didn't cost much. For $20,000 the conniver assured him, he could control the new invention. "It'll put me in a position to rival General Electric," Rubinstein told Schulz enthusiastically. "Serge . . ." Teddy helplessly said. But Rubinstein went ahead and gave the man the money.

Promptly that worthy vanished, never to be seen again at 814 Fifth. Another of the same ilk soon appeared. He had a great oil lease out West, he announced. For only $15,000 Rubinstein could have it. Invoking the shades of Panhandle's past glories, Rubinstein sent Schulz out to survey the world-beating field. Schulz returned saying that if salt water could be marketed the field would be a wonderful buy. But Rubinstein saw only that a small sum was needed. He paid out the $15,000 and it joined the $20,000 as one more business loss. Broadway theatrical producers filtered into his life, each with a miraculous hit play for him to finance. Rubinstein bit; the hit plays lasted a week, two weeks. But when the backers of *Guys and Dolls* asked him to join them, he declined.

His judgment of people also seemed to be fading. All his life he had boasted of how he could read men's minds. "I have special dreams and feelings," he said many times, "and I can tell what people are thinking. I can read the quiver of a nostril or the droop of an eyelash; I can sense things." But when a sleazy and fawning man he had known at Lewisburg appeared at 814 Fifth he took him in and announced to his people that he, Rubinstein, would now rejuvenate this ex-convict and make a man of him. He gave the man a charge account in a clothing store and a few dollars and a room in his home and a place at the dining-room table. There one day the man was introduced to Mrs. Pearl Murray, a public relations woman and the wife of the theatrical personality Jan Murray. She thought the fellow looked and acted the part of an ex-convict and crook, but Rubinstein assured her that he had looked deep into the man's heart and soul and found there only a great need for guidance and aid from above. Some weeks later Mrs. Murray was again in the house when news came that the ex-convict had disappeared leaving behind him a long list of bills for his protector to pay. (He also took a few valuables which turned up later in cheap pawnshops.) That his protégé had so decamped threw Rubinstein into a frenzy. He began to stalk up and down the room, hands behind him, talking more and more excitedly about how you couldn't trust anyone and that even when you tried to help people they turned against you. He switched to the subject of Laurette, crying out that even she had knifed him in the back; he had worked his hands to the bone for her and she had repaid him by leaving him in the lurch. His voice rose and soon he was screaming. A servant went to get Madame and she joined Mrs. Murray in trying to calm Rubinstein down. But he was quite out of control. "Everyone is against me!" he shouted. "I try my best but still they want to crucify me. Everyone! The whole world!" He was sobbing. "Serge, Serge," his mother said. He flung himself on the floor

203

in front of her, weeping unrestrainedly. Stella sank into a chair and cradled his head in her lap. His tears stained her dress. "Serge," she crooned, "I know you're kind and good, and Serge, God in heaven also knows it." Mrs. Murray stood by the kneeling man and he reached his hand out to her. She took it and held it. So they were for a long time: the mother, the visitor, the master of the house.

Pearl Murray was not the only public relations expert to be consulted. To most of them Rubinstein said that he needed an intensive campaign to get the New York newspapers on his side, and that as was the custom in Europe, he would be willing to make regular payments to editors and reporters. Most of the public relations people told him that was not the way to go around reshaping his image, and that a better method was to simply forego the pleasures of the big well-publicized night clubs. (Some of the other experts, however, gladly took him up on the suggestion that things could be arranged with various newspapermen, and relieved him of doled-out cash payments in exchange for promises that certainly, of course, everything would be taken care of now but that it would take a little time and just a little bit more money—in small bills, please.) Even as money was passed out to the members of the second group, the advice of the first was ignored. He was going around in a circle, appearing in night clubs with a splashy display which got him bad publicity which caused him to want even more to show them all by going out, which brought more newspaper items which made him even more defiantly eager to show himself. And he never went alone. There was always a group with him composed for the most part of various hangers-on anxious for a free meal and drinks. Some of the hangers-on hoped for more, however. They were girls of that segment of New York known as café society, most of them wearing their hair up for the occasion because it was said of Rubinstein that he liked that style. There is no real definition of "café society" and no real definition of the lives of such girls. But if you go at night to the East Side places you will see them in profusion. One night they will be with a sixty-year-old man, one night with a twenty-five-year-old. They are, many of them, girls with ordinary jobs, secretaries, clerks. The others live by working part-time as models, or as some-time call girls, or as kept women. Café society calls them semi-pros or light hookers, which means they must be taken to the best places for dinner before you go to bed with them and that they do not ask you for money in the morning. But that they do not ask does not mean that you do not give them a bill, saying buy yourself a new dress, dear, or here, use this for cab fare. (If there is no bill they don't go out with you again.)

But Rubinstein did not like giving bills so he gave promises and gifts. The promises were all couched in terms of stardom in the movies (I created Ava Gardner; I created Linda Darnell) and the gifts were secondhand furs and compacts bought $50 a dozen. He also specialized in giving out a kind of V-shaped cultured pearl ring. All his girls, save for the very quick one-night stands, got the ring. He bought them from a downtown jeweler at a literally wholesale rate, ordering ten at a time and paying $25 apiece. Most of the girls in his life did not last for more than a week or two—"Screw it and get rid of it," he said—but those that did were all somewhat jolted when they found that at a dinner for twenty at least five or six guests wore the identical ring. In the background to all of this was Betty Reed, looking on helplessly and asking all of Serge's friends if they didn't think he ought to marry her. None of them thought he would although it was a standing joke that Serge would meet a girl and a day or so later become "engaged to marry for two hours, upstairs in the bedroom." Actually few such "fiancées" could have believed marriage was going to result. But they could hope for other things from a man reputed to have at least $20,000,000, a man who often remarked that he was worth $50,000,000. His treatment of such girls was quite remarkable in the eyes of many people who observed it. On the first night he met one he would take her hands and look into her eyes and say Darling, tell me all about yourself, and be perfectly capable of meeting her on her own level, which was usually that of a kid two or three years out of high school and either in modeling or trying to get started in it while she worked part-time in a store. He was amazing on small talk and could go on for an hour with a girl about the world of modeling, asking one question after another about how many changes she'd made during a session, and how the arrangements were and what kind of make-up was used for the winter scene with furs and the summer one in play clothes, and how she'd gotten from one engagement to another. He had, it seemed, an infinite ability to stay interested in her descriptions of how she had been able to be at this photographer at 10 A.M. and that one at noon because she knew a stand-up place where they served a quick lunch . . . and so on. "Well," he would ask, "how did you get uptown, then?" And she would tell him on the Seventh Avenue to 34th Street. And he would ask but what about her hair——it was a windy day. And she would tell him Jerome gave her a comb-out at his salon even though she didn't have an appointment. "Oh, that was good!" he would say. Then he would warn her about various photographers, about how she must be careful; they were wolves. He and the girl would chatter on and then there would be the visit upstairs. After that everything would be changed for the girl. When next they met he would ask, "Well, how's the pretty girl today?"—a favorite phrase—but before she answered he had turned away to talk business or make a pass at something else. If it was a business conference it would go on and on, deportation proceedings analyzed, propositions evaluated, investments considered, but through it all the girl would be totally ignored, mutely sitting by and completely out of things, never asked to join in the talk, just another face to the lawyers and hangers-on. Occasionally he might pat her hand and say to Wolchok or Ennis or Katz, "Isn't she beautiful?" but that would be all; she might just as well not have existed until Rubinstein would turn to her and say, "Let's go," and take her upstairs to his bedroom with two immense beds once the property of the French financier Jacques Neckar, both joined to a great headboard and covered with black satin sheets delicately embroidered. (One he slept in; the other he called "my workshop.") An hour or so later he would be back again downstairs, the girl again sitting by like a flower on a table or perhaps gone, dismissed from his life. The next day another might be in her place, ignored—if it were not their first time together—and taking no part in what went on. Sometimes during morning working hours he would slip away from his secretaries and Schulz and the promoters coming to see him and go to his bedroom. He would emerge after a while and tell William Morter, the butler, to get rid of what was upstairs, get it out of the house: a new one was expected after lunch. Or if Morter was not around Rubinstein used a favorite and dependable gambit. "The market is just opening in Tokyo." (Or London, or Paris.) "I have to make some big purchases there—have to send out cables and telephone my agents. I'm sorry, dear, but you must go." After lunch the new one would arrive, be ushered in, given a cocktail and told to wait; Mr. Rubinstein would be with her directly. The girl, who in most cases was from something other than the highest levels of American social life, would sit alone and intimidated by the sight of great heroic paintings and statuary until her host would march in apologizing for his tardiness but explaining that he had been tied up in vast business undertakings aimed at developing oil empires or electrical trusts or whatever he was dealing with that week. Many of the rooms in 814 Fifth were either closed or very sparsely furnished, but the girl would not know that—nor would she know that Rembrandt didn't paint "The Notary"— and she would be terribly impressed. How had she originally met Rubinstein? She had been at a night club, or someone had taken her to dinner at his place, or a girl friend had introduced her to him at a bar, and they had gotten to talking and he had invited her to come over after lunch this day for a drink. And she had gone and seen butler and house and furnishing and now he was saying Darling, tell me about yourself and whispering of how smitten he was with her. Nothing would seem impossible for the mistress or wife of such a man; so thinking, an hour, two hours later, she would be with him in the bedroom. The next day she might be invited to come again, or she might be taken out for lunch or dinner along with ten other people, to find herself completely ignored until it came time to go again to the bedroom. Then perhaps once more, perhaps twice, she would be back again and then that would be the end of it. She would have the special cultured pearl ring, anyway.

Most days Rubinstein lunched in a restaurant that became known as his hangout. It was called Monsignore and later became famous as the place which Frank Costello left one night to go to the lobby of his home where he was surprised by an unknown assailant who took a shot at him, creasing his skull and greatly disturbing the balance of things in the underworld. Monsignore was run by Vincent Aufiero di Vettamena, known more familiarly as Jimmy Aufiero, a suave and dark man who met Rubinstein through a cousin who served time in Lewisburg for writing bad checks. After the cousin, whose name was Armando, came out of prison, he joined with Aufiero in outfitting a small but elegant East Side restaurant, Monsignore. The night before the place was to open, Armando telephoned his former co-inmate to ask that he give Monsignore a little of his business. Not every restaurant even tolerated Rubinstein, and there had been none that specifically requested his attendance, so he was pleased at Armando's invitation. He came with eleven guests to be the first customers Monsignore ever had. There were, besides Aufiero and Armando, only three employees, and all jumped forward to arrange a couple of tables in a row. Rubinstein sat at the head end with Madame at the foot and the ten others between them. Drinks were ordered and immediately Monsignore faced a problem. Rubinstein never drank liquor and her request was for a glass of Seven-Up, which the just-beginning restaurant did not have in stock. The waiter consulted with Aufiero and it was decided to give Madame ginger ale in the hope she would not know the difference. But Madame had a sensitive palate. She took one sip and immediately said she had not been given her Seven-Up, but ginger ale instead. Rubinstein got up and stalked over to sniff the glass and darkly ask the waiter just what Madame had been served. The waiter had to admit it was ginger ale. The news threw Rubinstein into a quick fit of temper. He took the glass, offending ginger ale and all, and flung it against the wall. But from this rocky beginning, Rubinstein and Aufiero grew to be friends, with Rubinstein the place's best patron. "See," he often said to Aufiero, "I was your first customer and I brought you luck." "That's right, Sergay," Aufiero would answer, pronouncing the name as Armando the ex-convict did. Rubinstein shortly gave Betty Reed a charge account at Monsignore and word of that spread around and became wonderously magnified so that many persons who should have known better believed that a whole string of girls were buying dresses and furs and eating well on Rubinstein's unlimited generosity. Actually the idea was completely off base. While Betty Reed might have *carte blanche* at Monsignore, and while Rubinstein would often grandly ask Aufiero to give him $200 from the cash register to be transferred to Betty's purse, in the process making sure that as many people as possible saw the act, other girls got nothing of the sort. Sometimes, to be sure, with three or four girls, he would sweep into the dress shop of his first post-Lewisburg girl friend—they had remained on good terms after the romance died—and buy a dress for each girl, but there was always an exact limit to the amount of money to be spent. His ex-girl was taken aside and told that girl over there gets a $50 dress, no more, while the other two could have $75 dresses. The dress shop was very intime; few men came in and fewer still with a stable of girls in tow, all with corsages bought in the restaurant from which en masse they had come with their benefactor. But when Rubinstein and company arrived, the intime atmosphere tended to vanish. While the girls looked at dresses Rubinstein took the shop's telephone to call his home and loudly ask whether London had called; had Paris been heard from? At home his switchboard operator, Billie Kane, would dutifully give negative answers to these rhetorical questions for which a more logical response would be to ask what in hell her employer was talking about—what in the world would London or Paris be calling *for?* Back in the dress shop the girls looking at themselves in the try-on rooms would hear the exciting Mr. Rubinstein carrying on about far-off places and think to themselves that here was a horn of plenty that seemed unlimited. But all they ever got were the dresses, the inevitable $25 ring and, after a very little while, the quick brush-off. No one of them took him; he took them. And having done so he would laugh about it to Gordon Foster or Spencer Samuels or Konrad or Aufiero. Those girls who tried to hang on to him in the hope of getting more than what he was willing to give found his quick temper flare-ups came with little warning. Many times a past plaything

208

would seek him out at Monsignore but he did not like that at all—I tell them when to come; they don't tell me—and there would be an unpretty little scene during which Rubinstein would snarl at the girl to make herself scarce, he didn't want to see her, couldn't she get that, what was so difficult to understand about it? The girl might cry a bit in a corner or go out with a handkerchief to her face, but neither Monsignore's proprietor nor anyone else took the whole thing very seriously, saying to themselves that the girl was a smart enough little cookie who'd gambled nothing beyond a quick roll in the hay and that now, having found the gamble hadn't paid off, she ought to be a good loser about it. She'd gone out with him of her own free will, hadn't she? Tears and all of that were very impressive, but actually what was she crying about? For the lost affections of a man who ignored her almost the entire duration of their relationship? Hardly. She was crying because while Linda and Ava were stars and other girls were supported by millionaires in style, she herself was back where she started from last week, before Serge asked her to tell him all about herself. Gordon Foster likened them to something nice to eat: you pick up a piece of candy, bite into it, one, two, and that's that, it's over and done with. Good-by. Let the girls think for a day or two that they were the one and only in his life—what did it matter what they thought? They didn't mean a damn anyway. A week after he had met them nothing of them would be left in his life but a picture or two, each picture just exactly the same: Serge and the girl, smiling, sitting at a night-club table in evening dress, dozens of girls, always the same Serge. The pictures mounted in the folder supplied by the night-club photographer went into a special file.

His appetite seemed truly insatiable. It was quite normal for him to take a three-day supply of girls with him to Lake Placid; each day another one of them was sent home and on the fourth day he came back alone. He regularly took girls on flights to Florida, but there was never a return trip ticket purchased for the girl in New York. Her return was contingent upon good behavior. Most of the time, however, he traveled alone—girls found him when he arrived at wherever he was going, particularly in Florida and California. (Each winter he went to Florida after letting it be known that he was about to rent one of the largest homes in Palm Beach or the Keys for the season. Real estate agents came trooping to see him but there was never a rental and he always ended up with just a suite in a hotel. California was somewhat similar; he always let it be known he had a giant movie in the works. People came trooping to see him but there was never any movie.) But as time went by, just having a girl in bed was not enough for him. It is a cliché that the higher a man's social and financial level, the more exotic his sexual needs are likely to be. Rubinstein was a European man of affairs and a millionaire. His needs were a great deal different from those of the factory worker making love in the back seat of a car with his coat and tie still on. Rubinstein had a mirror which could be tilted over his bed so that he could see out of the corner of his eye the reflection of what was happening. He experimented with positions. He liked to make use of the soft rug on his bathroom floor. And, after a while, he came to want not one girl with him, but three or four. He had a masseur come to his home every day but Monday and Thursday, and there in the bedroom give a rubdown to the master of the house. As time went on, the masseur discovered that often he would be called upon not to massage one person but three or four. "It's the greatest pleasure in life to be in bed with two or three girls," Rubinstein said several times to the masseur as the man worked his way from one body to another. Lying surrounded by naked girls, Rubinstein would whisper to the masseur that the one on the end, she was a virgin. Sometimes this team play approach made a new girl balk but when that happened Rubinstein, although disappointed, did not insist. Once in Miami he was introduced to a young Southern girl by one of the most famous tennis professionals in America. The girl was a talented amateur tennis star anxious to make the circuit of the various tournaments, but she had no money to do it with and insufficient reputation to bring her financial assistance from the tennis clubs. The famed tennis pro introduced her to Rubinstein in the hope of easing her financial problems. Together the three of them volleyed on the court, and Rubinstein asked the girl to come to his hotel room that night. The girl agreed to do so and at eleven o'clock she tapped on his door. After a moment he opened it a crack, looked out, saw her, and flung it open. He was naked. The girl stepped into the room but pulled up short as soon as she was past the entranceway. Another girl, nude, was sitting up in the bed Rubinstein had just left. "Join us," said the host. The tennis player numbly shook her head and fled. Rubinstein grabbed a bathrobe, dashed after her and caught her in the corridor. "All right, all right," he said. "Come back in fifteen minutes." She did. The other girl had disappeared; the tennis player was alone with Rubinstein. And she got an airline ticket to the site of a California tournament.

But not all women were the same as the tennis player in their distaste for this unusual way of doing things. There was a girl in New York, very tall, very blond, very café society, who when sober was quite normal but who when drunk displayed violent Lesbian tendencies. She drifted into Rubinstein's life and learned to make use of his ways even as he made use of hers. The girl circulated a great deal in night clubs and after-hours drinking spots and met many women. Her gambit was to approach one—usually a married girl whose husband would be working downtown at a time when Rubinstein was free—with the suggestion that the girl come see "something interesting" one afternoon. The girl would be curious and would agree to come. Rubinstein's blond friend would take her to 814 Fifth. The trio would have a few drinks together and Rubinstein and his blonde would fall into one of the dual beds—the "workshop." The visitor would sit on the other. After a short performance not unlike those hawked by the Parisian entrepreneurs who pursue tourists speaking of "exhibitions," the blonde would have the girl-to-girl talk with the visitor. "You're married, comfortable," the blonde would say. "How about trying something new? Something different?" The married girl would generally hesitate. More drinks would be had. Rubinstein would join the blonde in trying to persuade the visitor to join in the doings. Almost always she would begin to waver. Well, maybe I could try it and if I don't like it . . . The blonde would be drunk by then. Soon the visitor would be undressed. She would have an experience not easily forgotten and then, somewhat numbly, would make her way home, never to be asked again. The blonde's instinct was almost infallible. Almost none of the women she invited to come see "something interesting" failed to switch from the role of spectator to active participant.

Rubinstein's desire to be with two or more women in this way was not unknown to many of the people he met in his nightly outings to the clubs, and it was freely said of him that he also liked to observe Lesbians in action. That news attracted women of such nature to him, their thinking like that of their more usual sisters being directed at separating this millionaire from some of what he had. In addition to the outright female homosexuals, there came filtering into his life more of those girls who, like his blond friend, were what café society calls "switch hitters" or "AC-DCers." With them came frank panderers offering to fix him up with something really nice. But Rubinstein did not care for out-and-out prostitutes—"They always want money; the hell with that," he explained—so the panderers had to take the tack that no crass money need be involved, but perhaps the powerful Mr. Rubinstein might someday give out a good tip on the market or something like that. Rubinstein was glad to hint that if the proffered girl was up to par, why then, something could surely be done for her agent: don't worry,

I take care of people who are nice to me. The panderer would then be invited to a dinner party at which hints were dropped that great things were in the works, lucrative deals which would call for the spreading around of much money to many favored Rubinstein intimates. There would be only the hint, never the actuality, but another dinner invitation would follow and after a while the panderer might come to be one of the regular guests. In return he would provide new girls in exchange for new reassuring promises, and would slowly become something of a "gofer"—go fer the car, go fer cigarettes, go fer a new girl. It would only be after six months or a year had passed before the hopeful new friend would start to ponder the question of when he would be getting the hinted-at wonders. By then, however, he would have found a niche in the parties and at the table and it would not be much to his advantage to break away. And there was still always the possibility that the worth-thirty-millions financial miracle man would yet come across with something really good. As for the call girls coming at the bidding of their agent, they too were sustained by promises. And they had the additional recompense of being grandly introduced as most illustrious persons by their elegant host. By the time they realized their normal rates for an evening were being dispensed with, it was too late to do anything about it; they were passé in the Rubinstein set-up. One such girl, however, cleverer than the others, did come to a mutually satisfactory arrangement with the master of 814. The girl, like Rubinstein, saw herself as an empire builder. Her empire was located in the Midwest, her original home, and consisted of a handful of gas stations. She envisioned herself as the eventual gas station queen of America. She was anxious to learn about the oil business from the former president of Panhandle Producing and Refining Company, and happy to have him lend her volumes from his oil library. They worked out a situation where it was perfectly normal and logical for Rubinstein to call her up and ask her to come over. If she were not otherwise engaged, she would go and be quickly taken to the bedroom where with no bothersome talk or complications she would fulfill her part of their business deal. Then would come his *quid pro quo*. They would adjourn to the downstairs living room or the basement kitchen and there, drinking cognac, talk over the oil business for hours at a time. Amorously directed in the direction of gas stations, the girl found his reminiscences about Panhandle and his advice to her very valuable, and partly aided by it she was able to fulfill, in degree, her cherished dreams. An aged man in a Westchester suburb for several years had been keeping her, but not with sufficient generosity to allow her to blossom out as she wished. Eventually, aided by Rubinstein's suggestions and her own shrewd investing, she was able to cast the Westchesterite adrift along with all of New York, and to return to her real loves, gasoline and oil, which at last report were profitably filling the tanks of many cars. At Christmastime she would always send a card to "Ruby," as she called her friend.

Her passing was hardly noticed by the other people who came to 814. For she looked like all the others; she acted like all the others. It seemed to Spencer Samuels, the art dealer, that everyone who came to the house was looking for something. He himself kept coming because Rubinstein kept proffering a sweet vision to him. "As soon as I do this next big deal," Rubinstein often told Samuels, "I'm going to do the house right." That would cost, Samuels pointed out, at least one million dollars. "I know," Rubinstein answered, "but I'm really going to make this a showplace." Samuels could not find it in himself to think that Rubinstein really would, but like the girls and the pimps he kept coming back, hoping. But in fact the house was going downhill. Things kept disappearing, never to be seen again. "Well, William," Jimmy Morse, the handyman, used to ask Morter, the butler, "what's missing today? More silverware? Some cuff links? A tie?" It must be those cheap little girls going into the closets and finding gifts to give their pimps, Morse thought. And the things that couldn't be stolen were allowed to get rundown. There was a set of chairs in the dining room that cost $500 apiece and which should have had slipcovers but didn't; the chairs were getting shabby. "You ought to make him get covers," Morse told Gordon Foster. "I know," Foster said, "but he won't spend the money." Millions to keep out of the Army, but no slipcovers, for God's sake, Foster thought to himself. The house's walls were all paneled and to polish them would have required gangs of servants, but the walls were always dull looking because Rubinstein would not enlarge his staff of five. Madame also complained that her son was getting stingy. For all that he was very solicitous to her and helped her up and straightened her dress even as he ignored the girls standing by, he was in her eyes hounding her about money. "He won't give me anything to give my charities," she often cried. "I haven't a cent and he won't help me at all." (Actually he gave her $250 a week spending money but she was always short.) Upstairs on her floor Madame gave her little tea parties with her guests sitting on long couches eating great gooey sweet goodies from a large table. An immense yellow diamond ring with correspondingly immense flaws glowed from Madame's finger and at least one guest was struck by how the aging Europeans were similarly tarnished and flawed by age and what they had been through. Her floor was adorned with dozens of little statuettes of pigs, which she had collected for years. Every afternoon she sallied forth, generally with her friend Robert I. Wyner, and went to Rumpelmayer's, a very chic Central Park South place, where she told the waitress to bring her just a little, little, tiny, piece of cake, not too big. The waitress would do so and Madame would gulp it down and order another and another until she had eaten perhaps half a dozen. Then she would make for a French pastry shop to pick up a little dessert for dinner and while there would sample a bite of half the things the shop had. "She eats more than she buys," the shop owner would moan. Sometimes Madame's guests were joined by the master of the house and a girl or two, and that made many people feel sorry for Madame—she could not have enjoyed receiving all kinds of women of the sort her son dallied with. But other people thought Madame was happy to have him going through dozens of women, happy to know he would never marry any of them. Only Betty Reed stuck, and for that Madame hated her and cursed the elevator meeting. Betty tried to keep out of Madame's way, nervously saying to people that gee, the old girl was really giving her the cold eye. (The name "Betty" rarely crossed Madame's lips; the Tennessee girl was instead referred to as "humph, Memphis-Schmemphis.") Very regularly Rubinstein called upon Betty to sing for the guests and Betty complied to his enthusiastic applause, but an hour later he was capable of asking friends to get Betty off his hands. "Do something for me," he said to a woman he knew. "Find somebody for Betty." The woman remonstrated with him, pointing out that Betty had been with him for a long time. "Yes," said Rubinstein, "that's the trouble. She's too old. She's twenty-three, twenty-four. I like them younger." "But she's so beautiful," the woman said. "She's too old for me," he said. Betty must have known what was in his mind and perhaps because of that she began to drink very heavily. He also was stepping up his drinking, but while on Betty it showed, on him it did not, save for a certain slurring of his words and a sloppiness at the table. His eating was even more uncontrolled; he would come in at night and, half-drunk, go down into the kitchen, pull an entire cold duck out of the refrigerator and eat it with his hands, wolfing it down in a matter of moments. Finished, he would spit on the floor where the duck bones already reposed, and reach for a tin of the best imported caviar which he larded into his mouth with a soup spoon. He might follow that with an unsalted eel. Along with the food went more cognac or champagne. If he had a girl with him, he would then take her upstairs; if he was alone he would make a telephone call or two and soon there would be a girl or girls either pushing the bell or opening the door with the keys he sometimes gave out along with the cultured pearl rings. He had always been notable for the early hour at which he arose each morning—never later than seven—but that began to change, what with his drinking and the never-ending parade of girls. His rising time became later and later and soon it was not uncommon for visitors coming to the house at two in the afternoon to find their host in his pajamas and bathrobe. At table he dominated the conversation in a most forceful manner. Most of the time you could not get a word in edgewise. Almost always he carried on a monologue with the subject under consideration being only the life of Serge Rubinstein. If a newcomer to the table managed to get the floor and hold it for a moment, his contribution would be ignored as soon as he closed his mouth; the host would act as if nothing had been said, and then would again launch into a speech on what he had done and what he would do. It was not a matter of give and take; it was Rubinstein alone drinking and talking and drinking some more and then of a sudden taking his leave with a girl—always a girl, one more girl, another pearl ring.

Chapter Seventeen

Twilight

In the nights of those years, sometimes, he lay awake in his bed, alone, afraid of the dark, thinking to himself that all his life had been for nothing, a waste. In the morning he would tell Pat Wray, an intelligent girl friend, that it had seemed to him that everything was closing in, that the very air around him was filled with gloom. He would ask her, begging her to do it, that she talk with him and try to help chase off the terrible depression which sat like death upon him. She would hold his hand as he asked her to, and say to him that everyone had problems in proportion to their own personalities and that as he had a very big personality he had correspondingly immense problems. Then for a while he would be calmer and more at ease. "My salvation," he called Pat. She was an ex-Copa girl who had appeared in summer stock and who painted and read a great deal; they had met when Teddy Howard, the Long Island beach club press agent, took her to dinner at 814 Fifth. She thought the house like a great gloomy museum filled with poor exhibits, but its master had been much taken with her and began to call her and call her. She did not react well to so much chasing, and so his bids had been turned down. Then, again with Howard, she ran into Rubinstein at the Rendezvous Room of the Hotel Plaza. The orchestra was playing a waltz when he came over to ask her to dance. She had never met a man who could really waltz, and so she enjoyed that. Seeing it, he went to the orchestra leader and gave him a bill to keep the waltzes coming. They waltzed on, the seated Howard furious, the dancing Rubinstein murmuring that Pat was like royalty, born to the purple, with so much dignity, with such a way of doing things. After that, they went out rather steadily. But of course she was not the only girl in his life although perhaps in his way he loved her.

The other girl he had loved, Laurette, remarried. Her second husband was a man who worked in the Las Vegas hotel at which she stayed while she got her divorce. After the marriage, Rubinstein was very generous, helping them financially so that they were able to go into the hotel business on their own. He said to the people around him that he was doing it so that his daughters could have a stepfather with resources. But he did not want the two little girls to forget him, and when he went to California, where Laurette and her new husband settled, he went laden down with gifts for Alexandra and Diana. Once Alexandra told him she wanted a microscope and he ran out to buy one for $400 to present along with the inevitable immense stuffed animals and dolls and boxes of candy. To many people it seemed that he was trying to show Laurette now, when it was too late, that he really could be a good and loving father; others, more kind, said of him that for all else you could say of him he did love his children. But he was not adroit in his handling of the two, and would be constantly after them, rolling on the floor and tickling them until they became irritated. He would be told to leave them alone for a moment, that if he would only sit down and let them rest they would come to him in good time, but he did not seem to understand that, and his meetings with them would usually end in their becoming cranky. That would make him lose his temper and he would yell at them. But no one else was allowed to say a word against them. At the Beverly Hills home he rented for the summer Bill Tilden once cursed at the children for running onto the tennis court and from that moment on Tilden was never allowed to come to the place again. He was not terribly missed. Other well-known tennis pros were ready to take Tilden's place in giving Rubinstein lessons and hustling him for bets on games. Rubinstein did not seem to mind parting with the money; it added a certain air to his play. Not everyone could speak casually of an afternoon date to play a set with Bobby Riggs. Yet before he played he always took a pep pill to charge himself up so that a good showing could be made.

During his stays in California he took Laurette and her husband and the children by storm. He gave tremendous parties for the children, with Punch and Judy shows, magic lanterns, fireworks, animal acts, professional clowns, and himself as master of ceremonies and king of the kids in a top hat giving orders to the neighborhood children about which one would now say the word for the trained dog to jump through the hoop. To the parties, totally out of place, he would always bring a Hollywood starlet or two who would posture and strut to show off the figure encased in an evening dress. Laurette would glare and then sigh that that was Serge; he always wanted to have his glamour; he would never grow up. After the kiddie party he would go back to his place for a party of a different sort. At one such he invited three starlets who argued about who had the first claim on their host. A New York magazine publisher sitting by watched with concern as the dispute got hotter and hotter. "Who asked you here, anyway?" one girl shouted at another. "Why don't you get out if you don't like it?" the other screamed back. "*You* get out," cried the first. The two girls rose and clutched at each other. The publisher jumped to his feet saying "Now, now," just as a bottle of champagne was raised and emptied on one blond head. The damp girl stalked off and the aggressor dissolved in tears. The publisher looked at the host, who wore a delighted grin. "Son-of-a-bitch," he said, "you're enjoying it!" Rubinstein broke into a peal of laughter that went on for perhaps five minutes straight. He took the only peaceful girl into the bedroom.

The next day he was back giving more gifts to his daughters. But he seemed to wonder about it, about all the gifts and extravagant parties. "Terrible," he said. "They look for me to give them something. It's going to be they'll love me only for the presents." He handed Diana a big, gaily wrapped package. "Don't like me just because I gave you this," he said. "Just like me because I'm your dad." The child took the present and ran off to open it.

Later, at the airport, the children were there with their mother to see him off for New York. The woman who was a friend of one of his lawyers, out West for a trip, was also there. "Kiss your daddy good-by," Laurette said to the children. But they ran off. Laurette caught them and brought them back. "Kiss your daddy."

"I don't like you," one of the children said to him, and Rubinstein smiled. The friend of the lawyer felt, wanted to feel, that he was embarrassed. But she did not know if it was so. He smiled and boarded the plane.

In New York he went on as he had before—more slights from more people, more unpleasant newspaper remarks ("Socialites feel that draft-dodger Serge Rubinstein doesn't want to stay in California because the Korean War is just a little too close to the West Coast") and more and more a turning to a way of life that was totally uncontrolled and filled with extremely shady characters. He had a romance with an heiress of sorts, but it ended when he welshed on paying her a finder's fee for a deal involving the transfer of some oil properties. It became his trade mark that he would break his word on the payment of any moneys. Even his tipping became something of a scandal. On one trip to California the airport bellhops refused to carry his luggage. Morter, the butler, couldn't understand it. "The man wants a bit of service," he said, but the bellhops replied that the last time Rubinstein flew he had ten bags and tipped a dime. Morter said there must be some mistake and produced a dollar bill so his master could get his bags carried from his limousine. Konrad Sztykgold tried to reason with Rubinstein about his ways, but Rubinstein, once at least a little willing to learn, had become intractable in all things. "Oh, this man," Sztykgold said to a friend, "he makes me so sick. The way he does a man out of a commission, the things he does . . . But it's fascinating to be with him; it's like drinking good champagne even if it makes you sick." (The friend remarked that this was an exceedingly good argument in favor of temperance.) Then came the day when after so many years Rubinstein even turned on Sztykgold. They had made a deal by which Sztykgold acted as broker in the sale of some $300,000 worth of oil lands Rubinstein owned, lands that could not have been sold by Rubinstein himself because no buyers would have done business with him. Before Konrad sold the lands he made it clear to their owner that he would not be told the names of the buyers—Konrad knew the buyers would be embarrassed to be told one day that Serge Rubinstein was letting it be known that he had been in a deal with them. Rubinstein agreed: he would pay Sztykgold ten per cent of the purchase price and would not ask the names of the buyers. But when the deal was consummated, Rubinstein refused to pay Sztykgold unless the names were revealed. "I won't pay you your $30,000," he bluntly said. "What are you going to do about it?" Sztykgold was stymied. He had not expected this. "You see, I put one over on you" Rubinstein said, and laughed. But there were those who did not find it funny that Sztykgold, even more ill than when he disregarded doctor's orders to testify for Rubinstein in the SEC case, had been jobbed of his money by a man who apparently did the jobbing because his sick, old victim was not likely to be of much more use. The two became estranged, but before each Russian New Year's Eve after that, Rubinstein called Sztykgold to ask that the older man come to his annual party even though he need not speak to his host— "It will bring me luck in the new year if you are there." Sztykgold would not come, and in fact went off oil-prospecting in Israel. Before he left, Rubinstein called him one more, last, time. "So now even you, even you, desert me in my hour of need," he bitterly said. The commission was never paid.

His man in Wall Street became a thin and nervous and darting-eyed little man with the symmetrical name of Stanley T. Stanley. Once, long ago in a different life, Stanley T. Stanley had been Stanislas Ruziewicz, Polish consul in Berlin and owner of a large and beautiful villa. Then came war and inflation and all of that and he drifted westward to Paris and to Holland, where he fell afoul of the law for selling unlisted American securities for a bonus of a dollar a share. He was thrown out of Holland but it did not matter; he went somewhere else. He wandered into the Near East and a few deals there, and thence to South America and thence to the United States via diplomatic immunity he picked up by becoming Portuguese consul. In America he became a stockbroker operating out of a midtown office and pushing questionable little issues, a weak man functioning with other people's money, a little man looking for a patron to whose lion he could play hyena. He ended up with Serge Rubinstein telling him what to do and when to do it, with Rubinstein setting him up in his own two-room brokerage house and using the board located in the bigger house next door, Stanley always deferring to Rubinstein, always getting very little for his pains but the promise of what was coming. It was always "Stanley, I want this; I want that," and "Yes, Serge; yes, Serge." And so they went together on a couple of deals. One was between Rubinstein and a group of people merging a couple of companies; Rubinstein pushed for the designation of Stanley as the finder entitled to the finder's fee and then took a kickback of half of that fee after the deal was over and there was nothing the other people could do about it. Then the two of them, Stanley and his master, moved in on a Canadian oil company called Trans-Era Oils Ltd., and Stanley became Chairman of the Board with Spencer Samuels as a board member. Pat Wray was installed as the company's secretary; Rubinstein had uncounted credit cards issued to Trans-Era and paying for practically everything he ate or drank away from 814 Fifth. They called the company the Princess in their conversations, which were only partly concerned about oil lands (the last thing that interested them was developing the company; that would cost

219

money) but were instead aimed at working Trans-Era for a little rise in the market. When the market rise did not materialize, they found another way to make some money. A client of Stanley's brokerage business was one Alexandre Saffian, an international construction man and financial operator in many far-off places. He had met Stanley years-earlier in Iran. Saffian was taken into Trans-Era and then offered, as a member of the company, the right to buy many thousands of Trans-Era options which he, Saffian, could then sell to friends and associates. This would save the company the price of a regular underwriting by an outside firm, it was explained. Saffian bought the options at the price Stanley named; the money changed hands and disappeared into the banks and accounts of Rubinstein's other companies where it remained secure until the day came when Saffian to his horror found that, relying upon Stanley's word, he had paid far more for his options than they were valued at; that he had sold them to friends for far more than they were worth; that in the company's office it was freely said that Rubinstein and Stanley had knifed Saffian and that Saffian had unknowingly knifed the friends who had bought. Saffian went to a lawyer; suit was begun.

Trans-Era went along with its people talking about finagling some deal to send the stock right through the roof—but keeping their hands out of their pockets when Pat Wray would ask for someone to ante up the money for coffee sent in to board meetings. (It was a perpetual annoyance to her and Teddy Schulz that no one would pay for the coffee and the money would have to be taken from Petty Cash and vouchers and statements made out.) That the company was going nowhere was obvious, but now and again Rubinstein resurrected his great oil dreams. He began a drive to merge Trans-Era with the Stanwell Oil & Gas Co. Ltd., of Toronto, an outfit holding Alberta wells and leases and controlled by Lee Brooks, a financier. The deal could not be entered into under the name of Serge Rubinstein, so it was done under cover through the offices of a Swiss banking firm linked to a California holding company controlled by Virgil Dardi, an operator who had married into the Giannini banking family. The machinations were incredibly complex and they came to nothing save for immense law suits by Brooks against Dardi, by Dardi against Rubinstein, by Rubinstein against Dardi, by Brooks against Rubinstein. The main idea of the *v. Rubinstein* suits was that the defendant had concealed his participation behind the façade of the Swiss banking firm, and that the plaintiffs would never have gone into any deal with the man they were now suing.

It was a song similar to the one sung after Rubinstein became involved in a proxy fight between opposing sets of stockholders in Decca Records, Inc. The record firm, which controlled Universal-International Pictures, was headed by Milton R. Rackmil. Seeking to oust Rackmil from the company was a group headed by George Lloyd and including among its members Spencer Samuels, the Rubinstein lawyer Michael F. Doyle of Philadelphia, who was one of the country's leading Catholic laymen, and George L. Noble, an old-time Rubinstein associate. Rackmil charged that the Lloyd group was financed by Rubinstein and the whole effort was, in fact, a kind of polite blackmail which Rubinstein had offered to call off in exchange for some personal position in Decca. In a letter to stockholders Rackmil thoroughly got across his point that Decca was now in danger of being swallowed whole by Serge Rubinstein. This terrified the stockholders, who rushed in great number to announce that they would join hands with Rackmil to defend Decca from the monster. Lloyd realized in turn that the very breath of the name was going to halt his campaign right in its tracks. He burst into print with statements that he was absolutely clear of any involvement with the detested draft-dodger. "I expected that Mr. Rackmil would try to smear me," he said. "I am only surprised he has not labeled me a Communist." But the stockholder belief that Rubinstein was involved was too great a cross for Lloyd to bear. His group was voted down; Rackmil retained control. It was all a strange business. The exact depth of Rubinstein's participation is unclear; he had meetings with Rackmil as he did with Lloyd even as he was having Rackmil's phone tapped in the weeks before the proxy vote. (It was not hard to arrange this; many of his new post-prison friends had contacts who made such projects quite simple.) Some people thought he wanted Decca in order to use its channels to make a great popular star of Betty Reed and thus show the world that like Pygmalion he had created gold from dross. Others believed a somewhat less romantic but more practical reason for his interest lay in the business of Decca's controlled company, Universal-International Pictures, a position which would have given Rubinstein entrée to hordes of stars, starlets, and would-be starlets. Even less dramatic—but perhaps most important in his thinking—was that Decca, which had not been doing well, could have been liquidated or sold for a very considerable amount by anyone getting control of it. But the whole thing came to nothing in the end—save for a brief romance with a Decca secretary.

He cast about for something new and found it in a television packaging firm called Rockhill Productions. It was run by a woman, Janet Taylor, and needed money to exploit two properties, one a pilot film for a proposed Claudette Colbert series to be called *Leave It to Liz*, and the other an early-day juvenile stratosphere drama, *Tom Corbett, Space Cadet*. Both shows were outstandingly good; both could not be put on the air because Rockhill did not have enough money to film sufficient installments which could be shown to prospective sponsors. Looking around for a source of financing, Miss Taylor met, one day, with Frank L. Miller, the Rubinstein lawyer that sister-in-law Valerie had hated so bitterly. Miller was most sympathetic to Miss Taylor and her problems. He told her he would arrange financing through a client of his. Someone would soon call Miss Taylor to see just what could be done. The next day someone did call. His name was Ed Leven, he announced, and he represented Serge Rubinstein. Mr. Rubinstein was very anxious to help Miss Taylor, Ed Leven said, adding that it would be no trouble at all for Mr. Rubinstein to establish, oh, say three-quarters of a million dollars worth of credit for Rockhill plus a couple of hundred thousand in cash. "Let's see a filming of *Liz*," Leven suggested. He watched it and exhibited rapture in technical television terms learned during a career of television producer of talent but also of a fatal tendency to lie to and cheat his sponsors. Miss Taylor (who did not know this last) was impressed with Leven, who immediately began drawing up great plans for Rockhill: it would be the biggest TV packager in America; it would branch into movie-making in Hollywood. "I work fast," Leven said when he left Miss Taylor, and it seemed he was right, for he was back in a day. "You got a deal," he said, "I told Rubinstein all about it and he'll go along. He works fast too."

The Toni Company was very interested in sponsoring *Leave It to Liz*, and Leven took command of the negotiations, telling Miss Taylor he knew people, he knew television, it was in the bag. Nothing to worry about. But meanwhile, Mr. Rubinstein wanted to bring a new board of directors into Rockhill, some of his own people. And about the $750,000 worth of credit and the $200,000 in cash—that was coming through in just a day or so. A big man in the Street, Stanley T. Stanley was his name, he was arranging it.

The new board was installed: Spencer Samuels, a few other Rubinstein friends. But the credit and cash was not as quickly forthcoming. Meanwhile the negotiations with the Toni people stalled over the question of whether Claudette Colbert would personally do the commercials, a thing the actress did not want to get into. Leven said he would fly to the coast and fix everything. He left, signing Rockhill checks he had lifted from the office as he did so, and returned to say Colbert was impossible but he'd get Ginger Rogers instead. Again he flew to California, again scattering

Rockhill checks everywhere. He was in Hollywood when the checks started coming back to Miss Taylor. She called him to ask what in God's name he was doing. "Keep your pants on," said Leven, "and sit down. I got big news. It'll bowl you over. Serge and I have rented Errol Flynn's house. It has a butler and a wonderful cook and a gigantic pool. It's fabulous. And it's all Rockhill's; now we've got a big California office."

Miss Taylor understood all that—it certainly was fabulous —but who was paying? When was she getting the credit and the money? The questions hurt Leven's feelings. Here he and Rubinstein had done all this for her and she was being ridiculous, acting like a female. But, asked Miss Taylor, what about all those checks Leven was signing, all this money pouring out? Oh, she was so ridiculous, sighed Leven. So female.

In a week, Leven was back. Miss Taylor was beside herself. Every day new checks were being drawn on Rockhill's account—shoes for $50, Cadillacs rented for weeks, hotel bills, night-club tabs. But no money and no credit. She called Leven and told him to be in her office the next morning. He said of course. But when she showed up in her office he seemed puzzled. "What are you doing here?" he asked.

"What am *I* doing here?" she cried. "It's my office."

"I don't understand," Leven said. "This isn't your office. It's my office. You're out. I'm in. We voted me the president of the company."

She fell apart and began to run through the drawers of what had been her desk, looking for her stock certificates in Rockhill, her papers, her records. They were gone. Leven ~~had been a bit~~ now and then that he and Serge was all clear: she was ~~a bit~~ suspicious of this female and now it them a good screwing. Now ~~an~~ embezzler and had tried to give and Serge had caught on to her game.

Miss Taylor tottered out. That night she took an overdose of sleeping pills and was rushed to Bellevue Hospital in a critical condition which lasted for many days. While she was gone Rockhill bank accounts were being liquidated, everything movable was being sold, great salaries were being paid out, bills were being run up all over New York and California. A month later, she was back in action, seeing lawyers, talking to the District Attorney. Suit was entered into—one more *v. Rubinstein.*

But Rockhill had been good for a ride, a little money. The resulting suit was not important. The really important suit —aside from the perpetual Justice Department attempt to get an order of deportation—was the one brought by Odie

223

Seagraves of Texas, an impressive financier and oil man who had once, reputedly, been worth hundreds of millions. In the long ago, before the war, Seagraves and Rubinstein had made an agreement about sharing some of the money derived from the sale of the Chosen Corporation's assets. Rubinstein had welshed, Seagraves claimed, and never paid. Their argument dragged on for years; finally Seagraves turned the claim over to a Bronx roughneck named Manny Lester. Lester did not believe in law suits; he held with direct action. He hired two men to attack Rubinstein on the street. In August 1954 the two men grabbed Rubinstein as he walked on Fifth Avenue a block from his home. "Pay your debts," they shouted; one of them began to belabor Rubinstein with his fists. It was a strange sight for anyone passing by: a man hitting another, the one being struck not hitting back but instead yelling over and over, "Police! Help! Police!" It ended after a minute, Lester's two men driving off, Rubinstein still shouting, "Help! Police!" and then hurrying to his home. That night a brick came sailing through the window. A note was attached: *You have your warning. Next time you won't walk away.* Then a telegram was delivered: BE NICE AND LET'S SETTLE OUR DEBTS.

Rubinstein called his lawyers; they called the police and the District Attorney. An appointment was made between Sonny Wolchok and the insistent Lester, who told Wolchok, among other things, that he had been arrested a total of fifty-six times and that the last man who failed to pay him money had ended with "every tooth in his head knocked out." This did not stampede Sonny, who remarked that Mr. Lester would have to find different means of arriving at an arrangement with Mr. Rubinstein. Another appointment was made for Lester to see Wolchok in person. Lester came and announced to Rubinstein that unless the money was handed over Rubinstein would conduct his "business in a hospital for a year." "Why should I pay?" Rubinstein shouted back. "I owe nothing." Lester became more and more threatening, predicting dire consequences and speaking of his connections with big mobsters who, although now very peaceful, had not forgotten all they had learned in their tough-guy days. The debate ended when detectives with drawn guns marched in to tell Lester that Sonny had been concealing a tape-recorder microphone and that the whole dialogue was now going to be handed over to the District Attorney. Lester was hauled away to face extortion charges.

The summer ended, and fall came, and winter. For Christmas of that year, 1954, he went to California to be with the children and to confer with a West Coast attorney about having his deportation case transferred to that area's jurisdiction. In Laurette's home he again repeated to the people there what he had said so many times in the past: it was all a frame-up that made the world against him. Laurette's twin sister Betty was also out West for the holidays and the two of them, sitting together, spoke of premonitions. "I have a feeling I'm going to die soon," Rubinstein said to Betty. "I'm afraid to die." Then he said he was afraid to grow old, also. Afraid, afraid. Betty listened with half an ear: Serge with his crazy ideas that made some people call him the Mad Russian.

He went back to New York and gave his customary Russian New Year's party on January 13. It was very crowded with half the guests never having met their host, and more than half freely expressing their contempt for him. Waiters moved about distributing California champagne to most people but reserving some good French imports for specially selected persons singled out by the master. Sztykgold was not there, of course, nor was Gordon Foster, who had been deported because of his involvement with Rubinstein's draft-dodging. Pat Wray was there but perhaps there was some coolness in her attitude toward the host, who had upon his return from California revealed to her that he had caused a microphone to be placed under her bed during his absence, there to transmit to a distant tape-recorder every sound made in her room. "You talked about monkeys over the phone," he said. "Monkeys!" His mother's friend Robert Wyner was there, but perhaps with him also there was some coolness; just latterly he had arrived to sign some papers for Rubinstein while wearing open sandals, red nail-polish, powder and lipstick, and had been told to "God-damn it, go home and dress like a man!" Madame was of course in a place of honor behind a Louis XVI table loaded with cookies and cakes, but most of the guests pushed by her to rush for the real food on the buffet table. Afterward there was dancing, with the host the most active of anyone present, continually dancing with first one girl and then another, his clothes, however, never showing the effect because every two hours he went upstairs to change his shirt and spray himself with cologne. One woman complimented him on his great energy, saying it made him attractive even though he was not good looking. That threw him into a rage. "Why must I be insulted?" he shouted. "Many women find me very attractive, very handsome." She apologized but he stalked off to dance with someone else. There were several new girls at the party —there always were—and one of them was Estelle Gardner, a dark-haired ex-movie hopeful from The Bronx who had come back from Hollywood to settle with her mother in a very modest apartment on the Lower East Side. She was introduced to her host by Peter Crosby, a handsome young man from a wealthy family who had married and broken off with the French actress Denise Darcel—a good friend of Rubinstein's—and who was generally considered to be a Rubinstein "gofer" but whose relations with his patron were not always of the best. In 1953 Rubinstein grandly spoke of buying one hundred thousand dollars worth of oil lands Crosby was promoting, but when it came time to write a check, decided to plunge for only $3,000. Crosby called him a welsher and, it is thought, authored a note which was delivered to 814 Fifth with the information that as Rubinstein had knifed Crosby, who had thereupon been forced to knife the Mafia, which was behind the oil deal, the Mafia intended to take revenge upon Rubinstein unless the additional $97,000 was put up. The note was ignored and Crosby and Rubinstein patched up their differences to the extent that Crosby came to the party with Miss Gardner, who impressed Rubinstein enough so that an early get-together was suggested and agreed to. The party ended and the guests left, one of them thinking to herself that with Serge everything was very interesting but there were always too many people, too much of a rush, too much going on, and that in the end you never talked about anything at his place but only alluded to it because there was never enough time to talk. Funny, she thought. Never enough time. After you left him you always realized that.

A couple of days later he called Estelle Gardner to invite her to come to dinner at the house along with a dozen other people. Afterward the whole party went to the theater and later still Estelle and Rubinstein went back to 814 Fifth where Morter prepared two steaks for them. It was three in the morning when she went home. A few days after that Estelle went to lunch at the Colony with Rubinstein and then to his third-floor study where she sat reading his scrapbook while he made a few business calls. She was taken aback to see the newspaper clippings so uncomplimentary in tone but he seemed proud of them, explaining that some people read the news and others make the news, and that he was one of those who made it. Then he said to her that making a million dollars a day was, after all, not everything in life. "What good is it," he asked her, "if you don't have anyone you love to share it? What I really want in life is to have somebody to come to and just relax with. I am a very lonesome man. Are you in love with me?"

She was jolted. "How can I tell in such a short while?" she asked.

"I am not in love with you yet," he replied, "but I could

226

fall very much in love with you. Have I got you on my side? I think I have—am I right?"

She smiled.

Another few days passed. He made a date to go out with Estelle on the night of January 26, 1955. On that day he lunched at Monsignore with three other men. "I want to eat very lightly today," he said to Jimmy Aufiero. "I'm gaining too much weight. Give me two boiled eggs and a cucumber salad, that's all. Maybe a little sliced tomato." After his group left there was a call to Monsignore from his secretary, Billie Kane. One of the men had taken the wrong coat. She would send it back; would Jimmy please try to find the man's right coat? Jimmy would.

Later that afternoon he went to the Trans-Era office on Madison Avenue for a conference and after that to Stanley T. Stanley's office on Wall Street where he talked about his holdings in the Boeing Airplane Company. "I own what could be the controlling stock in Boeing," he said, "but I can't come out into the open and declare it because if I do the stock'll be sequestered on the grounds that I'm an alien." Stanley listened and made sympathetic noises at this oft-repeated recital which heavily implied that Rubinstein must have at least twenty million dollars in Boeing stock. A little after seven Stanley's Cadillac (paid for by Trans-Era) arrived and the two men went to 814 Fifth where Rubinstein got out. Teddy Schulz was there, working on the books and papers. Rubinstein remarked that he had intended to order a car and chauffeur for the evening but that he had forgotten. However, it didn't matter. Estelle was coming over to pick him up; she could come by cab. Schulz left. It was about eight. Rubinstein placed a call to the hotel of his lawyer's lady friend; she was not in. He left word for her to call him back. In the third-floor study which adjoined his bedroom it was announced to him that Miss Gardner had arrived. She was shown up and they were alone for a while. Then Morter, downstairs, was telephoned on the intercom and told to bring two martinis to the bedroom.

A little later, dressed in a tuxedo and evening coat with a velvet collar, Rubinstein talked for a moment with his mother and Aunt Genia, who were bound for the Metropolitan Opera House to see a performance of *Tannhäuser*. He started to leave them and then remembered that his former mother-in-law's birthday was coming up in a week. "Laurette said her mother needs a nice umbrella," he told Madame. "Go out and get her one." Madame said she would attend to it; Rubinstein left, wrapping a white muffler around his neck. His mind was still on his mother when he and Estelle went to dinner at Nino's La Rue, a posh eating place on East 58th

Street. "My mother said to me today that I'm a lost soul," he told Estelle. "She said that with all my money, I'm still a lost soul." He dwelt on that for a few minutes, how having millions and millions didn't mean everything, and then switched the conversation to suggest that Estelle fly to Florida with him that weekend. Estelle demurred, saying she had to go to work at her department store job—cosmetics demonstration department—that Saturday. "Quit the job," he said. "Why go on working at a measly salary?" He began to talk of making her a big movie star but she repeated that the answer was no. (Another girl, a few days earlier, had been a different answer; a Florida hotel already had confirmed a reservation for two.)

At Nino's the maître d'hôtel offered a table that did not meet with Rubinstein's approval. The maître d'hôtel, Joseph Peruzzi, then found a better table near the bandstand. Rubinstein and Estelle ate and drank, Peruzzi's attention being caught by the fact that Rubinstein was not drinking his usual Pommery Brut pink champagne, but instead was swigging martinis—too many. Some three hours passed; at midnight a group at the best table in the house left and Peruzzi invited Estelle and Rubinstein to take their place. They did so, staying at the new table for about an hour. At 1:15 Rubinstein asked for the check, which was a little more than $40. He signed it, adding very mediocre tips for the waiter and captain. As he passed Peruzzi en route to the door he stopped and handed over three one-dollar bills. A cab was unloading across the street; the La Rue doorman signaled it and it came up. The driver was Ernest LaMedica, a fifty-three-year-old moon-faced man. "Give me a quarter," Rubinstein said to him, indicating he wanted to tip the doorman. The cabbie did so and Rubinstein passed the coin on. They went to 814 Fifth. The fare was forty cents. Rubinstein paid with a five-dollar bill, gave back the quarter he had borrowed, and added a quarter tip.

He and Estelle went into the house. It was perhaps 1:30 in the morning, January 27. Rubinstein took off his coat and dropped it on a couch by the entrance; Estelle put on a table the red silk cape she had borrowed for the evening from a friend. They went up to Rubinstein's study and he went to a set-up chessboard there moodily to move one piece, which made Estelle think to herself that he was like that with people too, always wanting to move them and control their destinies. He mixed a drink for both of them.

He went to her and embraced her. He grabbed her shoulders. "You love me!" He was sloppy about his movements. "You're drunk," she said. He lurched at her but she pulled away. He fell onto his hands and knees and began to kiss her

228

toes. "What are you, queer for feet?" she asked. He stood up, hurt, and went to a telephone and called Pat Wray, who had just gone to bed and was not happy at being awakened. It came to Estelle that he wanted her to leave and so she said she would be off. He said all right, he would go down and put her in a cab. They took one of the house's two elevators downstairs, he still in his tuxedo but without a coat, and went out into Fifth Avenue. It was freezing and she said to him that he'd better go back inside; he'd catch cold. He said he was all right; he'd find her a cab. But no cabs came along. They stood for a few minutes and then he said that perhaps she was right; it was too cold for him to be out without a coat. He reached into a side pocket of his tuxedo jacket and brought out a five-dollar bill which he gave to her for cab fare. Then he went back into his house. It was nearly two o'clock.

In his room were big address books generally kept in Billie Kane's office; by his bed was a telephone. He called Pat again; she hung up. Perhaps he made other calls. He took off his clothes, throwing them on the floor, and brushed his teeth, leaving the brush as usual on the sink to be washed by Morter in the morning. The night passed; cold dawn came. A little after eight, Spencer Samuels' wife called from Rye to say Spencer would be a little late in getting to 814 Fifth to pick Rubinstein up for the trip to the Trans-Era offices and a conference there. Morter took the call and said he would transmit the message. Then he put breakfast on a tray and went up in the elevator and tapped on the bedroom door.

Chapter Eighteen

Finis

There was no answer to Morter's inquiring tap on the slightly opened door. The butler knocked again. There was no response from within the room. It came to Morter that it was strange that the door should be slightly ajar; at all other times it had been closed. He pushed it a trifle and looked into the bedroom. The first thing he saw was that the mattress and bedding were half off one of the beds and resting on the floor.

The next thing he saw was his master.

Serge Rubinstein was lying at his butler's feet. He was in black mandarin silk pajamas, his feet were tied, his hands were tied, a great swatch of adhesive tape wound up from around his neck to just below his nose, and he was dead.

229

His face was very much darker than it had been in life. He was lying very straight, as if at attention. His eyes were open.

Morter turned on the chandelier lights. He put down his tray of coffee, juice, and an apple and bent over his master. He reached down and began to undo the tape that covered the mouth; after he had worked a moment he stopped, dazedly stood, picked up a hanger that was lying on the floor and hooked it into the handle of a dresser, and went out of the room.

He went down the stairs from the third floor to the basement kitchen. Jimmy Morse, the handyman, sat there drinking a cup of coffee. "Jimmy," Morter said, "come upstairs. Mr. Rubinstein is on the floor. I don't know if he's dead or not."

Morse leaped to his feet; the two men went up the stairs and into the bedroom. Morse bent over the master, touched the tape, saw the lips were blue, and knew a corpse was before him. He stood up and looked down. How dark his face is! Morse thought. And such an angry look—as if to say, how dare anyone do this to me! Morse reached for the telephone by the bed and telephoned the New York City Police Department. He explained to the police operator that he was calling from 814 Fifth Avenue and that a man was dead, it must be a murder, the man was all tied up and with tape across the lower part of his face. The police operator simply took note of the fact that a man was dead and gave the information to the patrol car dispatcher. The dispatcher put it over the police radio as a Signal 32, the most common police signal, which calls for a car to go to the named address for investigation. A roving patrol car came on the air to say its occupants would go to 814 Fifth. It was about 8:25 A.M.

At that moment, in a shabby reconverted tenement opposite Police Headquarters in Centre Street, far downtown, Richard Piperno, a reporter for the New York *Journal-American*, sat dozing in a tiny room. The room was his paper's office in the little building, which is known as the police shack, and in which all New York papers station reporters who listen, night and day, to the police calls blaring out over the shack's police radio. Although Piperno was almost asleep, with head resting on folded arms across a desk, he did not miss catching the address given. Had the address been located in Harlem, the reporter would not have moved an inch. A Signal 32 for crime-ridden Harlem is nothing. But for a good Fifth Avenue address it is something else. Piperno got up, looked through a city index, and found that the only resident of 814 Fifth was listed as Serge Rubinstein. That made the Signal 32 even a little more interesting. Piperno put through a call to the office of the radio dispatcher and asked what the 32 seemed to be about. He was told that the report was that a dead man was in the house; that was all the dispatcher knew.

A man dead. That could mean a servant with a heart attack—nothing. On the other hand . . . Piperno told the Associated Press man, who had been out of the shack when the signal came over. The AP man called his office and was told to go up and take a look.

At about this time the responding patrol car drew up before 814 Fifth. Its two officers were met at the door by Morter, who led them to an elevator and up to the bedroom. The first cop, not knowing but that someone might be waiting, hidden, took out his revolver, pushed open the door, took a look around, put away his weapon, and called the local precinct. He got the detective squad room and announced he had a murder here, Serge Rubinstein.

The local precinct was the 17th, which covers an area encompassing some of the best hotels, shops, and residences in New York City. Crimes of violence are relatively rare in the 17th, and in any case, the detectives of the 17th were, like all other precinct men, not specialists. For that reason, before they dashed to the black unmarked cars the city provides for their use, the detectives of the 17th put through a call to the Homicide Squad of Borough Headquarters Manhattan East, which works with the precinct men on murders throughout the entire East Side. Even as the precinct men left East 51st Street, the homicide men started leaving East 67th Street.

It took only a few moments before the precinct and homicide men arrived at their destination. Only a few moments later the AP man arrived, found out what had happened, and telephoned his office. Perhaps twenty seconds after his call came in, an AP bulletin went out advising all city editors that Serge Rubinstein had been found dead, apparently murdered. From that moment on, 814 Fifth was as active as it had been during the biggest parties given by its late master. All the top brass of the city administration arrived to bustle importantly by the cops at the door, view the body, and pose for the newspaper and television cameramen. Upstairs, in the bedroom, men were constantly coming and going, detectives, officials, high police officers, Rubinstein friends and associates, and a slew of working Third Grade detectives. Among the visitors was the Police Commissioner, Francis Adams, who stood for a long while gazing down at the body of the man of whose defense staff he had been a member during the draft-dodging trial. Commissioner Adams observed the cords tying the wrists and ankles and turned to the Rubinstein lawyer Eddie Ennis, who was standing nearby. "Eddie," said the Commissioner, "you think there was some funny stuff going on in here—I mean some fairy business?" "Why do you ask that?" asked Ennis. "I don't know," said Adams, "the position of the body, maybe. It looks like there might have been some sex business here." Ennis said he doubted that.

Also among the visitors were representatives of the office of the District Attorney of New York County. Normally that office does not take part in the investigation of a crime, but for "heavy" or important ones, the District Attorney will help out. For this crime, the head of the homicide division, Alexander Herman, came up. He was accompanied by Courtlandt Nicoll, a Princeton man who had also gone to Harvard and Columbia Law Schools. The system in the homicide division was that one Assistant District Attorney would be on call for a straight twenty-four-hour spell, ready to pick up any case for which he was needed. Nicoll was the assistant at the time the Rubinstein case came in; he would handle it, take statements, do everything necessary, always keeping in mind the trial that would follow apprehension of a culprit, and carry the case through to presentation to a grand jury. As, however, there was no suspect in police hands, Nicoll joined in with the policemen and worked along the lines of a detective with them. Although Nicoll had been an ADA for only a couple of years and was not very experienced in homicide work, the sight of the body did not upset him unduly. His first case had jolted him far more—it was that of a grandmother who had been raped and strangled on a rooftop by a youth who habitually attacked older women. The youth died in the electric chair.

Outside, the chill January wind that blew across Central Park and onto Fifth Avenue froze the growing crowd of newspaper and TV people kept waiting before 814's glass and iron door. They sent in word that they were dying—couldn't they be let into the house? It was decided to let them in on provision that they not be allowed above the ground floor. There were about seventy-five of them; they came in with a rush, the TV cameramen scrambling to jump up on tables where their tripods could be secure, the technicians rushing to attach floodlights to the cases which held Russian ikons. Their coming, and that of the other men, awoke Madame in her bedroom one flight above that of her son. She got up, wandered out into the hall, and saw bedlam below, people running around, police photographers carrying equipment, fingerprint specialists dusting walls. Jimmy Morse came upon her and led her back to her bedroom. She asked him what was going on, what was all the noise. "It's

232

nothing, nothing," he said soothingly. Madame's maid took her into her bedroom.

Meanwhile, the news of the crime was reaching the people who had known its victim in life. At a modest boarding house on East 68th Street, Princess Valerie, the widow of Serge's brother, was called to the downstairs phone. A woman friend was on the wire. "Did you know Serge was murdered?" asked the woman. Valerie was dazed. Still holding the phone, she sank down on the flight of stairs down which she had walked. "Didn't I tell you he'd get what was coming to him?" jubilantly asked the friend. Valerie could not answer. No, she said to herself, it's not possible. The way he lives he can do anything he wants. It will go on forever. But the friend was still on the line. "Aren't you happy?" asked the friend. Valerie found her voice. "Yes," she said, "oh, yes."

At the Trans-Era office Pat Wray sat with a container of coffee brought up from the drugstore below. It was about nine o'clock; a meeting was scheduled for 9:15. The phone rang. It was some unimportant person who had done a little business with Trans-Era; as he came on the wire Pat remembered that she had not yet thanked him for the small Christmas gift the man had sent her in her capacity of Trans-Era secretary. "Miss Wray," asked the man, "have you heard the news?" "What news?" Pat asked. "By the way, I want to thank you for your lovely gift." He repeated his question and she again asked him what he meant—what news? She was thinking he was going to tell her the company's stock had gone sky-high; that was what was always being discussed around the office. His news was different. "Serge Rubinstein is dead," said the man. Pat stood up. Stanley T. Stanley came in and took her to his home where his wife, a nurse, gave her a glass of brandy and a couple of tranquilizer pills. She was in a daze. At Stanley's home someone asked her if she knew anyone who would want to kill Serge. "Kill?" she cried out. "Nobody told me he was *killed*. The man that called said he was dead. He didn't say Serge was *killed*." Pat began to cry.

In California, Laurette's twin sister Betty, staying in Laurette's home, awoke to the sound of a ringing phone. Her husband was calling from some miles away, where he had gone on a business trip. "I have something terrible to tell you," he said. "What now?" asked Betty, remembering a quarrel of the previous night. "This is really awful," said her husband. "Well?" asked Betty, and he told her Serge was murdered, it was on the radio. Betty suddenly felt as if hundreds of needles were being jammed into her flesh. She went upstairs and sat down on the sleeping Laurette's bed. Laurette awoke. Her hair, so blond when she was Mrs. Serge Rubinstein, had grown dark again; she was far from slim. She looked nothing like the girl he had married fourteen years previously. "I'm going to tell you something difficult," Betty said. "You must not send the kids to school today. Serge was murdered." Laurette said nothing, but sat a moment. Then she jumped out of bed and went into the bathroom to run water on her face before she came back, fell into a chair and cried. She and Betty were thirty-two and Serge was the first person in either of their lives, the first one ever, who died. They had gotten to be that old and no one ever died before.

At the Monsignore Restaurant, Jimmy Aufiero heard the news and felt cold all over. That very morning, at about 3:30, he had walked past 814 Fifth with a girl whose car was parked at Fifth and 66th Street. As Aufiero and the girl went by 814, Aufiero pointed to the house and told the girl how, a few weeks previously, its owner had come into the restaurant with a group of twelve other persons besides himself. When the group sat down, Rubinstein counted them and realized, with horror, that their total was thirteen. "My God," he said to Aufiero, "I can't eat at a table where the number is thirteen." He looked around the restaurant and at the bar, where a girl sat alone. "Jimmy," he said, "who is this girl here? If she eats with us, we'll be fourteen. Have her come to my table." Aufiero did so and the guest stayed to have a good time. Telling the story as he walked by Rubinstein's house, Aufiero smiled. But hearing the news of the murder some hours later he said to himself that it was possible the murder was going on even at that very moment when, strolling by, he was telling the story to his friend. "Jesus Christ," Aufiero whispered.

In far-off Israel, Konrad Sztykgold, hunting for oil, heard the news via a telegram sent him by his daughter. Shortly after, a reporter for a Tel-Aviv paper, acting in behalf of the New York *Post*, sought him out. "Most of what was said about Rubinstein and much of what he invented to dazzle other people's minds, is fantasy," Sztykgold told the reporter. It was true. But it was also true that a homicide had been committed, that the homicide had a title—Case 432, 1955—and that the New York Police Department wanted it solved.

In charge of the solving of that case was Deputy Chief Inspector Edward Feeley, commanding officer of all Manhattan East detectives. Feeley at that time had put in a round twenty-five years on the police force. One of fifteen children raised in a poor New York neighborhood, Feeley had joined the force at the age of twenty-nine. He had seen in his police years all the things a detective sees—the dead junkie dumped near the seashore where a roving band of wild dogs, aban-

234

doned by the summer people, finds him and rips him open; the man arrested for asking a woman on the street to beat him with a whip; the kid proud of himself for emptying a shotgun into the member of a rival gang. But for all these things, and more, Feeley retained a certain gentleness and ability to get outraged about what he considered violations of society's codes. "My old neighborhood was tough, sure," he would declaim, "but you have to say it different. If a fella's mother passed you by, you tipped your hat; if his sister passed you in the street, you said hello. That's the way we lived. We had respect for others and we were polite. Now some of the fellas were German and they went in for this goose grease on that pumpernickel bread. Now you and I might say, Jeeze, what the hell is that? But when you went up to a fella's house—say a fella you hung around with, he said come on up to my place—and his mother gave you the bread with the goose grease, you would take it to be polite. Outside you might take just one bite and say to him, here, you take it, but at least you'd been polite. Today it makes me sick to see the way kids call their parents by their first names. A girl calls her mother Florence or Jane, it makes me sick. You ask why they let them and they say, well, that's modern. And when I ride in the subway I give a woman my seat. I don't mean some young girl, but when a woman comes in, I get up right away. I don't like it the way most men don't do that anymore."

This was the man in charge of investigating Case 432, 1955. He knew, on January 27, 1955, little about the man whose murder he was investigating—little beyond what anyone who read the papers would know. Perhaps Feeley might remember the business of having detectives in to tape-record the threats of the extortionist Manny Lester, this having been done by men under his command, but of personal acquaintance with Rubinstein he had none. It did not matter. He attacked his case. His first questions were about who had last seen the victim alive. The answer, supplied by Teddy Schulz, who had arrived to begin his day's work, was that it must have been Estelle Gardner. Detectives were sent to Estelle's mother's apartment on East 15th Street, where they found the girl asleep. They woke her, gave her the news, heard her account of the evening. Had the door been left open when Rubinstein returned to the house? She didn't know —she had not seen him go inside, being occupied in looking for a cab. How long had it taken her to get the cab? A few minutes. What did the ride cost? One dollar and thirty cents, including tip, paid for out of the five-dollar bill Serge gave her. The detectives immediately went through her purse, finding just $3.70. Just whom had Rubinstein called while she was in the house? She didn't know. Feeley was called at the house: Gardner had dropped no blockbusters. Feeley told the men to bring her in for more questioning. Then he talked with Morter, the other servants, very briefly with Madame, with Eddie Ennis and Sonny Wolchok. Perhaps three hours had gone by since Morter first tapped on the door before Feeley's case was clearly shaped up. Here was a man, apparently choked, lying in a room that looked as if it had not really been fought in—no broken window, no overturned chairs, no real disarrangement of furniture save for the mattress dragged off the bed. The man's hands were tied with a thin cord known as Dandy Cord, but they were tied very loosely, and in front of him, which was strange. When you tie a man, you usually tie his hands behind him. The man was taped up like a mummy, seven feet of tape around him, but the tape was not tightly wound on. The legs were tied, but very, very loosely. There was no evidence of any forced entry at any window of the house, nor at any door, nor on the skylight—and later detailed examination would show beyond question that nothing had been opened in any irregular way. All right. So it means the killer or killers got in either with a key, or the victim let them in, or the front door was somehow left open by Rubinstein when he re-entered the house after seeing Estelle off. Now the desk in the room had been opened and a few papers taken out and left lying about, but it had not been ransacked, not really. And the wall safe was locked. All right. So what had been taken? Nothing, evidently. Nothing seemed to be missing, save for a little purse Madame had once given her son. But who knew when the purse might have disappeared? It could have been six months before Juanuary 27. No one could be sure. So what's the motive? Well, maybe it was a kidnaping that went wrong. You get a couple of tough boys to go in and say, Serge, get outa the bed. You tie him up, tape his mouth so he can't sound off, and drop him in the back of a car and head for Canada. Once there you say, Serge, cough up a hell of a big bundle or we tell the immigration people you're here, they seal the border against you, and you never see New York again, you never get to do any business there, you never see an East Side club again, you never make an American girl ever again. Kidnaping. But why tie him so loosely and with the hands in front? And why tie his feet? If you want to take a man out of his house, a man weighing 184 pounds, you certainly would want to have him walk out. You wouldn't tie his feet. And all right —forgetting for the moment the problem of the kidnapers in getting into the house—why would they have let their man get into pajamas and into bed? Wouldn't they just have waited until Estelle left and grabbed him in his tux? They could have just waited in the hall outside the studio and grabbed him when he got off the elevator. Or they could have taken him on the street with a gun, one-two-three.

So, maybe it wasn't kidnaping. Maybe it was a shake-down. Again, assume a couple of tough boys figured he had a bundle of money or jewels or something in the safe in the bedroom. They could go in, find him in the bed, shake him. He wakes up. They stick the gun in his face. He freezes, the way people do at the sight of a gun. So say one tough boy figures the guy is a screamer—didn't he yell "Help! Police!" when Manny Lester's men attacked him in the street?—and the tough boy slaps a hand over his mouth. So say Rubinstein starts to wriggle across the bed to get away. Right away the other tough boy stands him up and puts the mug on him, holds him, and by mistake squeezes too hard and does him in. He drops. He's dead. The tough boys realize it, decide to throw the cops off by making like it was a bungled kidnaping, and tie him up and get out. All right. But first, would two shakedown boys come in with Dandy Cord and adhesive tape, all prepared for this? Well, maybe. Maybe they meant to tie him up in any event. But would they risk carrying a gun on Fifth Avenue in the middle of the night? That's terribly risky. Suppose a cop stops them just on suspicion and frisks them—which can happen to two rough-looking types walking Fifth Avenue at a late hour. If the cop doesn't find any evidence of evil, he lets them go. But if he finds a gun, the two boys get taken to the station house where they get questioned about every unsolved stick-up in the area for the past five years. A gun is very dangerous.

Now suppose it was a deliberate murder. Lots of people had it in for the guy. Manny Lester was one. But at the time of the murder Manny was safe and sound in a California hotel. Lee Brooks of Stanwell, the oil company Rubinstein tried to take over, also hated the guy. But at the time of the murder Brooks was in a New York hospital to which he had admitted himself twelve hours before for treatment of an old back injury. And anyway, if you're going to murder a man, why let him get undressed and all of that? Why not just shoot him down in the street and get going?

Time passed; a couple of more hours. Rubinstein's body lay where it had been left. Downstairs, reporters for the afternoon papers, whose edition times were coming due, set up an immense furore. No information was being given out and they hadn't even been told how the man had died. The District Attorney's homicide chief, Al Herman, went down to talk with the newspapermen. But he was exceedingly close-mouthed about everything. "We heard he was strangled," one reporter said, quoting a detective he knew. Herman said he could not answer the question, not being a doctor. The reporters hooted at that. For God's sake, they shouted, if the son-of-a-bitch was shot he was shot—if he was strangled he was strangled. Herman repeated he could say nothing and turned to go up the stairs. But one reporter cried out a request to ask just one more question. Herman turned. "Well?" The reporter, savoring it, drawled out an inquiry as to whether the butler done it. The whole roomful of newspaper and TV men burst into a roar of laughter. Herman looked angry, and then laughed—as did millions of viewers who that night saw the act on their television screens.

It was a strange way to act at a homicide scene. Here was a dead man, here was a murder, and here were a large group of men laughing and joking and saying the damned draft-dodger had it coming anyway. The whole thing was treated as a carnival—a very good story, a great story, but a carnival also. When William Morter came downstairs and ignored all the questions shouted at him, the reporters made a joke of him, asking in sympathetic tones if he had found any more bodies lately.

Early in the afternoon, it was decided to ship the body to the Medical Examiner for an autopsy. A large wicker basket was brought; Rubinstein was strapped into it and, covered with a gray blanket, left his house for the last time. A barrage of flashbulbs went off to light his final exit. At the same time it was decided to adjourn all proceedings to the Manhattan East Headquarters on the third floor of the 19th Precinct house on East 67th Street. Before it was done the police consented to allow two reporters, one from a morning paper and one from an afternoon, to go up and view the murder room. (The two promised to give descriptions to their colleagues on the other papers.) Drawn by lot, a reporter from the *Post* and one from the *Mirror* were chosen. They went up and memorized everything, the English hunting scenes on the walls, the thick green rug, the picture on the marble-topped night table of Rubinstein in his Napoleon ensemble surrounded by four girls in period costume. They gave it all to their fellow reporters and then the whole crew went to East 67th Street. Also there went a detective who had some information for Feeley. Some weeks ago, he said, he had heard a couple of men at a bar talking about the kidnaping schemes of a Queens car-for-hire chauffeur named Herman J. Scholtz, a mousy little man. The detective had filed away in his memory the information that this Scholtz was hoping to tie up and kidnap and hold for ransom one of two rich men, the first being Frank Costello and the second Serge Rubinstein. As soon as he heard this news, Feeley put a

238

twenty-four-hour-a-day tail on Herman J. Scholtz. It was a lead that sounded good, very good. But it was by no means a sure thing, and so Feeley kept asking questions of the people in Rubinstein's life. It was not hard to figure out who they were, for in the large black loose-leaf books found near the dead man were listed the names and addresses and telephone numbers of 2700 persons, the compilation of everyone, practically, that Rubinstein had talked to in the years since he came to America. The owners of those names started getting called in—a lawyer who had a drink with Rubinstein ten years earlier in California and had never seen him again, a stockbroker approached on a transaction in 1950, a leading member of the city's Russian *émigré* group, a Count, a Marquise, an English Earl, several ex-convicts met in Lewisburg, some public relations people, a slew of Wall Street men, a Catholic priest often at 814's big parties, a few newspapermen, loads of lawyers and, of course, a perfect swarm of girls, almost all of whom arrived for questioning looking scared and unhappy and anxious not to be photographed—which they were, many times. The girls, it seemed to Feeley and his men, could well be the instruments for cracking the case. For Rubinstein had not had many men in his room at any time. So the girls were the first people questioned. The approach to them was a gentle one. "We're sorry to have to drag you down here," Feeley would say, "sorry to put you out, take up your time. How about a cup of coffee? Cigarette? Okay. Now, just tell us—now there's no need to get excited, plenty of time—just tell us what you knew about Serge. All right?" The atmosphere the cops wanted was a relaxed and friendly one that would be something like that existing between strangers on a train who get to exchanging confidences. When sexual details came up, Feeley would take pains to say that the girl's private life was her own but that for the sake of his investigation it was necessary that the girl answer certain questions about the habits of the victim of Case 432, 1955. "Now, when you'd be in bed there, say, and he'd send for another girl, would he go down when she came, or just leave the door downstairs unlocked so she could come in by herself? Now say you'd be leaving in the middle of the night—would he tell you to make sure the door was locked, or wouldn't he say anything about it? Now, did he talk much about his enemies, people trying to do him harm? Well, okay, if you can't remember, just take it easy and maybe it'll come to you. How about we all send down for a sandwich, what do you say?" Such questioning periods would take two, three, four hours. Then there would be another and then perhaps Feeley, Assistant District Attorney Nicoll and the others would grab an hour's sleep on a couch before going back to work. No notes were taken at any time—Feeley had always felt note-taking inhibits the person answering questions.

Meanwhile, even as some of the names were being questioned, others were being picked up. Assigned to bring in Betty Reed was Detective William J. Whelan, an amiable and likable Irishman with a quarter century on the force. He went to Betty's apartment on Central Park West and found she was gone. From the janitor he learned that Betty had a good woman friend who lived in Yonkers; it was the janitor's guess that she'd gone there. Whelan went to Yonkers and to the woman's house, and found it besieged by newspapermen who'd also talked to the janitor. He was told Betty was out cold from sedatives; he viewed her lying unconscious and announced he'd be back. The next morning he went to Yonkers again and informed the revived Betty that she was coming in. Outside, the reporters and photographers were waiting, but Whelan felt he could better gain Betty's confidence if he helped her avoid the many loaded cameras and poised notebooks. He recruited a friend of the Yonkers woman, a young girl, put a coat with a high collar on her and had her stalk majestically out of the house toward a parked car. The girl did so and the swarm of newspapermen came roaring after her even as Whelan and Betty dashed out of a side entrance and into a car which headed downtown. But the ruse didn't really mean much, for at 67th Street a different crowd was ready to scream questions and blast off flashbulbs. Inside, Betty seemed confused and unable to think straight. The cops outdid themselves in being nice to her but she had little to offer about Rubinstein's business affairs or enemies. Feeley was not satisfied. After all, she'd been the guy's chief girl friend for more than five years, ever since Lewisburg. She *had* to know something. He told Whelan to keep cultivating Betty; this Whelan did, getting quite close to her and seeing her regularly—but only with other people present. (Many times women cry rape when they want to be left alone in the future.) But for all Whelan's work, Betty had nothing to offer that seemed material. That last night, the night of January 26, she had gone to the Roxy Theater with a girl friend to see *There's No Business Like Show Business* and then had gone home. No, Serge had not called her.

While Betty was perfectly co-operative—or seemed to be —other girls were not as helpful. One such was Dorothea McCarthy, a model whose resemblance to Jacqueline Kennedy would, in later years, gain her quite a big name in modeling circles. Detective Vincent X. Murphy, Whelan's long-time partner, was sent to bring in Dorothea. "I don't want to waste my time on all this," Dorothea told Murphy, who in return told her this wasn't a case of some guy being punched in the nose or something, this was a murder, and if she didn't come in on her own, she'd be subpoenaed. She came, told the cops that Serge had said to her that the thing he wanted most was someone to love, someone who would love him in return, and exited, trailed by photographers and reporters—one of whom printed a report that she was a close relative of Senator Joseph R. McCarthy, which she was not. (She did not like the report and called Feeley to complain.) Dorothea was not the only girl who felt herself maltreated by the newspapers. Pat Wray was haunted by reporters who waylaid her in the elevator of her apartment building and trailed her everywhere she went. They lurked in the corridor of her house like a pack of wolves; they tramped down the street like a herd of elephants. (Or such were the animals she compared them to.) "When are you going to leave me alone?" she cried at them; they in return asked to know the truth— "Who really killed him?" After a day or so she told them she would grant an interview if they would then let her alone. She opened the door of her apartment and said they could come in and look around. "Come on in," she said bitterly. "Look at whatever you want to. Get your fill. Go on, go into the bathroom. Don't be shy." They came in with a rush and poured through her small place. The photographers took uncounted pictures of her, a somber-looking twenty-four-year-old standing by her desk upon which there was a photograph of Serge Rubinstein. For years thereafter she was bitter against all newspapers. Only one scrap was given her: when the *Times* commented on some paintings of hers, scenes of oil derricks and such, which hung in the Trans-Era office, the paper remarked that the work showed "above average talent." Pat managed to laugh at that, saying to her friends that it was really better than opening at the best 57th Street gallery.

Late on the afternoon of the murder, the autopsy report came through: The victim had suffered an injury to the larynx, a fracture of the hyoid bone, a fracture of the cricoid cartilage (the sound box), scratches on one finger of each hand. Death came between four and five A.M. There was found a discoloration about the mouth which, it was later determined, came from hard rubbing by a garment, specifically a brown tweed topcoat. Death had resulted from the pressure applied to the neck, the pressure that had broken the bones there. The autopsy went into the growing police file on the case, and copies of it were studied by all the men involved in searching for the killer. Another report came in:

There were eighteen fingerprints in the room, six of unknown persons.

After a while Madame and Aunt Genia recovered enough from their shock to be questioned intensively. Both had bombshells for the police. Madame, in fact, had two. She had been awakened that night, she said, by the sound of men's voices arguing below her on the third floor, Serge's floor. She said she got up, looked down the stairway, and shouted "Serge!" several times. The voices then quieted. But wasn't Madame's hearing very bad? gently asked the police. Well, yes. But still she was sure she had heard voices and yelled down. And another thing. During the night she saw a girl in brown on the staircase. Aunt Genia volubly confirmed this matter of the girl in brown. She, too, had seen the girl. The girl had opened her door, turned on the light, turned it off, and gone out. What time had this happened? Genia didn't know. But it happened.

The police were doubtful about the stories of both aged women. They decided there was no girl in brown. Madame's girl had been an ambulance attendant who walked into the wrong room; Genia's was William the butler checking on the room Genia occupied for the night. William was quizzed intensively on the question, as well as on all his actions of the night. He said he had gone to a bar on Third Avenue, watched a prize fight on television, gone home around midnight and to bed immediately. The cops went after him about his drinking habits. Didn't he like to take a drop now and then? Yes, he did. Was it possible he had been drunk and someone at the bar had helped him home and that the someone had thus gained entrance to the house? No, said William. Absolutely not.

The other servants were grilled. One maid said she heard noises on the roof around 4:30 A.M., but that they stopped after a moment. Noises on the roof? But there had been no forced entry from the roof. And all windows were locked. Entrance *must* have been made through the front door. So the cops set about to locate all the keys to that door. There had been, they found, eight keys. The lock had been changed in September 1954 because a couple of girls to whom Rubinstein gave keys became troublesome. So there were eight known keys. Where were they? Seven were held by servants, secretaries, Teddy Schulz, Madame, and so forth. But the eighth was missing. It was the key of one of the maids. She lost it, she said, on a day a few weeks previous when her daughter and son-in-law came to visit her from another city. Feeley had one hundred detectives working full-time on the case; he detailed half a dozen to find the key. They went over every minute of the maid's day with her relatives. She

242

had eaten breakfast at this tearoom, then she had gone to the beauty parlor, then to the hotel room of her visitors, then to the theater for a matinee, then for dinner. The police went everywhere she had been. In the beauty parlor, they found the key. An employee giving a hairset had found the key by a chair in which the maid sat and it had reposed, those weeks, in the cash register of the shop. Feeley took the half dozen men off the key. There was work for them elsewhere.

Despite the appeals in the newspapers, the cabby whom Estelle said took her home did not show up. Where was he? Estelle said he had never turned toward her; hence she could not describe him. Of his cab she remembered only that there was an ashtray in the door and that it was her impression the vehicle was far from new. She was asked to pick out the kind of cab it was and settled on a 1948 De Soto. But she could not be sure. So detectives set out to check the trip-sheets of every cabby on the streets during the early morning hours of January 27. In time they went through 3000 trip-sheets; 3000 reports were filed saying that So-and-so, hack license number such-and-such, had apparently not taken a fare from the East 60s to East 15th Street. As for Ernest LaMedica, who took Rubinstein and Estelle from Nino's La Rue to 814, he showed up, found himself the object of two dozen press cameras, told his story, which checked with what Estelle and the La Rue doorman said, and went back to his hacking.

The days went on. The case was a newspaperman's dream in one way, embodying murder, money, girls—everything. In another way it was a nightmare because there was little hard fact to go on. So the papers started running stories the headlines of which ended in question marks. "Was Serge In Tavern After Estelle Left?" asked one columnist, saying that a certain television executive was positive that a man drinking next to him in a bar at 2:30 A.M. was Rubinstein. The cops went to the executive, who recanted. Well, he wasn't sure. He'd never seen Rubinstein, but the man next to him did look like the pictures of the dead man in the papers. The story died. Other stories asked Was Serge Killed For Dominican Money Deal? "Café society is saying," said the stories, that Rubinstein was killed for speculating against Dominican Republic money. Teddy Schulz knocked the story down; there had been no such speculation. But Teddy also casually mentioned to Detective Whelan that there was a memo in the files, dictated by Rubinstein a while back, in which was said something about who would be to blame if he, Rubinstein, were ever murdered. "For God's sake, why didn't you speak up earlier?" Whelan demanded. He felt like slugging Teddy. Teddy rummaged briefly through a file cabinet and came up with the memo, which was dated January 5, 1954, and concerned itself with the opinions of attorney Lowell Birrell, an old Rubinstein associate who later fled to Argentina with numerous indictments charging multi-million dollar frauds hanging over him. The memo indicated Birrell had spoken to Rubinstein about Rubinstein's troubles with Virgil Dardi, one of the participants in the Stanwell oil deal. As taken down by secretary Billie Kane, whose spelling was not of the best, it read: "Mr. Birrell then proceeded to say that you can drive the 'ginnies' up to a certain point, beyond that he knows how the 'ginnies' and Sicilians act and I just wouldn't be around to collect. A car would drive by the house and somebody would shoot me and it would be said it was a veteran of the war who was vindictive. I make this memorandum for the purpose in case something like this happens that it should be evidence as to the person who caused it."

The memo was rushed to Feeley, who began to take a considerable interest in Dardi. Dardi, as it turned out, had an iron-clad alibi for his whereabouts on the murder night, but he was quizzed rather meaningfully. He admitted he had no use for Rubinstein, but denied any violent tendencies, Italian ancestry or no Italian ancestry. (Another Italian angle came up a little later. Some poems of Pat Wray's were found in Rubinstein's papers; in one she made reference to an Italian artist of the Middle Ages. The detective reading the poems saw an Italian name and immediately started checking all Mafia sources. He ceased his inquiries when Pat pointed out that if the artist did the killing, he would have achieved the feat of being the first 350-year-old murderer in history.)

Several days went by, the one hundred detectives working with no days off for any reason, and the newspaper stories getting wilder and wilder. One paper explained the vast collection of names and addresses and telephone numbers as part of Rubinstein's nightly "voodoo rites" which saw him brooding over whom he would destroy the next day. When a man was destroyed, the paper said, Rubinstein crossed his name off his list. (Not all of the 2700 persons were meant to be destroyed, however. Only some.) Another paper printed an item saying an unnamed mystery girl ran off with Rubinstein's immense assets. A detective questioned the author of the story, who refused to identify the source that had supplied it. Lawyer Eddie Ennis poured cold water on the idea by saying there were no hidden assets. That did not kill the story, which appeared in other forms, all of which indicated enormous reserves of money scattered all around the world. Other tales said all Wall Street "trembled" at what might come out of this killing. This concept was fed by

Stanley T. Stanley, who said it was a "mob killing" and that he feared he was next on the list of the "mob." He added he was going to seek a gun permit. A reporter talking to him in his home noted the family dog, which appeared in print the next day under the description of a "ferocious canine killer" purchased by the "fearful, pasty-faced Rubinstein associate."

Meanwhile, hordes of people were still going to East 67th Street to run the day-and-night gauntlet of reporters and photographers. The stepfather of actress Tina Louise, a physician, was questioned about a threatening telegram he once sent the dead man, asking Rubinstein to keep out of the doctor's marital troubles. But at the time of the murder the doctor was in Florida. He was clean; the questioning ended. Miss Louise also appeared in the picture when John Sorrenti, a convict ex-boy friend of hers, wrote from prison to say he had known Manny Lester and that Manny had once asked him to get his father-in-law, the Washington figure Henry (The Dutchman) Grunewald, to apply pressure so that Rubinstein would quash the extortion case against Manny. The plan did not work out, but Manny, Sorrenti wrote, told him it didn't matter; he had obtained the services of a beautiful girl who looked twenty-one but was only sixteen and was happy to go to bed with Rubinstein so that Manny could blackmail Rubinstein on the basis that he had seduced an underage girl. The cops were interested in Sorrenti's reminiscences, but unfortunately for him, the convicts in his prison found out about his stool-pigeon act and made his life so miserable that the warden, in compassion, had him transferred to another prison.

The Dutchman's son-in-law was not the only convict or ex-con questioned. All the men Rubinstein was known to have associated with in Lewisburg were brought in to be questioned very, very carefully. A businessman enemy would think of driving Rubinstein to bankruptcy, but an ex-convict might think in terms of blood and gore. So the men with records received the most careful probing. "What cans you been in? Lewisburg and Sing Sing? Okay. Now, you got a girl friend? Where's she live? You go to church, shoot pool; you play any basketball? All right, you know why you're here. Now let's go. What about Serge?" But more and more Feeley began to wonder if he was really looking for a professional killer or killers. For God's sake, why didn't they just dump him in the street? Why all the hocus-pocus with cord and tape? The suspicion dawned that perhaps it was just a couple of small-time punks looking to score something but had happened upon a man who just wouldn't sit still for a stick-up, began to shout, and got himself killed as a result. But if that were so, why so few signs of a fracas in the room? And why tape and cord?

Days passed. The body, its face dark and tremendously puffed up, was taken to the Campbell Funeral Church on Madison Avenue where it lay on public view in a seamless bronze casket lined with mother-of-pearl satin and costing $6000. Madame picked it out; Madame sat in a corner of the funeral parlor as the people passed by to see her son. Among the visitors were curious children from a nearby public school, a great number of shabby, aging Europeans, and former mother-in-law Mrs. Kilborn, who put a sprig of myrtle by the body. Serge had once asked Laurette to do that if he ever died, she explained. It was an old Scandinavian custom, he had said. And as Laurette was not coming to the funeral, her mother would do it in her stead. On Monday, four days after the murder, the funeral was held. The officiating clergyman was Rabbi Julius Mark of Temple Emanu-El, where Madame was a regular worshiper. Rabbi Mark did not want to be the burier of Serge Rubinstein, and Temple Emanu-El's members did not want him to have anything to do with the last rites for a man who had in their minds thrown such a stain upon the record of achievement of the Jews in America. But Madame begged Dr. Mark to conduct the services and he finally consented, suggesting, however, that there be no eulogy, but simply the reading of a few psalms and the saying of a simple prayer. Madame would not hear of that. She insisted upon a eulogy of her son. That put Dr. Mark in a bind. He said to himself that he was not going to say such things as would make people look into the coffin to make sure it was Serge Rubinstein who was being talked about. He was not going to have it said of him that he whitewashed the man. He went to the funeral parlor and to the assemblage before the coffin he said:

"It is not my intention to defend or in any manner condone the actions of Serge Rubinstein during his lifetime. Others are in a better position to judge him and even they must not usurp the prerogative of God, to whom belongs the final judgment. The man is dead and therefore in the hands of God.

"The word 'paradox' best describes the strangely complex, ambiguous and unquestioned psychopathic personality of Serge Rubinstein. He possessed a brilliant mind, but was utterly lacking in wisdom. He had a genius for acquiring wealth, yet never learned the simple lesson that money is a good servant but a harsh master. He was a frustrated man because he wanted friends and never had them, since he never seemed to realize that to have friends one must be a friend. He wanted love, but never knew that love must be

246

earned and cannot be bought. He declared that America was the finest of all countries of the world, yet stubbornly scorned the counsel of those nearest to him who pleaded with him to answer America's call to service. He wanted security, a natural desire, but lacked what is more important —inner security. He feared death, because in his heart there was no faith. And the irony of his life was that death should have come to him in so brutal a guise.

"Our hearts go out in understanding sympathy to his beloved and adoring mother. We pray that she may find comfort in the thought that her gifted, impetuous son now rests in peace."

The eulogy was finished. Its listeners sat in horror at such words. Mrs. Kilborn cried out, "Oh, what terrible things to say about Serge!" Jimmy Aufiero leaped up as if to rush at the rabbi, and then forced himself to sit down. Estelle Gardner, hands covering her mouth, rushed out into the street. Madame sat stricken; everyone was afraid to look at her.

The funeral cars filled up and drove to Woodlawn Cemetery in The Bronx. It was a nonsectarian cemetery, which seemed the appropriate place for a man upon whose body, hanging from a silver chain around his neck, were a Jewish mezuzah and a Christian cross side by side. Afterward, there was a funeral luncheon at 814 Fifth for some fifty of the mourners. "He was so courageous," Madame said. "Such a good son. I wish every woman would have such a good son as I had." When the company sat down to eat she did not sit at her customary place at the foot of the table. She sat at the head, where Serge had always been. And she did not speak of how she called him a "lost soul." In the eyes of many of the guests there was something about her expression that spoke of relief that at last it was all over, all that she had been through with this son in whose place she now sat, supreme mistress at the head of the table.

The investigation went on; the wild newspaper stories (some too wild to be printed) went on. It was nosed about among the reporters that the reason Madame spoke in a funny way was because Rubinstein had refused to buy her a new set of teeth: he had been amused, it had given him a laugh, to hear her clacking away with the old ones. The story became accepted as hard fact. The most weird sex stories were accepted as equally hard fact. . . . The bastard used to strip naked, save for high cowboy boots, grab a long whip, and run screaming up and down the halls and stairways of the house, a one-man posse chasing a bevy of naked girls. And he was a fanatic for oral contact with every part of the female body; why, he preferred that to.

anything else. (This last story gained particular circulation when a reporter for a weekly scandal sheet dreamed up a new solution to the whole mystery. What happened, the reporter theorized, was that Rubinstein, in his ceaseless quest for new sex thrills, had a girl tie him and tape him before she gave him a tremendous hug. But the girl pressed too hard and so in this exotic way inadvertently murdered the man.) A somewhat similar story found its origin in the recognized abnormal practice, known to psychiatrists, of persons who find sexual gratification from an interference with normal breathing. A reporter pushing the theory made it all sound logical when he explained it to his colleagues. A girl ties up Serge at his request, tapes his mouth, and then squeezes his nose with two dainty fingers. Serge is beside himself with sexual excitement. Encouraged by his happy look, the girl squeezes harder. Suddenly Serge goes limp. Exit the girl, hurriedly.

A parallel story was put out by a reporter who had served in the Pacific war. Were the police aware, he wrote, of the Japanese practice of torturing Allied fliers by taping their mouths and then squeezing the nostrils shut? Couldn't this have been done to Serge by business rivals seeking information about a deal? (Whether the police knew about Japanese tortures or not, they certainly knew the theory did not go very far toward explaining the broken neck bones and the fact that the tape was rather loosely wound on Rubinstein.)

The reporters, undaunted by official nonco-operation in pushing their theories, kept working away. And when there was the smallest bit of hard news, it got the best kind of coverage. Out on the West Coast, a movie starlet who was a Rubinstein flame during several Hollywood visits held what she called a press conference. Wearing a dress so low-cut that artists had to touch up the AP photos sent across the country, she said that Rubinstein was a wonderful man who told her he needed love. The name and the picture in the New York papers, however, reminded Madame of something that happened a while back. Upon the occasion in question, the starlet called Rubinstein from California in connection with some broken promises of his. She said she was coming to New York to force him to make good, and flew in to confront him with a gun which he leveled at his chest. He took the gun away and tossed it in the East River. A girl with a gun? The police were interested. But the girl had been far away at the time of the murder. She was clean.

In the middle of all this, all the stories and leads, a flood of letters and telephone calls began to pour in. They took up valuable time, but Feeley was afraid to ignore them. So they were all checked out . . . An anonymous caller said the murderer could be found at a certain downtown address. Vince Murphy went there and found he had arrived at a home for emotionally disturbed boys. One of the boys admitted making the call for a joke . . . A call came into the funeral parlor telling the attendant to take down a telephone number; the killer would be found there. Whelan was given the number and checked it out to a Bronx supermarket the employees of which were totally clean . . . A gibberish telegram arrived telling Feeley not to waste his time looking for the Rubinstein killer, but to investigate all the abortions in the city—"hundreds of pure girls are being killed." The sender of the telegram was a recently released mental patient . . . A man came in asking to speak to a detective on the case. Raymond Seiler talked to him and heard a recital of how the woman living upstairs was shooting acid through the floor, could see through walls, and made the club soda in the icebox taste funny . . . A West Point cadet wrote in that perhaps Rubinstein had had a woman three times that night and that "no matter how good a man is in shape, he can't take three times a night and still retain his energy, therefore it would have been easy for the woman to physically overpower him" . . . A Costa Rican businessman told of a dream about the murderer. "He looks like the one I saw in my sleep before, walking those long blue decorated corridors after he emerged seemingly from the bathroom where I heard the muffled voices." The man asked for something Rubinstein wore at the moment of death . . . A whole series of four-page letters came in from a tortured soul writing of voices taunting him and threatening that he would be killed as was Rubinstein.

Madame also received letters and calls. One such was from a medium who was invited to the house and revealed, in a trance, that Serge was killed because of fourteen letters someone wrote him. Madame was sure the medium had the facts, and asked Feeley to come watch a second séance. Feeley obliged by sending Whelan and Captain Daniel Mahoney of the 17th Precinct. They sat while the medium went into his trance and spoke of how happy Serge was in heaven. The Madame was called to the telephone, leaving the three men alone. The medium was seemingly in his trance, his eyes tightly shut. Mahoney leaned over to Whelan, covered his mouth and said—not as quietly as he had hoped—"What a load of crap!" The medium's eyes popped open at once, but when Madame came back he returned to his trancelike state. Speaking in sepulchral tones but glancing at Dan Mahoney through his eyelashes, the medium intoned, "Madame Rubinstein . . . Madame Rubinstein . . . It was D. M. who killed your son." Mahoney leaped up in a rage and de-

249

voted a couple of hours to finding out if the medium ever predicted the future, a crime for which Mahoney could have joyfully arrested him. (The medium, however, only specialized in interpreting the past and never ventured into the future.)

Eddie Ennis was also bothered by calls, including one from a man who promised to tell all but who, arrested by Vince Murphy, admitted he had nothing to offer and only called Ennis to see if he could con a few dollars out of him. At least Ennis's caller had a logical reason for his call; many of the other letters and calls seemed to be made with no rational thought whatsoever. They directed the police to fictitious addresses, to persons dead five years, to children; they involved the police in feuds where one party would write in that the other was the murderer. Meanwhile, Herman J. Scholtz, the would-be kidnaper, was under steady surveillance. A month after the murder, he was arrested. In his home the police found an armory of weapons including a sub-machine gun, a .45 pistol, a .38 and a .32. Also found was a supply of tape and cord. A small man who suffered from ulcers, Scholtz readily admitted his kidnaping plans, but said he had been unable to go through with them because his chief co-conspirator, one Elesano Troiani, a small-time bookie, had been arrested a few months earlier on a concealed weapons charge. The police went to Sing Sing to interview Troiani, who proved to be a burly and rough-looking customer with nothing at all to say. Scholtz was grilled and grilled again about whom else he had talked to about the proposed kidnap, but every man he implicated had an air-tight alibi. Had he given the scheme to someone who gave it to someone who gave it to someone who tried it and bungled it? Scholtz was grilled some more; his friends were grilled some more.

The case seemed to have no end. Names of new women bobbed up every day. "There was a married woman up on Fifth Avenue, she was in bed with Serge and me. . . ." Sergeant Sol Fuchs of the 17th went to check it out. The woman named bade him welcome and told the maid to get him a Scotch and soda. Fuchs asked the woman what she knew about Serge Rubinstein. "Serge Rubinstein?" asked the woman. "The fellow that was murdered? Why, I don't know anything about him. I never met him." Fuchs uncrossed his legs, crossed them again. "We heard different," he said. "Different?" asked the woman. "Why, what do you mean?" "What I mean," said Fuchs, "is that six months ago you and a certain blonde and Serge spent four hours in bed together having a little party. That's what I mean." The woman looked at Fuchs intently. "Will this go no further?"

He assured her it would not. And so they talked. The woman got no money or furs or anything like that. Young, married to a man whose work demanded that he be downtown at a time when Rubinstein was conveniently free, the woman had already had male whores and lovers, and this was something different. Plain curiosity accounted for her visit to Rubinstein's bedroom. But she knew nothing that could help the police. Fuchs thanked her and went on his way. There were many such married women in good addresses denying any liaison at first but ending up, each and every one, by saying that yes, they had been in the bed with Serge and another woman and that it had been so disgusting, ugh—but they wouldn't have missed it.

For the detectives assigned to it, the case was exciting. It had great flavor and style. This wasn't some Harlem knife job or a storekeeper on the East Side where it's simply a matter of talking to a few neighbors and then looking around for a couple of days until the killer drops into your hands. In most murders it's always the same thing, a common law couple fighting, or two guys having it out over dope or policy, or two winos in an alley somewhere. The precinct guys have sources and they tell you what they know, give you leads, and you pull in the guy who did it. It's not a hard thing. But with this case there were interesting angles all the time . . . A woman said that once Peter Crosby told her he had a special key to Rubinstein's place. Crosby was grilled pretty well. He insisted he had never had a key and knew nothing. No, he never wondered about how much money Serge might have in the bedroom safe. No, absolutely not.

Letters and leads kept coming in. An anonymous letter spoke of munitions shipments. A well-connected Wall Street man said he had heard rumors Rubinstein was a Soviet spy knocked off by order of Moscow. Another Wall Street said he understood a Justice Department man had been on the take from Rubinstein for years in exchange for a promise that there would never be a deportation, but that of late the man's demands for money had been excessive and that Rubinstein, angry, had threatened to make known to the man's superiors the whole story of all the pay-offs. That was interesting. Justice Department men had been at many Rubinstein parties. They were checked out. Not so interesting, however, was the never-ending search for Estelle's cabby. Where was he? Thousands of man-hours piled up but the only thing that came out of it was that on the murder night a cab had stayed parked near Nino's La Rue for about an hour, not responding to calls although its light was on. The questioning of cabbies went on. Also a continuing thing was the searching of the Bureau of Criminal Identification personnel for any information on any Rubinstein associates including the elevator repairman, the rug cleaner, and the electrician. Nothing material turned up.

Weeks passed; months. The story slipped off the front pages and into the back sections, and then there came a time when there was nothing more to be said. There was a brief flurry when the estate offered a $25,000 reward for the killer's arrest and conviction, but the flurry died when nothing but a new flood of crank letters came in. And so, after a while, the interest and the excitement died and the case became a matter of routine. Sometimes it would revive for a moment and then the police would think that now they had the tinkle that would put the killer in their hands. Once a detective not on the case remarked to Whelan that he had a case involving the robbery of a homosexual and that the victim had been tied up with cord. Cord. That was a tinkle. Whelan kept an eye on the other man's case and when one of the two robbers was picked up, Whelan questioned him. The robber, a young man who said he made his living hustling queers, said that certainly, he and another guy had tied up the fairy while they robbed his apartment, but they had never murdered anybody. He was clean. There was another tinkle when Morter found the murder room ransacked one morning. A horde of detectives rushed over, thinking that the murderer always returns to the scene of the crime, but deciding after they had seen the room that it was just a simple attempt at a burglary. (The house next door was looted, on the night in question, of $30,000.) At about the same time a woman tourist strolling down Fifth Avenue paused to look at the famous 814 of which she had read so much. As she gazed at it, a young man passing by grabbed her purse and ran off into Central Park. There seemed no connection with Rubinstein.

Months passed; years. Detectives were put on other assignments; Feeley went back to taking days off. But still men labored over Case 432, 1955, checking a murder in Chicago where tape was used, looking into shakedowns in Canada, reading the countless letters sent to Feeley, Betty Reed, Madame, Stanley T. Stanley and Eddie Ennis, and searching for someone to fit the six unknown fingerprints. More detectives were dropped and soon only a handful of policemen continued to wonder about who killed Serge Rubinstein. More years passed. The estate withdrew its offer of a reward. Vince Murphy retired from the Department. Only Whelan and Ray Seiler were left working full-time. Whelan retired. Assistant District Attorney Cortlandt Nicoll went into private practice. Chief Feeley was shifted to command Bronx detectives. Only Seiler was left. Then a police administrative shakeup took place and the case came under the jurisdiction of Manhattan South Homicide. Seiler was with Manhattan East; the shift ended his long association with what had begun for him at 8:45 in the morning of January 27, 1955. The loads of files were carted down from East 67th Street to Manhattan South Homicide in the West 20th Street station and there, along with a dozen other old homicides, turned over to Detective James Fallace, his to control until a perpetrator was convicted. Among the other dozen cases were some that were thirty years old but were still listed as open. Fallace is a young man, but if thirty years, or twenty, or forty, pass by and he retires, and the case is still open, someone else will wind up with the files and aging blue detective reports on Case 432, 1955. Fallace looked through the files, picking up one here and there, but what else could he do? One hundred detectives' work led to nothing but files and memories. All the long days and nights of work had not produced a culprit. And why had they worked so hard and spent so many thousands of dollars of New York City's money? Because it was a homicide.

And so, the case is still listed as open. Still, in theory, the Police Department waits for the tinkle that would allow Whelan with his private detective agency, and Murphy in the hotel where he commands the house staff, and Feeley in The Bronx, and Seiler in a new precinct, and Sol Fuchs in Brooklyn, and all the others, the many others—would allow them to say, Ah, so that is how it was. So that is why he died. Oh, yes. Rubinstein. Now we see. So that is what it was that morning long ago in that house.

But will the tinkle ever come? Really, is it likely? Will someone one day walk in saying I can tell you who got Serge Rubinstein? Not likely. Maybe someday someone will. But not likely.

So we are where we were a moment after Morter knocked on the bedroom door. The man was killed; no one knows why.

Epilogue

A Grave in the Weeds

The young man mentioned in the prologue of this book, who probably did not kill Serge Rubinstein, has lived on all these years with the firm conviction that a few months of his life were made miserable by one of the great villains of all time. Assistant Chief Inspector Edward Feeley, who as a Deputy Chief Inspector led the investigation of Rubinstein's murder, shares the young man's opinion. Certainly during Rubinstein's later years he was considered to be outside the pale of decency and honor. When, not long before his death, he appeared on the television show of the columnist Hy Gardner, Gardner introduced him as "the most unpopular man in America." After his death, a minister addressing his congregation remarked that "the public revulsion to the man is one of the healthy signs of the moral integrity of our nation."

To be so eminent a personage, Mephistopheles sitting at a night-club table fondling a girl, Rubinstein would have had to have a certain stature. Did he? Most of the people who knew him well considered him the most lonely, unhappy, lost man they ever saw. In his eyes he was all of that. But in the eyes of his world, which meant substantially those who read the New York City papers, Rubinstein was an important, big, meaningful if evil man. Was he? If he were, it would have shown up in his bank accounts and financial holdings, for they were what he devoted his extraordinary mind to.

It is of interest, then, to note that the size of his estate was exactly $1,281,668, most of it realized from the sale of 814 Fifth Avenue * and the apartment house at 19 East 88th Street that he owned. He had come to America with more money than that in 1938. There are people with many times his million and a quarter whose names never appear in newspapers, who never go to night clubs, who are not known beyond the smallest circles.

That he did not have the $20,000,000 he constantly spoke of, nor even ten, nor even five, came as a shock to many people. They were, for the most part, people who tried to take him for something. Or they were newspaper readers who believed he was the fabulous financier the papers always said he was. In the end, when he died, such people found it hard to believe there were no assets in foreign countries. Having believed his legend in life, they continued his legend in death, repeating the utter fiction that he was a sensational, incredible, miracle worker.

In fact, he was not. He could have been. That was the tragedy of his life. And the word "tragedy," which is applied to large sorrows, is applicable here. For Rubinstein was a one-in-a-million individual whose life, if it has any interest at all, is interesting mostly because it is the life of someone who could have been something but ended up as worse than a nothing, as a negative force.

Just as there were no foreign assets left behind, nothing else of him remained past the time of his death. The people

---

* As of this writing 814 has been scheduled for demolition. A giant apartment house is to be erected on the site.

around him dispersed very quickly. Stanley T. Stanley died. Pat Wray got married. Madame died. Estelle Gardner got married. Aunt Genia died. Betty Reed went back to Memphis. Teddy Schulz went to an average job and a very quiet mode of life. Sonny Wolchok moved to a small office. Sztykgold died. Ed Leven, the participant in the Rockhill television matter, went to jail for another offense—selling what did not belong to him. Peter Crosby also went to jail, for stock fraud. Gordon Foster, deported for his aid to Rubinstein in avoiding the draft, was allowed back into the United States. Laurette, with several new children, was entirely apart from the remains of her former husband's empire. And in fact there was no empire past January 27, 1955, because very few of Serge's people ever saw each other again. For years men and women had been circulating around him but when he was gone, they all vanished from one another's sight. Serge with his great drive to dominate would have enjoyed seeing how without him there was nothing left.

As for the million and a quarter, save for small amounts left to Schulz, Betty Reed, two secretaries and some servants, it went to the Rubinstein girls, Alexandra and Diana—who are not being brought up under their father's name. The method by which it was left to them was astonishing. By the terms of the will, which was taken down by lawyer Eddie Ennis one day as he and Rubinstein rode to La Guardia Airport, the two girls will not receive a penny of the money, save for a rather meager monthly allowance, until they reach the age of fifty years—at which time a good tax bite will be removed. In the thirty-five years remaining before they turn fifty, the estate is held in trust. However, if one or more of the suits pending against it is adjudicated in favor of the plaintiff, there will be no estate left. Manny Lester's claim is still alive—even though his violent prosecution of that claim earned him a jail term for extortion—and so is Princess Valerie's. Several other suits, including one by Alexandre Saffian of Trans-Era and one by Rockhill Productions, have already depleted what Serge Rubinstein left. (A flood of other suits, most of them based on claims that the dead man had promised things not delivered, have been disposed of during the years since Rubinstein's death.)

Rubinstein, it seems to the writer of this book, failed so dismally in life, in relations with people and with the world, primarily because it was his fate to own a background that not half a dozen persons in our time possessed, and which no one will ever possess again. He was a small legacy of a Europe now disappeared, and of a way of life well out of touch with the twentieth century. He never seemed to understand what America was all about, and that Imperial

Russia and Imperial Austria were over and done with. Had he gone into the Army he today might likely be known as a sharp but very rich man, but being Rubinstein the self-created nobleman, it was impossible for him to go into the Army and impossible to not do so quietly. Because of that he went to jail and began the series of later self-destructive moves from which murder quite naturally arose and as naturally acted as rescuer from a destiny become intolerable.

In psychoanalytic theory, men such as he devote the days of their lives to surpassing their fathers; in symbol it might be said Serge Rubinstein strove, pathetically also, to surpass Old Europe with its Grand Dukes and divine right. It was an unequal fight and one that he could not win. He was doomed by being born when he was and where he was. He said so often that the world was against him, and he was right. The world and history went beyond him; he stayed behind.

Jimmy Morse, the handyman, had a last word on his former master. Several years after Rubinstein died, Morse attended a funeral in Woodlawn Cemetery. While there he decided to visit the Rubinstein grave. With some difficulty he found it—a great immense marble thing with an inscription on it: TO LIVE IN THE HEARTS OF THOSE WE LOVE IS NOT TO DIE. But the inscription could hardly be read, for the grave of Serge Rubinstein was all overgrown with weeds and creepers. Almost the largest stone in the cemetery, it was also the most unkempt. Morse, a subtle man, looked at it for a while and allowed himself to think that perhaps this was the whole story of the man's life. But it was too obvious and too pat. He rejected the idea and hurried away.